Ducks & Geese in your Backyard

Ducks & Geese in your Backyard

A BEGINNER'S GUIDE

by
Rick and Gail Luttmann

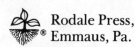 Rodale Press,
Emmaus, Pa.

Library of Congress Cataloging in Publication Data

Luttmann, Rick.
  Ducks & geese in your backyard.

  Bibliography: p.
  Includes index.
  1. Ducks.   2. Geese.   I. Luttmann, Gail, joint
author.   II. Title.
SF505.L87   636.5′97   78-14416
ISBN 0-87857-224-4

Printed in the United States of America on recycled paper, containing a high percentage of de-inked fiber.

4 6 8 10 9 7 5   paperback

Illustrations by Sidney Quinn and Jeana Farrar

We'd like to thank Danielle and Duncan Elliott for reading this manuscript to see that it covers all the questions beginners ask; Ralph Ernst of the University of California at Davis for helping us answer them accurately (any errors are, of course, entirely our own); and all of the people who have said to us, "So now that you've written *Chickens in your Backyard*, when are you going to write a book about ducks and geese in your backyard?"

Table of Contents

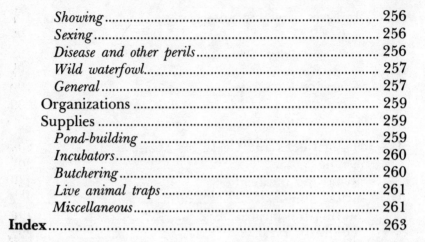

0

Introduction

This book was written to turn people on to the joys (and other benefits) of raising backyard waterfowl, and to provide the information needed for them to begin. We hope the book will also be of interest even to those who don't have waterfowl of their own—perhaps, for instance, it will enhance the enjoyment of Sunday afternoon strolls by ponds and lakes in local parks.

Those who have already read our book *Chickens in your Backyard* may find that certain portions of this book sound familiar. Of course, many common factors are involved in raising any kind of bird, but there are sufficient differences between waterfowl and poultry that a separate book was needed.

The scope of this book is limited to the raising of domestic ducks and geese. Although many people enjoy raising various species of wild waterfowl, these birds generally require very specialized care. We refer interested readers to the many fine sources of information on raising wild waterfowl listed in Chapter 16, "Resources."

It is essential to realize that your birds will be completely dependent on you for all their basic needs. Domestic birds have come to rely on their human keepers through many years of selective breeding for practical or aesthetic qualities. At the same time, many of their natural instincts for survival have been inevitably (though unintentionally) bred out. Therefore, it is unwise to turn them loose and expect them to fend for themselves. On the other hand, once their basic needs are met, ducks and geese are especially suited to domestication because they are so shamelessly healthy and hardy and easy to care for.

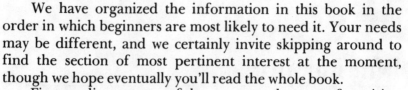

We have organized the information in this book in the order in which beginners are most likely to need it. Your needs may be different, and we certainly invite skipping around to find the section of most pertinent interest at the moment, though we hope eventually you'll read the whole book.

First we discuss some of the many good reasons for raising ducks and geese. We probably don't need to convince you, since you wouldn't be reading this book if you didn't already know some good reasons; but you may need some material to throw at your friends and neighbors (or even your family) in case they are still unenlightened. Next, since you should be familiar with many specialized words used in talking about waterfowl, we provide a narrative glossary. Then we introduce the waterfowl family and give a brief description of the most popular breeds of ducks and geese.

The majority of the book is devoted to the specific details of general care, such as ponds and feeding. Finally, after you've had a good close look at what's involved in raising waterfowl, we give you some tips on getting your flock started.

We hope you won't be put off by our numerous discussions of things that can go wrong, for it's by knowing what can go wrong that you are best able to avoid problems. As a well-informed keeper of waterfowl, you can justifiably expect that nothing will *ever* go wrong. (Well, *hardly* ever. . . .)

We give you as many alternatives as possible so that you can choose the combinations most suited to your particular situation. People have different goals, different kinds and numbers of birds, and a specific size yard to work with. They have to cope with their own local weather, terrain, availability of running water, and, of course, whatever facilities suited to waterfowl might already exist. Once you learn the fundamentals of waterfowl keeping, you will be able to make intelligent choices as questions come up, and to devise methods that fit your particular needs.

The multiplicity of choices may suggest at first glance that keeping ducks and geese is complicated. Quite the opposite is true. Once you have picked out the information which most pertains to your situation, the rest is literally as easy as duck soup.

There is a certain unpredictable element, though, since each duck and goose has its own personality and its own idiosyncrasies. This, after all, is what makes all of the fun of having ducks and geese in your backyard.

1

Why Raise Ducks and Geese?

Myths abound regarding ducks and geese. Here are some we've heard:

1. They are dirty and smelly.
2. They are unfriendly and stupid.
3. They require a lake and so are only for the rich.
4. Their eggs are unpalatable.
5. Their meat is greasy.
6. They are totally useless.

All of these statements are false. The keeping of small numbers of ducks and geese in suburban backyards is growing in popularity, perhaps because at last the many misconceptions about the nature of waterfowl are being replaced with accurate information about their proper care. People are learning that raising ducks and geese in the backyard is not only entirely feasible, but also positively delightful.

Waterfowl are hardy and relatively disease-free, as pets go, and will remain clean and odor-free as long as they are uncrowded. They need no elaborate facilities, although a bit of a place to bathe is recommended. Best of all, the cost of keeping them can be far less than that of a large dog or a persnickety cat, since they can forage for much of their own food where lawns, gardens, or meadows are available to them, and are thus inexpensive to maintain.

In addition to the many practical breeds of waterfowl, there are the more exotic and ornamental breeds that decorate backyard ponds or are simply left to wander about lawns, lending the elegant air of a country estate. Because of their aesthetic qualities, ducks and geese are popular for showing at poultry and waterfowl shows as well. Showing provides an opportunity to travel to different parts of the state or the country to meet others with a similar interest in waterfowl. Raising ducks and geese for show is a serious hobby, providing a practical rationale for exploring the fascinating fields of waterfowl genetics, environmental influences, bird nutrition, courtship displays, and so on.

Geese are known for their watchdog capabilities. Our own first experience with Chinese geese occurred many years ago when a friend invited us to her home to pick the blueberries growing in her backyard. Since she would not be home when we arrived, she instructed us to go right on around to the back to fill our baskets—failing, however, to mention her geese. No sooner were we through the gate of her neat picket fence, than the gaggle of honkers charged—arrogant and uncompromising, hissing snake-necked obscenities at us. We fell all over each other trying to get back out the gate, and would have gone away feeling foolish for having risked our lives for a measly handful

of blueberries if a sympathetic neighbor hadn't come along at the right moment to escort us through the yard.

Many people have learned to take advantage of this characteristic of geese. Several years ago an article in the papers told of an urban neighborhood that was experiencing numerous break-ins. The citizens formed a cooperative to purchase some geese and allowed them to roam at will throughout the neighborhood. Break-ins dropped off dramatically as word spread among the burglars that the gaggle was on the prowl. On many country farms geese are the sentinels who will holler and hiss at any prowler or intruder. Not long ago a fellow stopped by our place to get a goose to help him with his job as night watchman at a local apple cannery. In Dumbarton, Scotland, the famous Ballantine Scotch distillery is guarded at night by a patrol of roving geese. Rumors circulate about their fierce teeth and fiery breath. (But then there's a rumor of a monster in Loch Ness, too.)

Don't be so intimidated by stories of the ferocity of geese that you'll never want to own one. We hasten to assure you that the majority of geese quickly get used to their keepers and, like dogs, have their indignation aroused only when strangers come around. They are simply grazing doorbells. Also, if the truth be told, most geese are bullies who—again like dogs—come on tough but turn and run when their bluff is called. But don't tell this to a single soul, for as long as burglars don't know this, any goose can double as a night watchman.

Though it's geese that have the reputation as watchdogs, we've heard of at least one watch-duck. A friend tells us that her Pekin spends its days on the porch, watching for intruders. The duck silently allows familiar visitors to pass; but let a stranger come by and the duck sets up a din of quacking.

Ducks and geese may even serve as barometers, warning their owners of impending weather changes. We've noticed that our waterfowl become restless and noisy whenever a storm is brewing, even though we ourselves cannot yet detect any change. They're much more reliable than the official forecasts from the weather bureau!

Other interesting and imaginative uses for waterfowl have been reported. In a newspaper believe-it-or-not column we once read that during the big gold rush in Alaska, prospectors sometimes brought geese along when they wandered the river beds in search of gold. Since geese have a propensity for swallowing small shiny objects, when a prospector invited his feathered companions to their last supper he could count on finding a neat little packet of gold nuggets wrapped in the gizzard. (That's *almost* as good as the goose that laid golden eggs.)

Another believe-it-or-not column told us that the enterprising country people of Scotland—whose ingenuity we find breathtaking—utilize geese as surrogate shepherds to help guard sheep against danger. Flocks of sheep often panic for no apparent reason and, following one of their befuddled flockmates, may plunge over a cliff to their deaths or perpetrate some similar idiocy. Geese, on the other hand, are the epitome of rationality, intelligence, and level-headedness. The sheep, evidently heeding the wise counsel of the geese, keep calm and stay away from the edges of cliffs and other perilous places when in their company.

Cockfighting is a sport of which we all are no doubt aware, but it is not so well known that the Russians used to raise certain breeds of short-billed geese specifically for goose fighting. Once a recognized and enthusiastically followed Russian sport, goose fighting has gone the way of cockfighting in this country and was outlawed around the turn of the century.

Because they are active foragers and can glean much of their own diets from the growing vegetation, geese are often used as economical weeders for certain commercial crops. Both ducks and geese can be used to advantage in keeping down weeds and grass in empty lots and other areas, and are often kept on ponds to discourage an overgrowth of vegetation. Thus you have the unquestioned economic advantage of combining your lawn mower with your egg supply *and* making Thanksgiving dinner of the lot at season's end!

Waterfowl will control garden pests as well. Call ducks are active little birds frequently used in small gardens to search and destroy little crawly things; since they are small, they do scant damage to the vegetation. Muscovies, though somewhat bigger and clumsier, are famous for their vast appetites for slugs, snails, and other garden pests. We once heard on the radio that two enterprising young ladies in San Francisco provide a rent-a-duck service to gardeners who want Muscovy ducks temporarily for this purpose.

It is no secret to lovers of Chinese or continental cuisine that duck and goose make superb table fare. Duck is as well suited for the daily supper as goose for a holiday feast. Fat rendered in the roasting can be used as flavorful shortening. Goose liver pâté is a favorite delicacy, though the practice of artificially enlarging their livers through a force-feeding process known as noodling has fallen into disrepute. And, of course, these fowl are valued for the copious quantities of soft down and fluffy feathers for pillow-stuffing produced as a by-product of plucking.

For those who have ducks and geese as pets or who otherwise look on butchering as murder, perhaps eggs are their most significant product. Few commercial farms produce duck eggs, as the superior quality of these eggs has not become widely known in this country, much to the consumer's loss. Compared to chickens, ducks lay larger eggs with proportionally bigger yolks. Ducks also generally lay more eggs in a year, and some are more efficient at turning feed into eggs. They do need space and some water, which has discouraged their use for commercial egg production; like many other animals, ducks and geese don't thrive in overcrowded conditions that cause their quarters to become filthy and smelly. But given sufficient space they will remain happily clean and well preened, and as backyard egg producers they may be as practical, pleasing, and economical as chickens.

These marvelous virtues clearly show that ducks and geese are very far from useless. But ignoring practicality for a moment, ducks and geese may simply be enjoyed as pets. They live to ripe old ages when adequately cared for—ducks may live up to 20 years, while geese have been known to live as long as 40 years. Kept in the proper environment and fed an appropriate and nutritious diet, ducks and geese thus afford years of pleasure to the backyard fancier.

2

Words You Should Know

It is impossible to talk about raising waterfowl without using some specialized vocabulary, and the best time to get familiar with the words is right at the beginning. Some of these words are not in general usage; others that sound familiar are "false friends," with uses that have changed or become less precise in everyday speech.

You may wish to refer back to these pages as you read through the text or when you hear special words in conversing with other waterfowl breeders. Bear in mind that here we're giving only preliminary explanations; we'll elaborate later in the book.

It would be most fitting to start out with definitions of ducks and geese. We'll say here that they all love the water and have **webs** on their feet—extra skin spanning their toes so the water won't slip by so easily when they swim. But an accurate definition of ducks and geese is more subtle than generally supposed, so we've devoted the whole next chapter to the topic. Suffice it to say that the people who care about such matters are called **aviculturists,** which means people who have the pleasure of keeping birds. This name comes from the Latin word *avis,* which is what the Romans called birds.

Ducks and geese, like horses and dogs, come in different **breeds.** Those of a single breed share distinguishing characteristics that make them all alike. An offspring of two birds of the same breed will be of that breed, whereas an offspring of two birds of different breeds will be a **crossbreed,** and its characteristics will generally be the "average" of those of its parents. It is often difficult or impossible to predict what kind of offspring the crossbreeds will have. Very rarely a bird will differ unexplainably from its parents in some particularly obvious way. Such a bird is called a **sport.** Apparently these changes are caused by random genetic mutations. They are permanent and will be passed on to the bird's progeny.

Many breeds come in different **varieties,** usually distinguished only by color. The narrowest word in this classification scheme is **strain,** which describes a line of closely related birds of the same breed and variety. The birds in one strain are usually even more alike than those merely of the same breed and variety.

A **bantam** duck is any duck of a breed (including Mallards, Calls, Woods, and Mandarins) that is naturally small. To be called a bantam, the duck's live weight must be less than about 4 to 4½ pounds (2 kg).

The *Standard of Perfection* is a book published by the American Poultry Association that describes the color, weight, shape, feathering, and other characteristics of each breed and variety of fowl recognized by the A.P.A. One factor the *Standard* may prescribe is the **carriage** or stance of a bird, which describes how it carries itself. In waterfowl this may range from **low** (nearly horizontal) to **erect** (nearly vertical). If you want to show your waterfowl at a fair, they should conform to the *Standard,* for the extent to which they do determines the prizes they will get. **Standard-bred** waterfowl are those appearing in the *Standard. The Bantam Standard,* published by the American Bantam Association, includes detailed descriptions of the smaller breeds of duck. Both these books are fun to look through, even if you don't intend to show.

A bunch of birds is generally called a **flock,** but there are more specific words to refer to more specific flocks. A bunch of geese is called a **gaggle,** and a bunch of ducks is a **bevy.** A **pair** of birds doesn't mean just two of them—it means two of the opposite sex. A **trio** always means two females and one male.

Adult waterfowl form **pair-bonds** of varying strength and duration. This process, called **mating,** may take place anew every year, or it may take place once and last for the lifetime of the birds. An individual bird, especially a domestic one, may be involved in more than one pair-bond at one time. Such relationships are not stable unless acceptable to all parties involved. A collection of birds that has formed stable pair-bonds is called **mated.** The function of mating, of course, is reproduction, though the birds themselves may not be aware of it at the time. Domestic birds generally take mating much less seriously than wild ones do, but it depends somewhat on the breed and even on the strain.

The words mate and breed are not quite synonymous. **Breeding** refers specifically to the performance of the sexual act. It should not be presumed that just because birds are mated they will breed only with each other. Quite to the contrary, many breeds of birds are entirely promiscuous, and undesired fertilizations may result from such unions. Breeding is used also in another sense—to refer to the genetic control exercised by a keeper to ensure that offspring are produced only by pairs of birds he desires should do so.

A **breeding pen** is a place where a person who raises ducks or geese keeps his **breeders,** meaning adult stock that he is using for reproduction. Such a person is also referred to as a **breeder,** and this is not considered an insult.

A male goose is a **gander,** and a female goose is called a **goose.** This is confusing, to be sure, but what can *we* do about it? Some people call a female goose a hen, but this risks confusing geese with chickens. We're stuck with the fact that our language is simply deficient here. A male duck is a **drake,** and a female duck is a—**duck!** Context is the only way to determine whether in any given discussion "duck" and "goose" are being used to denote the whole species or just the female. (Maybe this confusion in ducks and geese explains why so many people think a "chicken" is a hen.)

Incidentally, **Mallard** does not denote the sex, as some people seem to think, but is a breed of duck. The source of this confusion could possibly be that male and female Mallards have completely different coloring, and someone who sees a lot of

9

ducks with green heads (the males) may think that they are all of one breed, while the all-brown ones (the females) are of another breed.

A baby goose is a **gosling.** A baby duck is a **duckling. Hatchling** is a general word referring either to ducklings or goslings or for that matter any young bird that has just hatched. A peculiar kind of learning behavior called **imprint** happens to waterfowl hatchlings during their first hours after hatch. The first large moving object they see becomes mom. To the day they die they will bear a particular affection toward whatever they imprint. This abrupt, unreinforced learning is only dimly understood. It is apparently the mechanism by which hatchlings are supposed to learn what species they are. But if their natural mother or another of their own species doesn't happen to be around at the right moment, they may have the misfortune to imprint on a human, or a teddy bear, or even a passing Ping-Pong ball.

When a hatchling is several weeks old and beginning to grow its feathers, it is described as **started.** In plain English, this

Drake feathers

means it's past the critical period. A duck or goose is called **young** during its first year. After that it is **old** even though it may still live a very long time. A bird is called **mature** when it is old enough to reproduce. This may be as early as the fourth month for domestic ducks, but may not be until the second, third, or even fourth year for larger waterfowl.

Since male and female waterfowl have very different economic functions, it is often desirable to be able to **sex** them, meaning determine their sex, at an early age. Some say it is easy to do this, although unless you have exceptional eyesight and lots of hatchlings to practice on, sexing is best left to the professionals. All mature domestic ducks except Muscovies can be sexed by looking for the **drake feather,** which is actually three feathers that curl up and forward in the tails of drakes. Usually it is possible to **voice** young ducks, that is sex them by the sound they make, before the drake feathers show up: the maturing males gradually lose their voices, and with a little practice they can be distinguished by their weakening quacks.

When drakes are just mumbling about nothing in particular, they emit a soft two-syllable call. This may sound like "quack-quack" to you, but it is really the **two-syllable rabe** call. (Rabe should be spelled räb but who can pronounce that?) The call is so named because the most famous aviculturists are German, and in Germany drakes don't say "quack," they say "räb." When drakes are distressed they make a more desperate sound of one syllable repeated over and over. Oddly enough this is known as the **one-syllable rabe.**

The collection of all a bird's feathers is its **plumage.** The process of getting the plumage organized after a swim is called **preening,** and they'll bask in the sun and do it by the hour. Birds are said to be **loosely** or **tightly** feathered according to how closely the feathers are held to the body. The long feathers on the wing are called **primaries** or **flight feathers.** These feathers are also called **quills,** especially when plucked and used for purposes other than flying. When feathers are just starting to grow they come through the skin in tiny hard sheaths. These are called **pinfeathers,** and pluckers absolutely detest them. Finicky eaters don't usually like pinfeathers, either, unless they can't see them: pinfeathers are harmless and tasteless. **Pluckers,** by the way, are the same thing as **pickers,** since the process of removing the feathers is called both picking and plucking. **A custom plucker** is somebody who will pluck birds as a service to those who raise them for meat but don't care to do the work themselves.

The very tip of a bird's wing is called the **pinion.** Sometimes people deliberately cut the pinion of one wing when a bird is a few days old and the bone is still soft. This prevents the bird from flying away when it grows up, and it is usually done only to wild birds. It is called **pinioning.** There are other techniques for restricting flight, including **clipping** some of the primaries of one wing. This is temporary and has to be repeated when the feathers grow back, whereas pinioning is lifelong.

Waterfowl have an additional layer of feathering called **down,** generally missing from other birds. It's like thermal underwear, serving to keep them warm and dry by trapping a layer of air between water and their skin. The measure of the ability of plucked down to fluff up and retain warmth is called its **loft.** It is the loft of down that makes it useful in parkas and sleeping bags. Hatchlings are covered only with soft down when they hatch, but the down is soon supplemented by feathers. This process is called **feathering out.**

Once or twice a year (depending on the species) the feathers are renewed in a process called the **moult,** or if you go in for four-letter words, the **molt.** A maturing duck or goose goes through two closely consecutive molts shortly after getting its first full set of feathers. A bird just going into the first of these is called a **junior,** or **green.** These terms are of special significance to pluckers, who like to avoid plucking at the time of a molt.

Species that re-form their pair-bonds each year generally have elaborate annual **courtship rituals** during which mates are chosen, and they generally have molts both before and after the spring rites. The one before is called the **nuptial** molt and brings them into their brilliant mating plumage. The other one is called the **eclipse** molt and brings them into the generally more drab plumage they need for camouflage after the honeymoon is over. The brilliant nuptial plumage of the males is useful in providing the females a means by which to choose a mate. In species that mate permanently, the romantic flamboyance of bright colors is unnecessary, so the males and females are usually the same color and they stay that color all year around. Presumably, this is the same reason that jewelry and fancy clothes appeal more to young unmarried persons than to older wedded couples.

Both ducks and geese can be **crested** or **tufted,** which means having a clump of feathers on their heads like a frilly bonnet. A crest is a large, well-defined clump; a tuft is a half-hearted bulge more like a cowlick. **Caruncles** are warty folds of skin around the eyes and head. They are usually seen only on Muscovies, and theirs are red. Some breeds of geese have a **dewlap,** a large extra fold of skin that hangs under the bill like a double chin; it would be a double chin except that geese don't have chins. Some also have a **knob,** which is a roundish protrusion between the eyes at the base of the bill. (The common white swan also has this knob.)

Waterfowl do not have beaks—they have **bills.** At the tip of the bill is a **bean,** a little spot that may or may not be the same color as the rest of the bill. Bills do not have teeth, but tiny little serrations (called **lamellae**) used to strain food out of a mouthful of water. The digestive system of a bird starts with its **crop,** where swallowed food is initially stored. From there it goes into a tough organ known as the **gizzard** to be ground up. This is the bird's jaw, but there are no teeth here either; the grinding agent is **grit,** which consists of little rocks and other sharp objects that birds eat. These particles also become ground up after a while and must be renewed. This grit is not the same kind people eat for breakfast; it can be purchased at a feed or pet shop if coarse sand is not available naturally to the birds. The rest of the guts are officially called the **entrails,** or the **viscera,** and removing them is called **evisceration.**

At the other end of the digestive system is an opening called the **vent,** terminating a short tube called the **cloaca.** The copulatory organs are located within this tube. Through this all-purpose orifice the bird eliminates, and if of the appropriate sex also lays eggs. The eggs are generated in the **ovary** (there are two but only the left one works) and come down a track called the **oviduct** as they grow larger, receive a shell, and are finally laid. They will also get fertilized along the way if the hen has been bred recently. If an egg is not fertilized it will still be good to eat, but it is incapable of producing an embryo. **Embryo** is the name given to a young bird as it is developing inside the egg. The embryo grows out of the spot on the side of the yolk where fertilization took place. This spot is visible when the egg is broken out. It is called the **germinal disc.** Many people confuse this with the two stringy whitish **chalazae** on either side of the yolk, which serve more or less to keep the yolk in a stabilized location within the egg.

In order for an embryo to develop, eggs must be **incubated,** or subjected for a period of time to a certain warmth and humidity. Incubation may be done artificially in a device called an **incubator.** Somebody who owns an incubator and hatches eggs for other people is called a **custom hatcher.** In nature, incubation is accomplished by a hen, who is said to **set** her eggs. A collection of eggs in a nest is called a **clutch.** When a hen gets in the mood to set she is **broody.** Any broody hen may be called a **broody** for short. A keeper who doesn't want his females to be broody has to **break up** his hens, which means to discourage broodiness in some way.

Even if an egg is fertile it may not produce a hatchling, due to various factors both internal and external. The **hatchability** of an egg is its fitness for producing a strong healthy hatchling. A powerful light can be shined through an egg to see how it is doing during incubation. This process is called **candling,** although it is seldom done with candles any longer.

When young are about to hatch they **pip** the egg, meaning they make a hole in it. The hole is also called a **pip,** and from this point hatchlings stage the whole operation of extricating themselves from the egg. A mother's collection of babies is called her **brood.** The baby ducklings or goslings hatched in an incubator must be given the same protection the mother would naturally have given them. This is done in a device known as a **brooder,** where the young hatchlings are kept warm and safe. To keep the brooder sanitary, absorbent material such as peat moss, rice hulls, peanut hulls, straw, or wood shavings is strewn about the floor; this is called **litter.**

So now we've come full circle. Another flock of young ducks and geese is growing up, and we still haven't made clear the thing that seems at first the simplest: What exactly is a duck and what is a goose?

3

MEET the WATERFOWL FAMiLY

What exactly is a duck and what is a goose? The more ducks and geese you look at, the greater the diversity of characteristics you see and the less certain you are. Of course, despite their incredible diversity, waterfowl must have some characteristics in common to distinguish them from other birds, and yet they must have some differences too to distinguish them from each other. Unfortunately, it is necessary to get quite technical in order to make such distinctions properly, considering such matters as details of feather and bone structure. We won't go into the intricate details here, but instead refer you to the classical books on waterfowl taxonomy, some of which are listed in Chapter 16, "Resources."

So that you can have some idea where domestic waterfowl fit into the picture, we will begin this chapter with a brief description of the family relationships among the wild waterfowl. The birds commonly known as ducks, geese, and swans collectively comprise the official category called "waterfowl" or, if you speak Latin, the *Anatidae* family. There are over 140 different species in this family, grouped together in various subclassifications that reflect their similarities and differences. All of them, however, are web-footed swimming birds; they all have a row of toothlike serrations along the edges of their bills to help strain goodies out of the water; and they all have downy young that, like the young of chickens and their relatives, are "precocial," meaning they're able to walk, see, eat, run around, and even "talk" within a few hours of hatching, unlike the naked and helpless young of many other bird species.

The waterfowl family is divided into two main subfamilies, one of which comprises swans, geese, and the whistling ducks.

These birds are alike in the following interconnected ways: the two sexes have the same plumage patterns and the same voice, they molt only once each year, they mate permanently, and the male helps with incubation and the care of the young. They tend to be rather large and so are necessarily conspicuous while nesting. Therefore, they must rely on aggression rather than hiding to protect the nest. They brood small clutches of eggs. Their young are slow to reach maturity and are vulnerable for a long period.

The chief difference between geese and swans is that geese are land feeders whereas swans are aquatic feeders. Swans have short legs and are awkward on land, but their long necks and sleek bills are suited for bottom feeding in shallow ponds. Geese have short, stout bills for grazing on pasturage and longer legs for easier walking.

The fourteen species of geese are classified into two groups. One group includes, among others, the two species known as the greylag goose and the swan goose. It is believed that all domestic geese developed from these two species—the Chinese and African geese coming from the swan goose, and all others from the greylag.

The second major subfamily of waterfowl includes all the remaining kinds of ducks. The plumage and voices of these ducks are different in the male and female; they mate for only a single season and go through elaborate courtship rituals; they experience two molts each year, the nuptial and the eclipse; the male leaves the female after she begins to brood and thereafter has no association with her or their offspring. Nests are well hidden and broods tend to be large. The young reach maturity quickly and are vulnerable to predators for only a short time.

Roughly speaking, there are three types of ducks in this subfamily: the diving ducks, the dabbling or surface-feeding ducks, and the perching or wood ducks. Among the perching ducks is the Muscovy of Central and South America, which has been domesticated since the time of the Incas. All other domestic ducks apparently were derived from the common mallard, one of the eleven species in the dabbling group. Such domestic breeds, including domesticated Mallards themselves, are referred to as mallard-derivatives. Some strains of domesticated Mallards have not been as genetically tampered with as their derivative breeds have been, and tend to retain their natural behavior patterns. The wild mallard is perhaps the most numerous of all wild waterfowl species and certainly seems to be the best known.

There is evidence that the domestication of ducks and geese goes back at least to 2500 B.C. Although certain species of wild waterfowl with aesthetic appeal have always been bred and raised just for pleasure, through the ages the most compelling reason for keeping waterfowl was their value as a supply of meat and eggs. In the course of time keepers of waterfowl have selectively bred for characteristics that are desirable for meat and egg production. It is therefore no surprise that modern breeds of waterfowl are substantially different from—and for human purposes superior to—the wild breeds. Most of the major differences between the two subfamilies, being irrelevant to these economic considerations, have been inadvertently preserved—plumage patterns, molt cycles, and aggressiveness among them.

It would be impractical to try to list all varieties of domestic waterfowl, since new ones are continually being created (such as

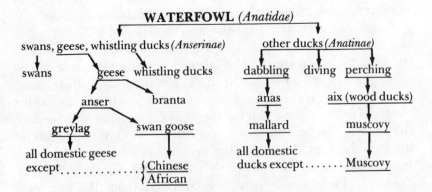

(The underlined classifications include the birds dealt with in this book.)

the Penguin duck we have been developing for several years). Furthermore, there is little point in listing rare breeds, as they are difficult to find and in some cases may even have disappeared entirely. Therefore, we will describe here only the most common domestic varieties. Because domestic ducks and geese come in such a wide assortment of colors, sexes, and other characteristics, it should be possible for you to choose a breed that is aesthetically pleasing to you and fits exactly your particular needs.

Some strains may not have been bred to conform to the standard for their breed, so don't be surprised to find exceptions to our description or those in the *Standard*. Furthermore, factors such as egg-laying ability and the weights of individual birds depend on several matters in addition to breeding, and these are discussed in succeeding chapters.

Breeds of ducks

In this section we will describe in alphabetical order the eight most common domestic breeds of ducks. Two of them are usually considered strictly ornamental, one is generally raised specifically for eggs and four others for meat, and one duck serves as a dual-purpose meat-and-egg type. In order to help you sort out their various characteristics, we have provided a chart at the end of the section delineating those virtues important to choosing a breed of duck.

Aylesbury. This large white duck may weigh as much as 8 or 9 pounds (3.5 to 4 kg), and its principal use is as a table fowl. Aylesburies are fairly poor layers, as is often true of the heavy meat breeds, and are also poor setters. Because of their large size they have difficulty breeding and so their fertility rate is often low. The Aylesbury is named for the town in Buckinghamshire, England, where it originated. It is as common a meat duck in England as the Pekin is in the United States. This provides an interesting study in the development of cultural preferences, for the chief difference between the Aylesbury and the Pekin as meat ducks is the color of their respective

19

Aylesbury

skins—the Aylesbury dresses out white, while the Pekin is yellow-skinned. The British consumer has been brought up to prefer the former, while the American duck-eater has been conditioned to prefer the latter.

Call. Call ducks are generally considered ornamental, being too small to be of economic value. On the other hand, their small size makes them desirable to duck lovers with limited facilities and tight budgets. Calls require less space than the larger breeds, and being among the most active of foragers, they can be relatively inexpensive to feed. They do, however, tend to get larger through overfeeding as well as careless breeding, and may lose their characteristic compactness unless selectively bred for smallness. While Calls are quite prolific, the young are delicate and often require special care in order to get them through the first three or four critical days after they hatch. Calls are considered particularly friendly and docile but are known for their tendencies to fly.

These bantam ducks, which usually weigh 2 pounds (1 kg) or less, were once used by hunters to call in wild game ducks until a federal law of 1934 made the use of live decoys illegal. The breed's name reflects this former function. In Britain they

Call

are usually called decoy ducks. They can make noise all out of proportion to their size and appropriately are also sometimes known as quack ducks. Their quacking is persistent and high-pitched, and this must be reckoned with by anyone hoping to own them happily. They are no breed for the nervous person—or anyone with nervous neighbors!

Calls commonly come in two color varieties, the white and the grey, although others have been developed by Call breeders. The grey was the original and is nearly identical to the Mallard in color pattern.

Campbell. Originally bred in England out of a desire for a good laying duck that would also have a full body suitable for table use and light plumage for easy plucking, Campbells are among the best general-purpose ducks. The breed was developed around 1904 by Mrs. Adele Campbell of Ulay, Gloucestershire, by crossing Mallards, Rouens, and Fawn-and-White Runners. Unfortunately, not all strains of Campbell available today have retained the laying ability for which the breed is known. Campbells weigh around 4½ pounds (2 kg) and come in three varieties. The original and still most common variety is the khaki. The female of this variety is a uniform seal-brown

21

Campbell

color, while the male has the same general body color touched with darker bronze in some sections of the plumage. In fact, the Khaki Campbell drake's plumage pattern closely resembles that of the Mallard drake, but in sepia tones instead of green, grey, and rust. Other varieties of Campbell include the white, which is rarely seen today, and the dark, whose body coloring is similar to the khaki but somewhat darker. The Dark Campbell, also called the German Campbell, is popular in Germany where it was developed. Darks are sometimes seen in Canada but are not often bred in the United States and have not yet been admitted to the A.P.A. *Standard.*

Campbells acquired an upright carriage, along with their prolific egg-laying ability, from their Indian Runner ancestry. They are fairly active foragers and can withstand cool climates.

Indian Runner. Indian Runners are a small (4 to 4½ pounds or 2 kg) breed of duck, developed in Scotland from stock originating in the East Indies. Their unique carriage appeals to those who enjoy the unusual—they look like walking wine bottles, and when they have someplace to go they scamper rather than waddle. The varieties most commonly seen are white, pencilled, and fawn-and-white, although there are at least half-a-dozen other color varieties. Runners are well known for their ability to produce large eggs in copious quantities. Because they are lightweight and therefore do not eat much, the breed is a favorite of commercial duck egg producers. Runners are an active breed and tend to be somewhat nervous.

Runner

23

Mallard

Mallard. Probably more is known about the wild mallard than about any other duck, since it is the progenitor of most domestic breeds and is also of interest to hunters and bird-watchers in virtually all areas of the world (except South America where it doesn't naturally occur). The shiny green head of the slate-grey drake is legendary and has earned this fowl the nickname of greenhead duck. Novices are often confused by the fact that the color pattern of the female (shades of brown and dark pencilling) differs from that of the male, and they sometimes think that the birds are of two different breeds. While the male and female plumage patterns are different, they have in common an electric-blue band of feathers on the wing, called the speculum after the Latin word for mirror. The plumage color of Mallard drakes changes during the year: for two months during their eclipse molt they take on the brown hues of the female. In addition, the young of both sexes have the plumage pattern of their mother until the first molt at about five months when the young males change abruptly into their familiar brilliant adult plumage.

Domestic Mallards generally lose the characteristic raciness and gamey flavor of their wild relatives. They may also lose their tendency to fly, though this happens over years of domestication, so pinioning may be necessary in the meantime. Mallards have an amazing ability to spring into flight from a standing start, even when in water, and do not require a long runway take-off as many other birds do. For this reason, they are especially difficult to confine.

While mallards have long been prized for their delicious meat, they are fairly small by domestic duck standards, generally weighing between 2½ and 3 pounds (1 to 1.5 kg). The egg-laying of domestic strains of Mallards, like that of their wild relatives, is highly seasonal. The duck stops laying and begins setting as soon as a clutch has been gathered in the spring. For these reasons the domestic Mallard is generally considered an ornamental breed.

Muscovy. Originally found in the wooded areas of Central and South America, Muscovies were domesticated in Peru by the Incas. Muscovies are also known as Pato, which is Spanish for duck. They are sometimes called mute ducks or quackless ducks. The males are almost totally mute. The only sound they make is a voiceless hiss. The females are capable of making a loud noise when thoroughly frightened or distressed, but ordinarily make only a soft musical sound, a sweet whimper rather than the loud abrasive quacking of the females of other breeds. It is for this reason that they are very popular among suburbanites who do not wish to incur the wrath of their neighbors or bring themselves to the attention of zoning authorities by keeping noisy pets! The propensity of the males to develop a musky (but not offensive) odor with age has earned them the additional nickname of musk duck.

Some people are put off by Muscovies because they find the caruncles or red warty mask on the faces are ugly. But beauty is only skin deep after all, and the friendliness, natural curiosity, and intelligence of these birds endear them to many people. Among the ducks, they make the best pets.

Muscovies are a very large breed. The male and female are quite different in size, the male outweighing the female by nearly two to one. Females weigh around 7 pounds (3 kg) and males may grow as large as 12 pounds (5.5 kg). This is as large as many geese, and Muscovies therefore make exceptional meat birds.

Their delicious meat is quite different from that of other ducks. In fact it is so unlike other duck meat that even experts are sometimes fooled by it. We'll discuss some of the differences in Chapter 12, "Raising Ducks and Geese for Meat," along with methods of preparation.

The Dark or Colored Muscovy, iridescent greenish black and white patches on the wings, is the original variety. The pure white variety is a later development, bred out of a sport from the colored. Many young White Muscovies have a little black patch on their heads as a token of their dark ancestry. A proliferation of less common colors including chocolate, blue, buff, and silver also originated in the dark. These colors are strictly a result of selective breeding among Muscovies and were not developed by crossing Muscovies with other breeds of

Muscovy

domestic ducks, for propagation of such strains is an impossibility. As noted earlier, Muscovies are an entirely different branch of the waterfowl family from other domestic ducks. Although they often promiscuously breed with other domestic ducks, the resulting crossbred off-spring will be unable to reproduce. These sterile hybrids are appropriately known as mules.

Muscovies are arboreal in the natural state, roosting in trees and nesting in wide forks or in hollow trunks. Because they are perchers, they have sharply clawed toes in contrast to other ducks. They are also dandy flyers, especially the lighter females, though they rarely fly farther than to fence posts and roof gables. Pinioning may be required if confinement to a specific area is desired. While they are hardy in moderate zones, they are originally tropical birds and therefore prefer warmer areas, and, in fact, they do better in hot climates than do any of the mallard derivatives. Muscovies get along quite well on land and are considered semiterrestrial. They therefore do better than mallard derivatives in areas where water is scarce.

Muscovies have a rather curious habit of jerking their heads. When they walk or swim or just stand around with each other discussing the weather, they have a singular way of drawing their heads back, then thrusting them up and forward. One could almost believe it was a necessary accompaniment to their locomotion. A friend of ours, a crew enthusiast, used to amuse himself at the pond's edge by calling out a measured "Stroke! Stroke! Stroke!" as our imperious drake paddled his way across the water with his head-waving machinery turned on.

There is little or no pair-bonding among Muscovies, and their sexual activities are officially classified as rape. For this reason, Muscovies are regarded as primitive and even barbarous by other ducks.

Male Muscovies are extremely aggressive and tend to be rather bossy in the barnyard. They could even be said to be ill-tempered. Occasionally there are some very fierce battles between males for dominance, similar to those between chief roosters. Their powerful wings and sharp claws make them rather terrifying engines of destruction when their wrath is aroused, and these battles tend to be very bloody though rarely mortal. After the decision, the loser will be thoroughly intimidated and hang meekly around the edge of the bevy.

While Muscovies are quite large and can therefore be somewhat destructive in the garden, they do seem to have a greater appetite for slugs, snails, and other garden pests than the mallard derivatives, and so are commonly used to rid backyards of these pests. They can even be assigned to gopher patrol! One day we watched a sweet little Muscovy female eagerly devour one by one a whole nestful of baby gophers we had inadvertently spaded into. This was apparently such a treat that for months thereafter we couldn't reach for a shovel without her noticing. She would come running over to supervise whatever excavation we had planned and would impatiently peer down into any hole we dug as soon as there was the slightest alteration of the soil. As our original discovery was an unusual accident and never recurred, she eventually decided we were phonies and gave up her vigils. But she always makes a thorough investigation of each fresh mound that the gophers push up in the meadow, for she must sense the elusive treasure that lies below.

Pekin. This white breed, with its orange bill and feet, is often considered *the* farm duck in the United States. It is the duckiest of ducks, the one everybody thinks a duck should look like. Donald is a Pekin.

Pekins are poor layers and also poor setters. If a duck does take it upon herself to hatch a brood, she is likely to be an undependable mother. On the other hand, a body weight of 8 to 9 pounds (3.5 to 4 kg) makes the Pekin an ideal meat breed. It is most likely the type of duck you will eat if you order duck in a Chinese or French restaurant.

Note that the name of the breed is Pekin (pronounced PEE-kin), not Peking (pronounced pee-KING), the capital city of China. Peking duck is a certain way of cooking duck. However, the similarity is not accidental. The Pekin originated in China and its name came to us through the French language.

These ducks are sometimes called by their nickname Long Island duck, since large bevies of Pekin ducks for table use are traditionally raised on Long Island, New York. In fact, over half of all dressed duck marketed in the United States is grown there. Ironically, it is due solely to this large duck-growing industry on Long Island that we know as much as we do today about both the nutrition and the diseases of domestic waterfowl.

There is a tendency for the size of a strain of Pekins to decline with succeeding generations if care is not taken to prevent this through selective breeding. Strictly speaking, a duck is only a Pekin if it is up to the standard weights, but since many people use the term loosely, some breeders have introduced the term Giant Pekin to indicate that care has been taken in selectively breeding against degeneration of the characteristic size.

Pekin

Rouen. The Rouen bears the beautiful plumage pattern of the mallard, from which the French developed the breed long ago. It is named for a city in northern France, but the pronunciation is strictly Anglo-Saxon (ROW-en or sometimes ROO-en). It is a very large duck, usually weighing 9 to 11 pounds (4 to 5 kg) or sometimes more, and looks like a Mallard that's been stuffed with buckshot. Rouens drag their bulging bodies over the ground like a dinosaur, and one feels that if they scraped on a sharp rock they might puncture and explode! Rouens are not very active and are generally quite docile. The ducks are poor layers, and people who raise the breed often find their eggs are low in fertility. The Rouen is generally considered ornamental, but due to its size it is also suitable as a meat breed.

Rouen

Additional duck breeds. Among the less common breeds of duck enjoyed by many backyard fanciers are: the Cayuga duck, a black breed developed in upstate New York, whose eggs are sometimes black at the beginning of each season; the Buff duck, a dual-purpose meat-and-egg breed; the Blue Swedish, an attractive smoky-colored breed with a white bib; and Crested ducks, varieties of which have been developed in several different domestic breeds by the genetic addition of a powder-puff of feathers on the top of the head.

In addition, a few wild types are quite popular with backyard fanciers, and these include two bantam breeds: the beautiful oriental Mandarin and its cousin the exotic North

Breed	Colors (variety)	Average adult live weight	Egg shell color	Average number eggs per year	Disposition	Fly	Noisy	Broodiness	Generally recognized purpose
Aylesbury	white	8–9# (3.5–4 kg)	white	less than 100	calm	no	moderate	poor	meat
Call	1. grey (mallardlike) 2. white 3. others	2# (1 kg)	white or greenish	20–35	active	yes	yes	good	ornamental
Campbell	1. khaki 2. white 3. dark (German)	4½# (2 kg)	white	250–300	moderate	no	moderate	poor	meat/eggs
Indian Runner	1. white 2. fawn-and-white 3. pencilled 4. others	4–4½# (2 kg)	white	140–180	excitable	no	moderate	poor	eggs
Mallard	males: grey with green head females: shades of brown	2½–3# (1–1.5 kg)	greenish	20–30	active	yes	yes	good	ornamental
Muscovy	1. colored 2. white 3. others	male: 10–12# (5.5 kg) female: 7–8# (3 kg)	waxy white	40 or more*	moderate	yes	no	good	meat/eggs*
Pekin	white	8–9# (3.5–4 kg)	white	110–130	nervous	no	moderate	poor	meat
Rouen	mallardlike	9–11# (4–5 kg)	greenish	80–100	calm	no	moderate	good	meat/ornamental

*Our experience with Muscovies is that they lay more than the official estimates say they should.

Crested duck

American Wood Duck, both alert, agile, and brilliant in plumage. Mandarins and Woods are both flying breeds, requiring either confinement or pinioning. They are considered wild breeds and neither interbreeds freely with domestic ducks. In the United States a permit from the Fish and Wildlike Service is required to raise Wood Ducks, and state licenses may also be required. Since the care and feeding of wild birds differs from that of the usual domestics, information on them has not been included in this book but can be found in some of the books listed in Chapter 16, "Resources."

Breeds of geese

Just as all breeds of domestic ducks were developed from two wild species, the muscovy and the mallard, there are two species of geese from which the numerous varieties of domestic geese are thought to be derived. The swan goose is considered to be the forerunner of both the Chinese and the African, while the greylag goose of Europe is probably the progenitor of most other breeds, including the common Embden and Toulouse.

Chinese and African geese do better in warmer climates than do other breeds, presumably since the earth's more temperate zones were the natural habitats of their ancestors. In fact, because the knob toward the top of their bill is prone to frostbite, it is necessary to provide a winter shelter for these two breeds in colder areas.

At the end of this section we provide a chart delineating the outstanding features of each breed.

African. Although it originated in China, the Europeans named the African goose for the place from which it came to them. The African is a graceful breed, bearing close resemblance to its cousin the Chinese goose. Most breeders of Africans raise the brown variety, which has a black knob and bill and a rich brown stripe down the back of its long neck, but

African

there is also a rarely seen white variety with an orange knob and bill. Both varieties are distinctly dewlapped. Africans may weigh from 18 to 20 pounds (8 to 9 kg) and are considered good layers. They are fairly calm and are easily confined since they tend not to wander.

Chinese. As the name implies, the Chinese (or China) goose originated in eastern Asia. This breed is considered the best layer among geese. The females tend to be good setters as well as good mothers, an unusual combination in birds that lay well.

Like most good layers, the breed is lightweight, ranging from 10 to 12 pounds (4.5 to 5.5 kg). It is commonly used for meat because it's fast-growing and is an ideal size for small families. Nonetheless, Chinese goose makes a rather pathetic centerpiece for a holiday feast.

The breed is upright in carriage and has been developed in two varieties—white and brown. The latter, like the African, has a rich brown stripe down the back of the neck. It is no

Chinese

34

accident that the Chinese goose is often called the "poor man's swan," for it bears a striking resemblance to the common white mute swan. (As its name suggests, the swan goose from which the Chinese was derived has a very swanlike appearance even though it is technically classified as a goose.)

Chinese geese persistently call or exclaim in a high-pitched "doink!"—a sound some people find irritating. But this very characteristic has enhanced their reputations as watchdogs. In fact, the Chinas are probably the breed that gives geese their reputations as guardians. They are sensitive to disturbances and can appear quite fierce. Since many people are afraid of geese anyway, the tendency of Chinese to threaten intruders makes them invaluable protectors. They do attack and bite much more readily than other breeds, despite their smaller size. Among geese, it's the little guys who are the toughies. The big ones, like all bullies with and without feathers, tend to run away when their bluff is called.

Chinas are also commonly used as weeders because they are active foragers and, being fairly small and lightweight, do little damage to crops.

Also because of the relatively small size of Chinese geese, breeders experience a high rate of fertility, even when they don't provide much water for them to breed on.

Embden. The Embden, which was developed in Germany, is a large goose, sometimes weighing up to 30 pounds (14 kg) though usually closer to 20 or 25 pounds (9 to 11 kg). Due to its immense size, it is the most desirable goose for table use. Its white plumage makes it a practical meat bird, since the light-colored pinfeathers that are inevitably left on a plucked bird are difficult for a finicky diner to detect. But Embdens have the most incredibly appealing Nordic blue eyes, making them very impractical meat birds for those who already have jitters at the thought of a chopping block.

These geese are used in Europe as a perpetual source of down, but the plucking of down from live geese is considered inhumane in the United States. Though the adult plumage is pure white, the down of the goslings may show tinges of dark

35

Embden

coloring. As the yellowish green down of the newly hatched goslings is replaced by the developing feathers, spots of grey may persist, generally disappearing by the time they reach full maturity. While we don't know of anyone who has experimentally verified this, it is said that the darker-downed goslings are young females and the lighter ones are males.

Pilgrim. There is evidence that Pilgrim geese were brought over by the founding fathers of our country—hence their name. They were once quite common in early New England, so perhaps we could justifiably call them "the founding feathers" of our country. They were apparently the principal goose of the English countryside from as far back as the late Middle Ages. Weighing 12 to 14 pounds (5.5 to 6.5 kg), Pilgrims are a small breed, but on the other hand, they grow quickly and lay prolifically. They have been known to fly readily when excited or disturbed.

This breed's chief claim to fame is the unique distinction in the plumage color of the sexes. The Pilgrim gander is all white, with perhaps a trace of grey on the back, while the goose has grey coloring somewhat like the Toulouse. Older females often develop a whiteness in the feathers around the base of the bill. A gaggle of Pilgrims sometimes causes confusion for novices, who may think it's a mixed gaggle of young Toulouse and Embden.

Pilgrims can be distinguished by sex from the day of hatch on the basis of down color: the males are bright yellow while the females are a pale pea-green. The conjecture that down color in Embden goslings also varies with their sex has an interesting ramification—it supports the theory that English farmers of long ago bred the Pilgrim from the Embden of Germany by selectively breeding for ever greater down-color differentiation between the male and female young.

Pilgrim

Toulouse. In the south of France is a city named Toulouse, where this goose originated. Toulouse geese are grey in color, darker along the back and lighter in the breast, with white plumage at their lower posterior. This breed tends to be placid in disposition and has little tendency to roam. They are easy to raise, especially when ample forage is available. They

Toulouse

are an all-purpose goose, being satisfactory for both eggs and meat.

The *Standard* shows this breed to be massive in appearance, with loose feathering and a large dewlap. But geese neither as massive nor carrying a dewlap, though of the same color pattern, are also called Toulouse and are much more common in the barnyard. The *Standard* calls for a weight of 20 to 26 pounds (9 to 12 kg), but among the common strains this is rarely achieved. Apparently this goose, like the Pekin duck, tends to degenerate in size unless conscientiously bred for massiveness. To distinguish between the common grey barnyard goose and the one bred according to the *Standard,* the name Giant Dewlap Toulouse is sometimes used to designate the latter.

Additional goose breeds. In addition to these breeds, a few others are of interest to backyard fanciers though not as commonly seen. Some are kept mainly for their fanciful appearance. Among them is the Sebastopol, named for the Crimean seaport in the Soviet Union, and not the California town we live in. It is a white goose with a crinkle-cut plumage. Its wing feathers are curly and totally useless for flight. These

geese look like they got the Cinderella special from a misan-
thropic hairdresser.

Tufting is also an ornamental characteristic sometimes
bred for, and in fact nearly every breed of goose has a tufted
variety. This tuft is not as prominent as the crest on crested
ducks but is merely a noticeable bunching of feathers on the
head.

The somewhat popular Buff goose is an American sport
that shares the Toulouse's characteristics but is buff instead of
grey in color.

There are a few other breeds of geese that are often kept in
backyards, though they are not truly domesticated. Among the
most popular are the small, feisty Egyptian geese, prized for
their iridescent plumage and unusual body type, and the
celebrated "Honkers," or Canada geese of which there are a
number of kinds. Canadas require close confinement, and a
wildlife permit must be secured from the U.S. Fish and Wildlife
Service in order to keep them.

Sebastopol

CHART 2. GOOSE BREEDS

Breed	Color	Average weight	Disposition	Climate range	Average number eggs per year	Fly
African	1. brown 2. white (rare)	18–20# (8–9 kg)	moderate	mild to warm or provide shelter	around 40	may
Chinese	1. brown 2. white	10–12# (4.5–5.5 kg)	active	mild to warm or provide shelter	50 usual, but up to 100 reported	may
Embden	white	20–25# (9–11 kg)	moderate	cool	35–50	no
Pilgrim	male: white female: grey and white	12–14# (5.5–6.6 kg)	moderate	cool	20–40	may
Toulouse	grey and white	20–26# (9–12 kg)	calm	cool	35–45	no

4

Understanding your Ducks and Geese

Whatever your reason for having ducks or geese in your backyard, sooner or later you will undoubtedly decide you need some better understanding of what makes them tick. Most of their behavior, and all of the interesting part, is in one way or another associated with propagation and the attendant formation of nuptial allegiances.

Waterfowl have an incredibly complex system of social behavior. In order to appreciate fully its complexity, you must spend many hours sitting by the pond observing them. Once you are able to recognize the formalized behavior patterns, you will begin to understand their significance to the ducks and geese themselves. It is only through these simple stereotyped visual and vocal signals that they can communicate their innermost feelings. This is true for each type of waterfowl, and it is in fact true of other kinds of birds as well, though each has developed a set of communicating signals suited to its own peculiar traits.

The pledge of allegiance

Waterfowl have varying understandings of what constitutes a marriage contract, and it is important to know their biases and inclinations when organizing breeding pens. Mallards, for example, being closest to the wild, generally mate in pairs, though a drake may occasionally be persuaded to take two mates. Since a Mallard drake abandons his wife soon after she develops her motherly urges, this pair-forming must be

41

renewed each spring, and the same pairings may not necessarily be formed year after year.

Some strains of domestic Mallards mate in larger units, as do most of the mallard derivatives. This is desirable from the point of view of the breeder, since he can thereby make more efficient use of his males by spreading them around.

Most of the mallard-derived breeds show some attachment to their mates, but above all the Mallards themselves usually become very attached to one another during their short marital season. The drake stays close by his mate and will come to her defense if she is in danger or is harassed by another drake. She cools off the amorous attentions of other males that solicit her favors with her characteristic "dit-dit-dit-dit" sound and a poking of her head to one side—substitutes among ducks for wedding rings.

As short as their love lasts, it is clearly very compelling while the fires burn. One spring we lost a female Mallard in a storm accident. For several days her fiancé stood dolefully in a secluded corner of the yard, mourning his loss, oblivious to the several remaining unattached females in the yard. Eventually he decided to seek solace elsewhere, for early one morning he flew off, and we never saw him again.

We keep several breeds of ducks together during most of the year so that they may all enjoy swimming in the larger of our ponds, and we must be especially careful to separate the different breeds well before mating season commences. We usually do this in early January here where the climate is temperate so that when spring allegiances begin to form we have already exercised some control over who falls in love with whom. Should we be a little behind (which is all too often) and the ducks begin to pair off before we have separated them, we find that one or both members of a mismatched couple become useless as breeders for that season. In rapture's embrace, they pace the fence separating them, whispering sweet nothings about how cruel their people are, and napping together beside the fence, totally unmoved by the charm and allure of those of their own breed on the same side of the fence.

It happened one year that a Khaki Campbell drake fell in love with a Pekin duck. The drake got his exercise flying over the fence that separated him from his beloved, while we got our exercise that spring by catching him to return him to the Campbell side of the fence. Campbells supposedly never fly, but this fellow was an outstanding exception. It was apparently the strength of his love alone that made him capable of such super-duck feats as leaping tall fences at a single bound. Even after we relieved him of his flight feathers, the two would parade up and down the fence, talking out their woes. Since such unrequited love is nearly as traumatic for us as it seems to be for the ducks, we do our best to prevent its occurrence. These soap-opera tragedies can easily be avoided by organizing breeding pens well in advance of the pair-formation season.

Muscovies may be penned four or five females to a male; it is apparent from watching them that, unlike other domestic ducks, Muscovy drakes rarely get more sex than they can handle. Our neighbor, who is very pure, calls them "nasty, awful things" and continually entreats us to dispose of all the males and just raise the females, even though we have discreetly pointed out to her many times the impracticality of her proposal.

Muscovies do not seem to form any real nuptial allegiances. Instead, the sexes generally remain separated, or at least at formal distances from one another, until a male decides completely on his own that it's breeding time. Weighing only half as much, the targeted female has no choice in the matter, although in fact female Muscovies happen to be among the most strong-willed of creatures.

Unlike ducks, geese do not mate promiscuously. They need time to establish strong pair-bonds before breeding, so an unacquainted goose and gander should be placed together well in advance of breeding season to ensure that all eggs laid will be fertilized.

Geese generally mate in pairs, and their fidelity is much greater than that of ducks. They are commonly believed to mate for life and monogamously at that. Although this is not strictly true, it is heady and heroic stuff. The alleged fidelity of geese is so famous and so admired that people of many lands have made the goose a symbol of loyalty in their folklore and in some cases have even accorded it a central place in their sacred pantheon. In ancient China, a pair of geese was traditionally given at weddings as a symbol of faithfulness.

While geese do take mating very seriously, it isn't always monogamous nor is it always for life. Ganders may be successfully induced to take on two wives, especially if both are introduced to him at the same time. If a pair is already established before the second female is introduced, it is likely they will run her off, frustrating all her attempts to approach them. The simplest way to introduce a new wife into an already established partnership is to leave a female offspring with the pair that raised her.

While it is usually possible to remate yearling geese or adults which have not been together long, caution must definitely be exercised in attempting to split up a long-established pair, for so serious will the pair-bond have become to them that the separation may end in the death of one or both mates. Our first pair of Toulouse geese, whom we called Mr. and Mrs. Lautrec (and whom our unintellectual friends called Toulouse LaGoose), were obviously deeply devoted to one another. One day Mrs. Lautrec died in an unfortunate accident, and we found Mr. Lautrec sitting in a stupor by his dead mate. He never got over it. He languished for a couple of weeks, refusing to eat. The sorrowful gander finally wasted away to nothing and died of a broken heart.

The gander of a trio of our acquaintance suffered a long illness and finally died one night at 2:40 A.M. His owners know precisely at what hour he died, for they were awakened by the soulful and pathetic wailing of his two wives.

Poultry show managers have learned that when pairs of geese on exhibit are kept in adjacent show coops instead of being separated, the showroom no longer resounds to the calling of lonely geese who miss their mates.

A split-up pair will continue to call one another as long as they are within hearing. But once they are removed from each other's earshot, the chances become greater that in time either or both will forget the other and eventually accept a new mate. If for any reason it becomes necessary to split up a pair of geese for remating, then it is imperative to remove them totally from the sight and sound of one another, which for most backyard situations means that one must be entirely removed from the property.

Although ducks and geese lean toward the traditional heterosexual matings, they can also be terribly chic in their sexual activities. It is not at all uncommon to see two males or two females engaging in what otherwise appears to be a natural act of procreation. One of the ways that one male may establish his dominance over another is by attempting to mount the weaker drake or gander as though it were a female. Except in being less symbolic, it's the same principle as the Latin flair for driving a sword into a bull. Females also mount one another, though why they do so remains somewhat a mystery. Sometimes waterfowl actually form homosexual pair-bonds and develop the same mutual devotion normally associated with heterosexual pairings. It is not altogether unusual that one of them will take on the demeanor of the opposite sex.

Experiments have demonstrated the relative ease of turning ducks permanently homosexual. Ducklings were raised with the sexes totally separated from one another and only reunited in adulthood. These birds made no pairings with members of the opposite sex, and in fact had no social interaction at all with the other birds, seeming to regard them as a different species.

Such arrangements don't do much for the person whose primary interest is in a new crop of springtime baby birds, and they do less than nothing for the individual who is still coping with the problem of trying to distinguish between the sexes.

A goose or a duck may form an attachment to another type of animal if one of its own kind is not available. We receive

infrequent but regular requests for a mate for a lone pet duck which has formed an unnatural attachment to the family dog. But our favorite story concerns a cow and a gander that one of our neighbors kept in the same field. Much to the amusement of the whole neighborhood, the gander and the cow kept constant company, wandering the field and grazing together. The cow didn't have a lot to say but the gander apparently regarded her as a good listener, and they were the fastest of friends. When it became necessary to give the cow another home, no thought was given to the poor gander. But after the cow had been removed, the gander put up such an insistent fuss for the return of his friend that, in desperation, the entire neighborhood was driven to demand the return of the cow. When the gander saw his old sweetie coming down the road, he broke through the gate and ran in ecstasy to meet her.

As described in Chapter 11, "Bringing Up Ducklings and Goslings," young geese sometimes form strong attachments to their owners, particularly if imprinting has taken place. A local lady has a pet Chinese goose that follows her everywhere, just like a toddler. She takes him to poultry shows where he enjoys accompanying her up and down the aisles. Looking over the exhibits, he often pronounces very outspoken opinions regarding the quality of the birds on display. Be forewarned that although this kind of relationship can be fun to develop, there's no turning it off when it grows tiresome. It can become very annoying when a persistent goose just doesn't know when to get lost.

On aggression

Strong attachments between goslings and their keepers may eventually be the source of a different kind of annoyance, for the goslings grow up without fear of humans. That's fine as long as they love you. But a day may come, namely when they mate and establish a nest, when they will regard you as a threat, and in this circumstance their absence of fear of humans will make them much bolder and hence more dangerous than is normally the case. During the breeding season, when these geese choose mates and get on with hatching a family, woe be it to anyone who happens too close. The gander will come charging with neck stretched toward the intruder, hissing and

ruffling his feathers to ward off any penetration into his nesting ground. Although geese tend to be bullies, their bark is generally worse than their bite. They usually stop short of actually attacking a human, and may even run away from them. But those raised with no fear of people, or let's say lacking healthy respect for greater authority, can cause a mighty tense situation. People are often astounded that their pet goose will turn on them in this way, but it's certainly understandable that a goose would pledge its strongest allegiance to its own mate.

Though geese generally attack only when protecting their nests or their young, they sometimes attack when teased. Frankly, we have no sympathy with goose teasers, and it never ceases to delight us to see one, human or canine, surprised with a good nip.

The hissing threats with outstretched necks, so characteristic of geese, are often part of what aviculturists call the triumph ceremony. This is a ritual behavior that apparently strengthens and reaffirms the participants' attachment to one another. The gander first attacks a real or fancied intruder, then runs back to his goose with wings outstretched to tell her of his success. In celebration, the two gabble boastfully about his exploit. Goslings often join in this merrymaking, imitating the motions and sounds of their parents.

In addition to the lowered-head threat posture (one the intruder should learn to be wary of since it often indicates that a goose means business), a gander may take on another body attitude to show that somehow it has been offended: it rears its head back and stretches full height. We refer to this as the bullying stance, for the goose generally has its body partially turned and, looking at the fancied enemy out of one eye, seems to be planning a retreat with the other eye, not quite sure whether to choose fight or flight. We have found that geese assuming this posture are easily intimidated. When necessary we bully right back by charging and hissing at them until they run away. In general, the aggressions of a goose can be diverted by a good deal of hand-clapping and arm-waving. At the same

time you must run toward the aggressor, for if you are backing up he will take advantage of your insecurity.

Fighting among waterfowl sometimes occurs when new birds are put into an existing group. Often the new bird is ostracized or is chased away if it attempts to socialize with the others. Unless the bird is unhealthy, or unusual for the rest of the group (a different species, for instance), or unless a superfluous male is being introduced, the rest of the birds will in time eventually accept the new one. Young birds, especially, or those heavily outclassed in size should be watched carefully for the first days so that you can intervene if necessary.

Although ducks and geese don't exactly peck, they do nonetheless establish themselves in a pecking order of sorts, just as chickens and other birds do. Normally they do this peacefully and with dignity, especially when a flock has been raised together from the start. But sometimes there are altercations among the males, and even once in a while among the females. Reminding us of drunks at a bar, drakes may shove one another about by grabbing each other's chest feathers in their bills, or they may chase one another around. These bouts are usually inconsequential, if not actually comical. The scrapping of ganders and Muscovy drakes, on the other hand, must be taken more seriously. They may thrash each other with open wings, the same strong wings that once carried 20-pound birds on migratory flights of thousands of miles. We had a friend who tried to break up such a fight between two full-size Toulouse ganders, and she herself ended up black and blue from the beating while the ganders emerged unscathed and nearly unruffled.

Muscovy drakes have long, sharp claws as well as very powerful wings and often get fairly violent among themselves. We try to minimize this aggressive tendency by keeping no fewer than five ducks for each drake, and by giving plenty of room to bevies in which more than one drake is kept. In general, fights like this are an indication that conditions are too crowded and that some of the birds should be removed.

Though lots of people are afraid of Muscovy drakes, it is rare that they will attack a human. Somewhat of an exception to the rule, a drake we once acquired used to attack women. He never gave men a second thought, but he had an immediate and intense dislike for any woman who came into his yard. He would interrupt his activities and steam over in full battle posture, hissing and wagging his tail and craning his neck. When he was at point-blank range he would suddenly and without warning launch his attack. Needless to say, we had some startled visitors but happily no lawsuits. We never figured out the source of his selective hostility, but in all other cases we've heard of, it was clearly due to some sort of mistreatment in the early experiences of these drakes. Edgar Allan Poe would have been proud of Muscovy drakes—they really know how to carry a grudge.

The feathers on their heads rise when they are angered or otherwise aroused, perhaps to create a fearful appearance, though in principle this response is no different from the rising of the hairs on the back of your neck when something frightens you. The fearful appearance of Muscovies may be augmented by their habit of jerking their heads in and then bobbing them out. They do this when they are angry, it is true, and the frequency of the movement seems to indicate the intensity of anger. Head bobbing is also a sign of sexual interest. But the movement is repeated with such frequency in our yard without any subsequent overt expressions of either hostility or sexual arousal that we can only assume it is also a sign of recognition, or simply a pleasant way to pass the time.

Muscovies also periodically wag their tails. There is something distinctively canine about this and therefore we are glad to see it. But the emotions behind the wagging are apparently not those of a happy puppy. Tail wagging in Muscovies often accompanies mild displeasure and frequently occurs after a minor encounter has been successfully resolved. Nonetheless, we prefer to pretend that it just means they're glad to see us.

Catching and carrying waterfowl

Every owner of waterfowl has to catch them at one time or another, so it's handy to have an idea how to go about it. One of the main problems in attempting to catch ducks and geese is that they don't sleep through the night, which surprises those who have branched into waterfowl from raising chickens or other landfowl. Waterfowl sleep when they are tired and are active when they are ready to eat or play, so it is not at all unusual to find them wandering about the yard at any hour. They have no respect for those who sleep a civilized eight hours either. Nonetheless, it is somewhat easier to catch them at night, since they don't seem to move as rapidly then as in the daytime, and they don't see as well and are easily confused. It is sometimes possible to take advantage of one quirk of their nature—they will try to get away from the beam of a moving flashlight and may actually become so confused that they will walk into the source of the light. So, it is possible to guide them into a confined area by coaxing them along from behind with

51

the beam of the flashlight. If only a few individuals must be caught, it may be possible to grab them as they walk right into the flashlight.

We ourselves prefer to catch ducks or geese during the daytime because of the many trees, fences, and other obstacles in our yard in which we can get tangled up. Besides, it's easier to see the birds during the day, which is important if we are trying to sort them, such as for largest to butcher or best quality to show. If there are very few ducks or geese, and if they are used to being handled, there is often no difficulty in catching them. But in flocks of a half-dozen or more, the birds are inclined to stampede when approached.

If you can get them into a small confined area, it's easier to pick out the birds you want. We generally try to herd them into a corner where they have fewer directions in which to escape. Of course, this isn't a good idea when sorting through a large number of birds as they will trample each other. It's best to sort through small numbers at a time. For all but Muscovies, it is a simple matter to set up a corral of some sort and herd the birds into it. We have found it easier to herd them when there are at least two bird herders to help keep any from sneaking away.

Muscovies do not herd easily and are very canny about dead-end enclosures. On the other hand, they are normally less timid about people and do not run away as readily as the others. They are therefore easier for the quick and nimble to catch by the expedient of a sudden and unexpected tackle.

Ducks that can fly clearly present difficulties of a greater magnitude. It is important to move slowly and smoothly so that you won't frighten them into flight. You can tell when a duck is about to take off—it will crouch slightly just before it springs into the air. Sometimes a duck will hesitate first, and if you're quick you may be able to catch it just as it leaves the ground. If you choose to raise flying ducks you might wish to get a bird-catching net in order to try to snare the ducks in mid-flight. Another alternative is to pinion them as discussed below.

You've undoubtedly noticed how little we've said about catching your birds if they happen to be swimming in the pond at the time you want them. That's because we find this a very consternating problem, and we would be happy to hear of creative and effective solutions.

For very large ponds or very small ponds it's no problem, especially if you have a net. You go out on the large pond in a boat. You wade into the small pond with rubber boots, or you stand on the bank and intimidate the birds by shouting hysterically, waving tree branches, and otherwise conducting yourself in an uncivilized manner until the birds decide to shun your company by leaving the pond.

It's the in-between-size ponds we haven't figured out. Unfortunately, that's the kind we have.

If you are very strong, you may want to catch your duck or goose by clamping the wings down on either side of the body. The reason this takes strength is that the birds will often attempt to get away by flapping their wings, and you may find you really have your hands full. Geese and Muscovies have especially strong wings, making them difficult to hang on to.

As appalling as it may sound, the recommended way to grab waterfowl is by the lower neck. For many years we could not bring ourselves to do this but finally found that it really is the best way. After all, the neck is sticking right up there, providing a dandy handle! More to the point, the neck is very strong and tough and can withstand such treatment, even if the bird's dignity *is* slightly offended. We definitely recommend you don't catch or carry a duck or goose by its legs. People who are used to catching and carrying chickens generally grab for the legs, but it's too easy to break a leg of a duck or goose by putting pressure on it in the wrong direction.

The bird will flap its wings wildly, even when caught by the neck, so you may want to hold it away from your body to keep from getting black and blue. This is no joke; we have a friend who was beaten to a pulp by a pair of geese while she was holding one in each hand. This is one of those times when a second person comes in handy.

The most respectable way to carry a duck or goose is to hold it against you with one arm around its body to pin down its

Proper way to carry a duck or goose

wings and the other arm beneath it for support. The bird is then safely confined and cannot be injured in transit. If civility is not at issue—perhaps you're en route to the butcher block—the bird can be carried as it was caught, by the neck.

Transporting waterfowl

If you are planning to do a lot of transporting of your waterfowl, for instance to shows, then you might want to invest in a special carrying coop. This can be a small wire cage just big enough to contain one bird without crowding it, or a specially constructed wooden coop. Cardboard produce boxes aren't as luxurious as permanent carry-coops but work just fine if the right sizes can be found. Cardboard banana boxes, which have tops that slip over the bottoms and holes cut all around to let in air, are just perfect: they somewhat subdue the bird in a darkened environment and at the same time admit just enough light and air to keep the bird comfortable. Cardboard boxes are readily obtainable and easily disposed of, which solves by elimination the twin problems of finding storage room for carry-coops and having to clean them thoroughly after each use. Only one bird should be transported in each unit.

Waterfowl can also be transported in 100-pound burlap sacks. On hot days or when being taken far, ducks should be placed individually in sacks, but two or three ducks can be put into one sack for short rides on cool days. No more than one mature goose will fit easily into such a sack. These conveyances can be made more comfortable by cutting a small slit into one corner so that the bird can stick out its head and neck. The opening of the sack should be closed tightly around the body so that the goose cannot squirm around in the sack or stand up inside and try to walk around. Sacking waterfowl is not recommended for long trips or if it is important to keep their plumage clean, as when taking them to a show.

Incidentally, when purchasing waterfowl, it's a good idea to bring your own cages, boxes, or sacks for transporting the birds. Sellers are not always able to provide appropriate containers.

Geese and ducks can be transported in the backs of open pickup trucks, provided the containers are placed close to the

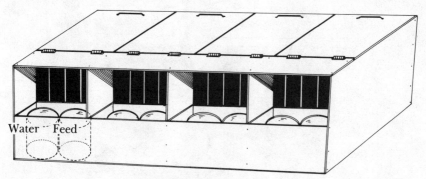

Wooden carry-coop

front where there is less draft. In cars, it is best to put them on the backseat or on the floor, and in any case caution should be exercised when placing them in a trunk: a leak in the exhaust can asphyxiate a bird.

One time some friends came on a motorcycle to pick up a duck. They insisted on taking the duck without a container, and we were certain that we would soon hear that the duck had gotten away during the ride home. The best news, we thought, would be that it had merely escaped; much more gruesome possibilities could be imagined. But as they sped down the driveway and into the street, it was apparent that the duck was ready to enjoy the trip as much as they. Riding between the driver and the passenger, and evidently enjoying the breeze, he sat gazing calmly and contentedly over the scene as he disappeared from our view.

Although some people like this idea of transporting a duck or a goose without benefit of a sack or a box, we think it's risky. The bird might become excited or frightened by unusual

surroundings and the confusion of travel and try to escape. This not only distracts the driver, who, of course, should be concentrating his fullest attention on the road, but also might cause injury to the bird. Should you nonetheless wish to carry a bird without confining it, we tactfully suggest that you at least prepare yourself with some newspapers, an old towel, or clean rags as protection against staining your clothing or upholstery. Very few waterfowl we know of have the discretion to wait for the driver to stop for gas.

Geese are fairly intelligent as birds go, and they do seem to enjoy car rides when they can see out of the window. One goose of our acquaintance was tied in a sack with its head and neck poking out of a hole as just described, and traveled on the lap of a passenger. The goose seemed quite enchanted by the view out the window and took special interest in watching pedestrians cross at intersections.

Nervous breakdown

Ducks and geese are prone to nervousness and can develop a condition akin to a nervous breakdown if unduly excited or disturbed. A bird just moping around, or that seems to be having trouble walking and instead uses its wings for mobility on land, might be the victim of such stress and its death could result. Perhaps the bird was recently excited or frightened. Nervous breakdowns can occur to ducks or geese if they are unaccustomed to being caught and carried around; if recently chased by owner or by predators; or if transported long distances, especially under unpleasant circumstances. To avoid overexciting your waterfowl, remain calm yourself, moving slowly and deliberately at all times, handling them gently, and making certain that they are comfortable in transit. If your duck or goose does seem to have been overly excited or frightened into a nervous depression, move it to a quiet, clean, comfortable area where it can relax and recover. The company of one other bird of the same kind, preferably of the opposite sex, is said to hasten recovery.

Pinioning

Many waterfowl owners are pleased when the wild birds migrating through their area are enticed by their own domestic birds to put down at the pond and refresh themselves awhile. But stories abound of such visits ending abruptly with the departure of the entire collection of birds, the stay-at-home branch of the family having apparently been persuaded to join the wanderers. This can happen suddenly, as when a pet has a love affair with a wild duck and decides to leave home to follow it during migration; or it can happen over a period of time if wild blood is mixed with domestic blood year after year through mating until the entire flock acquires the migratory instincts of the wild ones. This is one reason to pinion ducks, or at least remove a portion of the wing feathers so that they are unbalanced and cannot fly.

Ducks may fly away if frightened, especially if they are being chased either by the owner or by predators. They may also seek more comfortable surroundings if they do not like their environment, particularly if they are overcrowded. They may simply fly around, some for the sheer joy of it, others in search of greener grazing pastures, a secluded nesting place, or a neighbor's swimming pool. Pinioning can help keep neighborly relations neighborly.

Our Mallards enjoy flying test patterns in great circles around our neighborhood, landing suddenly with a great splash in the center of the pond. They seem to be congenitally incapable of flying slowly. On their first major flight many appear somewhat terrified, as if they never knew it would be so scary and aren't at all sure how to get down. At such speeds a novice flyer has a lot to worry about.

Sometimes one will take off and just keep right on going. We never see it again, and it doesn't even have the graciousness to drop us a postcard about how it's getting along. On the other hand, periodically someone else's duck flies in and joins our flock, so it all evens up in the end.

Not all stray ducks come here by air. Some are chauffeured in the family car and summarily dumped on our front lawn late at night. These orphans walk round and round our fenced yard trying to join our birds until eventually they discover our neighbor's swimming pool. Our neighbor always calls us very early the next morning, telling us to come get "our" duck.

Mallards and other small ducks are likelier to fly than the larger, more domesticated ducks. Most domestic ducks do not fly, either because of excessive weight or because of a disinclination bred into them. Muscovies are known to fly, but it is our experience that they don't fly away, they merely fly around. They are naturally arboreal and enjoy perching on rooftops and fence posts. This can be a nuisance. They may fly up to a perch and then inadvertently fly down on the other side. Or they may not like being moved to a new area of the yard and fly back to the place where they were formerly kept.

Among domestic geese only the smaller breeds can even think of flying and usually do so only when they have been excited or disturbed. Most geese like to think of themselves as fliers, however, and on windy days they may be seen standing on tiptoe flapping their wings against the wind as though airborne. In the absence of wind they may race downhill flapping and bellowing, a foot just touching the earth every few strokes. Gaggles of geese make a regular routine out of grazing slowly to the top of their yard, "flying" dramatically in such fashion to the lower end, and then grazing up again in a perpetual cycle. What could it all mean? Perhaps they are avian Walter Mittys, fantasizing about making a real migration someday.

Pinioning is accomplished by removing the last segment of one wing of a day-old bird, thereby imbalancing it when a different number of flight feathers develops on each wing. For day-old birds, the removal of the end of the wing does not seem traumatic, and the wound heals quite rapidly. It is possible to pinion older birds, but the older they get the more likely it is that the wound will bleed profusely or develop infection, and they might even die from the operation. Adult birds may be pinioned by snipping off the last segment of one wing with pruning shears or other sharp scissors. If you first tie

59

Pinioning a day-old

a tourniquet just above the part to be removed and apply a pinch of baking soda afterward, bleeding will be reduced. Pinioning older birds by this method often leaves a jagged bone that may continue to irritate the bird or otherwise cause it problems. The Philadelphia Zoo has developed a different method of pinioning older birds that they find quite satisfactory; should you have a surgical bent, you might wish to look it up in the article "Methods of Restricting Flight" included in the International Wild Waterfowl Association's book *Raising Wild Ducks in Captivity*.

If you happen to acquire a mature duck of a flying breed, you might wish to keep it completely confined. The ideal situation is a covered pen that is large enough to provide comfortable and sanitary conditions. If you would rather let it go loose, it would be a good idea to unbalance the flight feathers in order to keep the bird on the ground at least until it becomes adjusted to its new surroundings. This can be done by cutting the flight feathers short on just one wing or pulling out the first ten feathers of one wing. They come out easily and it doesn't seem to hurt the bird. Cutting is effective until the next molt, while the feathers that are pulled out will grow back fairly rapidly and must be checked relatively often.

Distinguishing the sexes

In order to ensure that breeding ducks and geese have been penned in the appropriate proportion by sex, it is important to know how to tell the sexes apart. Because the male and female Mallard plumage patterns are so radically different, any simpleton can sex them at sight with no difficulty, even if it's foggy and he's nearsighted and chewing gum. Unless, of course, it's late summer and the birds are in their eclipse plumage. At this time it is best not to rely on visual sexing, for the eclipse plumage of the Mallard drake is virtually identical to that of the female.

Fortunately, it is still trivial to sex Mallards, as long as they can be inspired to quack. The male voice is very soft and muted, a hoarse whisper, whereas the females have a stentorian quack that is raucous and brassy.

As long as the ducks are not actually in one of their two molts, it is also possible to sex them by checking for the presence or absence of the so-called drake feathers—the feathers that curl forward from the tails of drakes. Under normal circumstances, all the tail feathers on the female lie flat.

As young ducks reach maturity, their voice changes are the first clue to their sex. We receive many calls early each summer from concerned first-time duck owners who think that some of their ducks are developing laryngitis. At about two months the whistlelike peep of the ducklings gives way to the characteristic voice of the adult. For these teenagers, we usually determine their sex by catching them and attempting to make them quack in order to determine their sex. It is not until four months or so that the plumage forms are differentiated. About the same time, the curly tail feathers will show up on the young drakes.

All mallard-derived breeds can be sexed by any of the above methods, with the sole exception, of course, of the varieties in which the male and female plumage are identical, such as those that are all white. In these, the males do show the drake feather, however, and do have the muted voices, so there is still no difficulty in sexing them reliably.

Muscovies of both the white and the colored varieties have nearly identical plumage; the males lack the curved tail feather

61

that is characteristic of the mallard-derived breeds, and neither sex officially has a voice at all. Fortunately, it is still easy to sex adult Muscovies because the males are nearly twice the size of the females, and the caruncles or red warts around their eyes are generally much uglier and more prominent. In addition, the female makes a soft, musical, bubbling sound while the male's only noise is a hiss. (In honor of his rasping voice and her ladylike demeanor, we called our first pair of Muscovies Hissy and Missy.) Though Muscovy females rarely use their loud voices, they can quack like other types of ducks and do so when extremely frightened.

To visually sex maturing young Muscovies of the same age, it is necessary to wait until there is a noticeable distinction in size. In a flock of mixed ages, it is still possible to pick out the males with a little practice, since they will be long and gangly, obviously immature, and less well feathered out. Because Muscovy ducklings can peep shrilly with the best of them and are nowhere close to mute, there is theoretically some point at which a male Muscovy duckling loses his voice. But as far as we can tell, this occurs after it is already possible to sex them satisfactorily by size.

Most breeds of domestic geese are more difficult to distinguish sexually than adult ducks, for between the sexes there is very little difference in size, plumage coloration, or voice. The single exception is the Pilgrim goose, as the males are all white and the females are grey and white. For the other breeds, sexers looking at external features must rely on subtle differences in body postures and in the calls they make. The male's call is shrill and higher in pitch, while the female's voice is a sonorous tone, deeper and more relaxed. Both, however, hiss and honk sharply when disturbed or angry. Females generally carry their necks in the configuration of a question mark, while the ganders tend to walk with necks stretched tall and erect. Males generally have longer, thicker necks and larger, coarser heads, and in African and Chinese breeds their knobs tend to be larger, though these distinctions are not particularly pronounced. The goose, which is often slightly smaller, frequently precedes the gander in their strolls about the yard.

To be absolutely certain of the sex, however, you practically have to undress them. Novices and even experienced waterfowl raisers usually depend on vent-sexing when it is essential to make a reliable judgment. Because the sexes of adult ducks can generally be determined by external features as described above, it is usually unnecessary to vent-sex them, though this is possible.

To vent-sex a goose, the bird's private parts must be closely examined. The goose is turned on its back, preferably over a supporting knee or a table top, with the tail over the edge. One hand is placed on either side of the tail, the thumbs pulling against the two opposite sides of the vent while the fingers, rolling the tail slightly toward the ground, push upward from beneath to expose the copulatory organ. If the bird is a gander, his penis should unwind like a corkscrew from its protective enclosure. If a goose, the vent area will be all fancy and frilly with no one particularly obvious protrusion.

Large geese, especially those not amenable to being sexed (this includes all of them we've ever met), are best examined by two people working together, one holding the bird in position while the other does the sexing. In any case, the goose has six very sharp claws loaded and aimed directly at your face as you work, so you may wish to pay particular attention to restraining the feet.

Understandably a bird will sometimes be modest about displaying its attributes, and it may therefore be necessary to massage the area around the vent in order to relax the muscles. Insert one index finger into the vent and you will feel the sphincter muscles tighten around it. Keep up a steady counterpressure against them and you will soon tire them out, enabling you to get on with the sexing.

As tricky as vent-sexing a goose can be, there are additional complications in vent-sexing immature geese. Since the organ of a young gander is not fully developed, it is easy to confuse a female with a male whose penis simply did not get discovered.

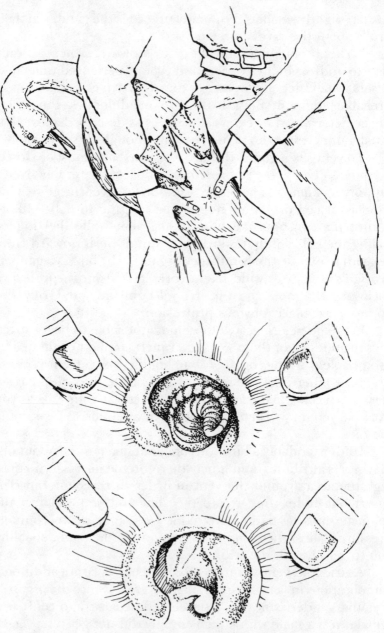

Sexing adult waterfowl

The rule is: if you see one, it's a male; if you don't, it could be either, so you'd best check again later.

Hustling our young male geese off to the butcher last Thanksgiving, we were selecting them out of the flock by size and posture and then vent-sexing as a double-check. One big bruiser showed no male organ even after we looked very hard for it, so we decided to keep "her" as a breeder in order to breed up the size of our stock. "She" ran with the older geese for several weeks and showed every conceivable social and behavioral indication of being a male. When it came time for the Christmas trip to the butcher, we checked the vent again and there was still no male organ in evidence. We ate him for Christmas dinner.

5

The Pond and Other Amenities

The pond

Of all the questions we hear from beginning waterfowl breeders, the one most frequently asked is "Don't I need a pond?" The answer to this question is not so simple. The most honest response is no, you don't really need one, but we certainly recommend a pond. They're really not as much trouble as you may think. A pond is no harder to construct or maintain than a chicken coop, and in the end it can be very much more aesthetic!

Waterfowl can get by without a pond, but there are several important reasons for providing them at least some minimal amount of swimming water: they keep themselves clean and pretty; they breed more frequently and effectively; they can endure weather extremes more comfortably; they have a better chance of evading predators; and last but not least, a pond makes them very happy.

Oh yes, and don't forget the Equal Rights Amendment. If every chicken gets its coop, then it's only fair that every duck should get its pond.

Commercial duck growers are not in complete agreement on whether swim water is necessary for raising ducks. Traditionally they have provided it, even though it's a nuisance. In recent years many commercial growers have tried to do without ponds entirely. They have had relative success and have substantially cut their costs. The current recommendation of the experts is that at least a very modest quantity of swim water should be provided, largely for general sanitation and to improve the quality of feathers so they are marketable as a by-product. Studies have shown that young waterfowl kept without benefit of swimming water gain weight less rapidly and have poorer feather growth compared to their swimming cousins.

Notice that these considerations are entirely economic. Backyarders may have other standards. A pond can be very pretty and certainly is more humane for the ducks. Our feeling is, if you can't provide a pond, you should consider raising something else. But a pond needn't be expensive or elaborate, as you shall soon see, and one is entirely within the means of the average person.

Swimming water helps waterfowl keep their plumage shiny clean. After taking a long splash bath, or even a quick swim, ducks and geese may spend literally hours preening in the sunshine while their feathers dry. This important activity helps them to reorganize feathers that have gotten into disarray and helps keep the plumage glossy and smooth. Preening serves an important function besides good looks, for it helps ducks and geese to remain waterproof. Waterfowl without swim water often become dirty and ragged and are more likely to get soaked in torrential downpours.

When a duck or a goose comes out of the water, it shakes itself off like a dog that has just come through a puddle, and flaps its wings to help remove the water. Then it begins to preen, meticulously pulling each feather through its bill to smooth it

out, and putting each in its place. During this preening, ducks and geese rub their bills against an oil gland at the base of their tails and then rub the oil over their feathers. It was once assumed that this oil makes birds waterproof, but recent investigation has suggested otherwise. It is the structure of the feathers themselves as well as their arrangement on a bird's body that causes air to be trapped between and beneath the feathers so that water cannot penetrate.

This research has, of course, left all the more perplexing the question of the function of the oil gland. One conjecture is that the oil gland is a mechanism for providing vitamin D. According to this theory, sun shining on the oil that has been spread thin over the feathers produces vitamin D, which is eventually consumed by the birds as they preen. Our own bodies obtain vitamin D from sunshine in a similar way except that, since our skin is not hidden from the sun by feathers, our glands are spread over our bodies, and it is not necessary for us to distribute secretions from one central gland.

It is known that both detergent and chlorine destroy the waterproofing of a bird's plumage. It was once assumed that these agents did so by dissolving away the oils. It now appears that they cause a slight change in the surface tension of water and allow it to penetrate more readily the fine structure of the feathers.

Preening does play a role in waterproofing a bird, not because of the spreading of oil attendant to it, but because through preening the feathers are kept properly arranged. The preening process restores the orderly structure of feathers that, through the bird's normal activities, have gotten disarrayed and thus lost some of their water repellency. Preening therefore plays more than the perfunctory role of keeping plumage pretty.

Waterfowl without benefit of swim water will stand around looking depressed and sullen, and their plumage will get ragged and unsightly. But let it start to rain and see them come to life! Even just the spray from a hose can set them frolicking like kids. Preening will begin almost at once, and in a short time they will have transformed themselves like dusty travelers after a bath.

The long hours spent at preening may suggest that waterfowl find it an enjoyable way to spend their time. Just as a cat taking a nap will suddenly awaken to give its bib a lick or two, resting ducks and geese during their one-eye-open, one-eye-shut naps will suddenly begin preening their breast feathers before tucking their heads back under a wing.

Preening also may start suddenly when two drakes or ganders get serious about pushing each other around. It seems entirely out of place in the middle of a fight, but in effect it is the loser's way of hollering "uncle." Called a displacement action by aviculturists, preening in this context helps ducks and geese avoid serious altercations. The main function of preening, though, seems to be to maintain the waterproof condition of the plumage.

Most types of geese are accustomed to breeding on water. The larger breeds find it especially difficult to mount on land and require buoyancy to give them a boost. Fertility may therefore be low in hatching-eggs if water is not available.

In areas where weather extremes can be expected, open water is helpful to the birds in maintaining their body temperatures. During hot days they like to splash in water to keep cool; where no pond is available, a simple garden sprinkler helps them to cool off, and they have fun playing in the spray. On cold winter days in northern climes, when everything else is frozen up, open water helps swimming ducks and geese keep from freezing their feet and legs. Open water is usually available on large, moving streams but can be provided in small, hand-built ponds with a circulating pond system, as described in Chapter 6, "Pond Construction." If an indoor shelter is provided for winter use, an open-water pond is not as essential for protection.

There is virtually no backyard anywhere, rural or urban, that is entirely free from every kind of predator. Though the pond isn't an all-purpose sanctuary, it does help the birds escape from some types of predation. Water is their element after all, and it is *not* the natural element of many of their predators—exceptions being swimmers such as raccoons and flyers such as hawks. If the pond is provided with an island of any kind, even a

69

floating platform or just the tip of a rock or a shallow place on which to stand, their watery world will be as fast as a moat-encircled fortress.

The argument which most impresses our questioners of the wisdom of providing a pond is that the ducks and geese themselves seem to enjoy water immensely and spend hours bathing, playing, or just floating tranquilly; their enjoyment of the swimming privilege adds to our enjoyment of them. At times their excitement rises to a peak, and they will beat their wings to send a shower of spray over their backs, then perhaps suddenly begin darting here and there, disappearing underwater and reappearing elsewhere, whirling in a kaleidoscope of color and spray. And on hot summery days it's comforting to know that our ducks and geese are placidly bobbing in green and golden waves in the cool shade of overhanging trees.

Suburbanites often ask if they might just let their ducks or geese swim in the family swimming pool. On reflection this turns out to be a thoroughly underwhelming idea. Most pool owners find it difficult enough to discourage their guests from fouling the pool, let alone an unhousebroken duck. Besides the obvious sanitary considerations, the chemicals used in swimming pools are not healthy for waterfowl.

Sometimes people ask if it is feasible to keep fish in the same pond with ducks and geese. In large, well-balanced bodies of water this may be possible, but it is unwise to keep them together in small backyard ponds. For one thing, fish are disturbed by frequent draining and cleaning of small ponds. Further, ducks foul shallow water, making it difficult for most fish to live. Unless the water is very deep, ducks and geese may keep the water too stirred up and murky for most breeds of fish, and the birds may even injure the fish with the paddling of their feet. Lastly, large fish such as bass sometimes eat ducklings and goslings, and conversely waterfowl sometimes eat small fish. One day we discovered our Muscovies had gotten into our ornamental fish pond and were thoroughly enjoying themselves, ripping up the water lilies, stirring up the bottom, and terrorizing our koi carp. After we shooed them back through the gate, one duck developed a persistent cough. Several hours later it coughed up one of our fish, which, of course, hadn't enjoyed the experience at all and was quite dead.

We once had over a hundred fish in that pond—until the day that someone, during our absence, opened the gate and let our ducks have at it. When we got home we had an uncharming little fish pond full of duck pucky and not a fish in sight.

Ideally, a waterfowl yard should have running streams or natural ponds, but alas, for most of us such luxury is an impractical dream, and we are forced to create that which nature has failed to provide. If it is your lot to create a pond for your waterfowl, we have provided explanations of several types, along with detailed directions for building them, in the next chapter, "Pond Construction."

SPACE

The unjustified notoriety of ducks and geese for being smelly is directly related to the prevalent practice of keeping them in areas that are entirely too small. One goose, a pair of regular-size ducks, or a trio of bantam ducks can be kept cleanly in a minimum area of about 13 feet (4 M) square. Of course, the larger the area the happier will be both the birds and the person who must keep the area sanitary and attractive. The more active breeds will also be happier in areas larger than the minimum (see charts in Chapter 3, "Meet the Waterfowl Family").

The best place to keep waterfowl is on a slightly sloped area that has sandy soil, since both the slope and the sand promote rapid drainage of moisture, thus keeping the area relatively free of disease-causing organisms. If the area is poorly drained, you should increase the amount of space per bird. The area should have both sun and shade so that the birds can choose a resting place most comfortable for them in the prevailing weather.

The dissipation of manure is a natural phenomenon: in the course of time it degenerates and becomes part of the soil. However, if it is being deposited at too rapid a rate onto each unit of soil, it will build up faster than the processes of time can remove it. In more crowded conditions the area soon becomes muddy and develops unpleasant odors. The misconceptions about pigs apply to ducks and geese as well—when forced to live in areas of inadequate size they will soon be wallowing in their own filth, but that doesn't mean they *like* it that way.

FENCING

Most backyard waterfowl keepers provide a fence around the area where ducks or geese are kept. This is an excellent idea, for fences keep the birds from being chased by each other or by neighborhood pets and from wandering off in search of tasty tidbits. Unlike chickens, waterfowl don't know where they live and don't come home each night to roost.

Fences also prevent dogs and cats from harassing or killing pet ducks and geese, and if suitably designed will keep out miscellaneous marauders—including wanderers-by who occasionally shoot domestic ducks and geese for sport or steal them for dinner. We have an elderly friend who watched helpless and dejected one New Year's Eve as two drunks staggered into the rain from a nearby bar, rounded up her pet geese from the puddle in which they were blissfully celebrating, and stuffed them into the trunk of their car, pleased at having so easily and cheaply come by their holiday dinner.

Ducks and geese are crafty about escaping through holes in fences but usually can't recall how to get back in, so fencing should be sound all around. The mesh need not be small unless it is important to protect vegetation growing close on the other side. Otherwise, expect vegetation to be cleared within approximately a duck- or goose-neck's length of the fence. Better yet, expect the vegetation to be cleared twice that far, since chances are an avaricious duck or goose can stretch its neck farther than you could imagine.

To keep ducklings and goslings from getting away, it is wise to add a strip of narrow gauge wire netting to the lower part of the fence. The little birds sometimes fail to heed their mama's stern warnings and sneak through fences to swim in the

72

neighbor's pool or to eat lunch on the lawn. Usually they are eaten for lunch themselves by a passing cat, drowned in the pool, or otherwise punished for their disobedience. A 12-inch (30 cm) strip of 1-inch (2.5 cm) mesh poultry netting will put an end to this.

Most waterfowl can be confined by a 3- or 4-foot (about 1 M) fence, though to protect them from predators, something more elaborate may be needed. Flying ducks can get over nearly any fence that could realistically be installed, so either they must be pinioned (see Chapter 4), or else their living area must be roofed or fenced over—quite a chore unless the area is very small. As we have noted, Mallards can spring into flight without even pausing to file a flight plan, and so are quite as capable of getting in and out of tight spots as any helicopter. Flying geese can be confidently confined in a pen open to the sky as long as the dimension of the pen is small, since these heavy birds require a long runway for take-off. In planning the height of your fence, take into account any special features of your yard, such as a particularly steep slope. The Pilgrim geese of one of our friends live on such a steep hill that they have no trouble getting sufficiently launched from the top of the hill to clear the 5-foot fence at the bottom.

Protection from predators

Domestic waterfowl have a host of enemies, and nearly everyone with ducks or geese must contend with losses due to predators, ranging from wild birds pecking holes in freshly laid eggs to raccoons doing in a mother attempting to defend her brood. The worst possible situation from a political standpoint is losing your pet to someone else's pet. Too often the owners of a dog or a cat do not take the loss of a pet bird very seriously, and in any case it is extremely unpleasant to confront a neighbor with evidence that their pet is a killer.

The best way to prevent loss to marauders is to provide secure conditions for your birds. Generally a 5- or 6-foot (150 to 180 cm) fence, with the bottom edge buried about 4 inches

(10 cm) below the surface, will keep out most predators. If burrowing animals are a special problem, discourage them by burying the fence straight down at the fence line to about 18 inches (45 cm). Coat the lower part of the fence with tar or asphalt emulsion to prevent it from rusting rapidly underground. Climbing animals can be deterred by an electrified wire around the top edge of the fence or a few rows of barbed wire at an angle to the main fence. Though a dreadful nuisance and expense, covered pens or electric fences are about the only effective ways to keep out raccoons and skunks. These animals can be a problem even in relatively built-up areas.

It is wise to be constantly on the alert for predators. Your neighbor's pets should not be allowed to wander freely about your property, for even a friendly and affectionate cat will be a likely suspect should your spring ducklings or goslings disappear. Playful dogs sometimes get a little too frisky and may innocently injure or even kill one of your birds, or they may turn into nocturnal killers and come around to perpetrate some villainy. A lot of people don't like to admit it, but domestic pets have a wild side, and often the calm and civilized Dr. Jekyll demeanor during the day will give way to a bloodthirsty Mr. Hyde streak when the moon comes up. Sad to say, even your own pet dog or cat should not be above suspicion when you're investigating homicide in your waterfowl yard. Stray pets should be reported to their owners or to your local animal control officer.

A perennial problem in trying to collect waterfowl eggs is beating the bluejays and other marauders to the nests each morning. Keeping away such egg-eaters is one good reason for providing ducks and geese an overnight shelter where they may lay their eggs in the early morning. Encouraging them to lay in hidden nests helps somewhat, but crafty marauders are often not easily fooled. We had a persistent scrub jay go after our eggs, pecking little holes in each one and making them useless for any purpose except cat food. We finally got hold of some stone eggs and placed quantities of them in the nests. The jay must have bent his beak trying to get them open, and in any case he did not bother the real eggs for several days. But eventually he learned to distinguish between the real and the fakes, for it wasn't long before we began finding holey eggs again.

You might wish to set a trap to catch egg or bird predators. A number of brands will capture animals without harming them. There is more to this than mere humane concern for wild creatures. If the predator turns out to be, for example, your neighbor's prize basenji, you will not only have certain proof of the guilt of the culprit, but you also will avoid an inevitable feud over harming the neighbor's pet. Should the culprit turn out to be your own pet, you might prefer to attempt to reform it rather than commit it to the jagged justice of a pair of steel jaws without so much as saying good-bye. Some wild animals caught in these traps are not easily dealt with, and your animal control officer may have to be called to remove the animal from the trap.

Some sources for live animal traps are listed in Chapter 16, "Resources." The traps generally come in a number of sizes, but if you do not wish to invest in a whole line, there is usually one that makes a fair compromise, suitable for most common enemies including raccoons, skunks, and scrub jays. The type of bait to use depends on the taste of your local predators. Each type of marauder has its own culinary preferences, so some amount of experimentation may be necessary before you learn what treats successfully lure your particular predators. Obviously eggs provide suitable bait for egg-eaters, but fresh or canned corn is also often used. Some animals will require a live bird as bait, while others are satisfied with a peanut butter sandwich on whole wheat.

What you do with your wildlife once caught is another question, and we'll leave that to your discretion. Please don't send any to us. It may be possible to donate such an animal to a museum or zoo, or to a local university or other school interested in wild animals. One beleaguered friend of ours just heaves the trap into his pond when no one is looking. Some people take the trap to remote areas to release the offending predator where it will presumably do no harm, but remember that animals have strong homing instincts. You may think you are ridding your area of enormous numbers of raccoons, for instance, when in fact you are simply giving the same raccoon the enjoyment of periodic rides in your car and the exercise of trotting back home again after each ride. A friend who lives on the west bank of a large river releases trapped raccoons on the east side of the toll bridge because he knows that they can't pay the toll to get back across. (One day at an auction we overheard a man from the east bank telling his friends that he always takes the raccoons he catches over to the west bank to release them because he knows they can't pay the toll to get back!)

Shelter

Waterfowl are remarkably immune to inclemencies in the weather. They're not sissy birds like chickens, and they certainly don't need a full-fledged coop. But some sort of protection is advisable in the event of extreme conditions. In those areas where nighttime predators are plentiful, you might wish to provide a sound but simple building in which to confine your ducks and geese at night. This may be as necessary in big cities as it is on isolated farms. Enterprising skunks or worse have been known to wander into town, and a big-city friend tells us that one day a puma came up through the sewer line near his home! During the day, a shelter can provide shade from scorching sun or protection from cold, wind, storms, or heavy snow.

If you are lucky enough not to have spells of intensely cold weather or marauder problems, all that's needed is a simple low roof on four posts, with a thick layer of litter for the birds to sit on. A windbreak can readily be provided by adding a row of shrubbery or a few stacked bales of straw.

Should you decide that predators or weather make an enclosed shelter necessary, it need not be larger than 6 square feet (.6 sq. M) of floor space per duck and about 10 (1) for each goose. For only a pair or trio of birds, a small shelter with a low roof is both inexpensive and easy to keep clean. If the floor space must be larger, raise the roof so that you can easily enter and exit when cleaning. The floor may simply be hard-packed dirt; smaller shelters can thus be moved to a clean area when the floor gets dirty. The floor in a larger shelter may be made of concrete to facilitate hosing out periodically. Remember that while adequate ventilation is a necessity in a waterfowl shelter, it is equally important to be sure that birds can avoid heavy drafts.

Use a thick layer of good litter on the floor to help keep the building clean, whether birds are confined for long periods or just overnight. Litter helps absorb not only water spills but also moisture from droppings; waterfowl droppings are much less cohesive than those of chickens and may be up to 90 percent liquid. Fresh litter helps to keep eggs clean that are laid inside the shelter. Litter should be a durable material that does not pack easily and that dries out quickly when wet, such as straw, pine needles, peat moss, wood shavings, sawdust, rice hulls, peanut hulls, and a host of things perhaps more readily available in your area. Litter is easily removed and replaced as it becomes soiled. Fouled litter should be exchanged before it becomes moldy, as it may cause sickness.

To keep the shelter from becoming messy and unsanitary, feed and water should not be provided during nighttime confinement. It's especially critical not to provide feed when water is unavailable, since the birds tend to choke on dry grains or pellets. But they really don't need feed or water at night anyway, and if they have water they'll just play in it and make a mess.

If ducks and geese are kept inside at night, it is likely that most of their eggs will be laid in the building, since it is their custom to lay at dawn's early light. Eggs can then be gathered inside the building in the morning after the birds are let out for breakfast. Provide nesting boxes as described in Chapter 8, "The Golden Egg."

Waterfowl tend to be restless at night, and they will be active inside the building. Unlike some other types of domestic birds, they do a lot of their sleeping during the daytime and are

77

as fully awake at night as any other time. Since moonlight makes them particularly restless and noisy, the shelter should be built so that moonbeams can't shine in. Strange lights, such as shafts of moonlight, streetlamps, and back-porch lights, confuse and frighten ducks and geese at night and they may mill around or even stampede and injure themselves. An alternative to a complete blackout is to run some low-wattage bulbs in the shelter at night, arranged so as to avoid any casting of shadows.

Waterfowl don't do well indoors and should not be confined longer than necessary. But there are regions where the climate is severe enough to mandate keeping birds confined for several days during long cold spells. The shelter should then be somewhat larger and equipped with feeders and waterers of a design that will keep mess to a minimum. We describe types of feed and water containers in Chapter 7, "Feeding Your Ducks and Geese."

Where freezing weather is common, heat should be provided in the shelter so that the temperature drops no lower than 32°F. (0° C.). On no account should the building be warmed to more than 45° F. (7° C.), as otherwise the birds may catch cold when let outside again. South-facing windows of glass or clear plastic will let in winter light and help keep the building warm. You might install an infrared brooder lamp in the center of the building, far enough away from any source of water not to get splashed and high enough above the litter not to be a fire hazard—at least 18 inches (45 cm). The birds will have freedom to move closer to or away from the heat as they desire. Of course, any such heat source necessitates running electricity to the building.

You may find that your ducks or geese are reluctant to go in at night. Like mischievous children, they can delight in giving you trouble at bedtime. Two people and lots of psychology may be necessary to outwit them. You may wish to arrange fences so that the birds are funneled through the door when herded in that direction.

But ducks and geese may be entirely unpredictable in this matter. A friend of ours, returning home unusually late one night, expected to have the devil's own time rounding up her ducks and geese in the dark. After unsuccessfully searching the yard for them, the only place left to look was their nighttime shelter. There she found them snugly bedded down and wondering what was taking her so long about shutting the door.

6

Pond Construction

Types of ponds

Of the many kinds of ponds used for backyard ducks and geese, some are elaborate and time-consuming, while others are quick and inexpensive.

The simplest way we know to create a pond is to acquire a plastic kiddy wading pool (the hard plastic kind—the soft plastic is too easily torn), or an old-fashioned galvanized washtub, or even just an old dishpan, and bury it in a hole in the backyard. These are relatively common, particularly for just a pet duck or two, and install easily. Such ponds do have some obvious drawbacks, however, and we really don't recommend them except as a temporary measure. They require frequent scrubbing with a brush or broom to remove algae clinging to the inside walls, and dumping the water for cleaning can be a real chore. If your tub is small enough to pick up and dump, you probably have an overcrowding problem, as anything you could lift that's full of water is certainly too small for more than one duck. Some of the larger portable pools have drain plugs for rapid cleaning. Something of the sort is almost essential. If there's no plug you may have to rig up a siphon.

When we moved into our present home there was a duck pond in the yard consisting merely of a shallow hole formed by the large root system of a wind-felled tree. The dug-out dirt had been packed around the sides to form banks. This pond taught us a few of the thousand-and-one reasons why dirt ponds don't work. Since ducks like to dig in soft dirt with their bills, the copious holes they drilled along the edges needed constant patching. To make matters worse, whenever we had a rainstorm we could invariably expect overflow to wash part of the bank

80

away, not only creating a long afternoon's work for us, but also taking away more and more of the fast-disappearing banking soil. Ironically, the only practical way to clean the pond was to let the water out by chopping away a part of the bank. Like Sisyphus pushing his rock up the hill and watching it roll back down again, we spent countless hours redigging the pond and shoveling dirt out of the center that the ducks had managed to drag in from the edges.

We knew for a long time that someday we would have to find a better solution. The final impetus was provided by our first goose, an immense gander we named King Tut for his regal bearing and his propensity for bossing our ducks around. The first thing King Tut did on entering our yard was head straight for the pond. He waded across, pausing every few moments as if expecting to be able to lift his feet and begin swimming. He couldn't believe it was taking so long to reach deep water. After he had waded the full length of the pond, he turned around with an indignant sneer as if to say, "You call *that* a proper pond?" and pompously stalked off to check whether the rest of his new accommodations were of any higher class. So, on top of all the other problems we had with our little backyard pond, we now learned that it was too shallow for geese. Since it would have been impossible to maintain a deeper dirt pond with manual labor, we had no choice but to build a concrete one. This is the kind of pond we recommend and will shortly describe in detail.

For those who are unconvinced and want to give dirt a whirl anyway, we would at least suggest reinforcing the soil with a bit of cement. Mix about one part of cement to five parts soil, wet the mixture, and put it into place. Though this construction will not withstand great stress and will need periodic renewal due to weathering and traffic, it may be satisfactory until you decide you really ought to have a proper concrete pond.

A slightly more permanent compromise between dirt and concrete is a sandbag levee. Fill 25-pound sandbags with a mixture of dry sand and cement in about a five-to-one ratio. Pack the bags into place starting with a layer several bags wide at the bottom and tapering up to a single bag. Overlap the bags so each is cradled in the pocket formed by the bags beneath it. Soak the bags thoroughly with a fine mist as they are put into place. After a few days the concrete will harden in the bags and you will have a pretty solid semipermanent wall.

ACCESS

When planning a pond, it is essential to keep in mind the ease with which the birds can get in and out of water. Many ducklings and goslings, as well as their full-grown relatives, have drowned because they could not get out of the water. Bereaved duck owners have exclaimed that their ducks should have been able to get out of the water since they somehow managed to get into it all right. But it isn't so. A bird may have enough energy to spring or fly into an elevated pond and then become so thoroughly waterlogged and exhausted in searching for the exit that it cannot spring back out. Farmers who provide big tubs of

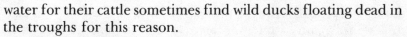

water for their cattle sometimes find wild ducks floating dead in the troughs for this reason.

The best plan is to make the sides of your pond gently sloping. If it is not possible to eliminate steep or slick sides so that the birds get in and out with ease, then provide a ramp of some sort, like the entrance to a freeway or a football stadium. It is as important to provide a ramp out of the pond as to provide one into it. Ramps should be no steeper than a quarter of a right angle, about 22½° to the horizontal, and should be covered with a nonskid material. Boards get slippery when wet, so thin slats should be nailed crosswise at intervals to provide a foothold.

Keeping it clean

Another important consideration when planning a pond is the ease with which it can be cleaned. Ducks and geese not only drag a lot of dirt into the pond with them, but they also do not have any discretion about fouling their own waters. Thus, it may not take long for a pretty little pond to turn into a cesspool.

The frequency of cleaning depends on how big the pond is and on how many birds are kept in it. Some people clean theirs daily, others once a year. No human intervention is required to keep free-flowing water or larger lakes clean. Nature, of course, has been successfully solving the contamination problem for millions of years, partially with the help of running water but also with the help of the various natural prophylactic agents that in their own time will keep clean any body of water not too badly fouled through overcrowding. These agents will be working on your side too, and the larger your pond volume per bird, the greater proportion of the burden they will assume. Deep water stays cleaner, but even it will foul in time if the pond is over-crowded.

If you're fortunate enough to have access to running water you should take full advantage of it. Contrive to use it to flush and fill your pond periodically, as does a friend of ours who has a small live creek flowing through his property. He has built a dam for his ducks and geese, and all he has to do to clean out the pond is pull the plug to let out all the water. Then he closes off the dam to let it fill again with fresh, clean water. He thus prevents sediment buildup from both the deposits of the stream itself and the daily activities of his flocks. We do have to caution you to check with your local authorities before proceeding with such plans, as there are usually restrictions of various sorts on your right to divert or pollute the water if this will adversely affect users downstream.

If you're among the majority who don't have the felicity of flowing water, you will have to find another solution to the drainage problem. Before we talk about getting the water out of the pond, let's have a brief think about where you're going to put it when it's out. The worst place to put it is on the neighbor's patio. But it's almost as bad to let it run into the gutter or storm sewer, for in truth you've got a precious commodity there, and it's a shame to let it go to waste. If at all possible you should run it onto your garden. The water from a pond is excellent fertilizer for gardens or lawns, and we use it to keep our young fruit trees irrigated in the summertime. Planning a garden close to the pond is ideal, for the water could be continually used to irrigate and fertilize the vegetables or flowers. The clean water you would normally have irrigated your garden with can instead be added continuously to freshen the pond.

There are essentially three methods of getting the water out of the pond and into the garden, or wherever you decide to put it. In order of desirability they are: drain it, siphon it, and pump it. If you must locate your pond in a low area, you may have no choice but to pump it; if your pond is high enough, you should be able to drain or siphon it. Siphoning is a big pain and not really efficient in cleaning sediment out of the bottom, so if at all possible a drain should be built in. An appropriately located drainage ditch could channel the water and flush out sediment to a location where it would do the most good.

In case you didn't or couldn't build a drain and instead have to rely on a siphon, here's how it works. Place one end of a garden hose in the pond and the other end where you want the water to run out. Then get another hose that's connected to a faucet. Turn it on and, holding it against the submerged end of the siphon hose, force water into the siphon hose until it starts to come out the other end. Turn off the faucet and your siphon should be functioning. You can check for steady flow at the outlet to make sure.

It doesn't matter to a siphon where the hose goes between its two ends. The siphon will work as long as the outlet end of the hose is lower than the surface of the water. The greater the height separation, the faster the flow. If the water level lowers to the height you are siphoning to, the flow will stop.

It does matter that the inlet end of the hose doesn't clog up with debris from the pond. If there's much at the bottom, make sure the hose opening isn't in it. This makes it hard to get the last little bit of water out, but that's hard anyway. You usually have to do it by hand-holding the hose like a vacuum cleaner, just below the water surface.

If you wish, you can put a filter over the siphon hose, and you definitely need one over your intake hose if you're using a pump. Just take a small piece of window screen, fold it over the end of the hose, and secure it with a hose clamp from a hardware store. It's better if it bulges out a bit so there's lots of screen surface for the water to move through, making it less likely that the screen will become completely clogged by debris.

Size

When planning the size of your pond, don't forget to allow for future expansion in your waterfowl empire. You may be in a lot deeper someday than you intend right now—and concrete ponds grow *very* slowly.

If frequent draining is a practical possibility, 12 inches (30 cm) is deep enough for ducks and twice that for geese. These figures are minimal, however. In a deeper pond, bottom sediments won't be continually stirred up, and the water will remain cleaner longer. The pond should be large enough that the birds are not crowded when all are swimming together. For deeper ponds, 25 square feet (2.5 sq. M) of surface area should be

provided per duck and twice that per goose. The shallower the pond, the more surface area will be required.

For ducks there is an advantage in having a pond that is no deeper than 18 inches (45 cm). The mallard-derived breeds are dabblers and so like to up-end and dig around in the bottom sediment. They may not find anything—ever—but they do it anyway. Where the pond bottom is firm-packed rather than soft and squishy, ducks enjoy up-ending for small amounts of whole grains tossed in once a day. We made our pond in two sections, with a submerged berm separating a small shallow area for dabbling from the larger, deeper section designed for general splashing around.

Making your own

While there are firms specializing in backyard pond-building, we felt that it would be great fun and less expense to make our own. You may be put off at first, as we were, by the thought that building a concrete pond must be a challenging and formidable task, and probably a great expense besides. It need not be any of these. Our pond is 30 inches (75 cm) deep and an irregular shape about 30 feet (9 M) long and 20 feet (6 M) wide. It cost less than a day at Disneyland and took only one Saturday's work by a committee of our friends, whom we bribed with free pizza and beer. Once you understand the principles involved you will be able to design an artful and imaginative pond whose size, shape, and mood are tailored to fit perfectly into your particular backyard. And if you make your pizzas with lots of pepperoni, our friends will be right over to help you.

On looking into it, we discovered that large concrete basins are expensive and tricky, as they require technical skill and know-how. Adequate thickness and proper reinforcement are required to prevent cracks due to ground movements that always accompany the changing of the seasons. Therefore, we chose to make only the banks of concrete. Such a structure is much less sensitive to stress from ground movements and is therefore easier to build. Only the edges of a pond really need concrete, to withstand the constant traffic in and out of the water. Nonetheless, the bottom must be effectively sealed and the sealing layer protected from gnawing rodents from below and prying bills from above.

Of course, a *small* pond can just as well be built in one solid piece without serious complications. Even a larger one can be built in one piece as long as there is proper reinforcement in the concrete.

We began our pond by digging a basin and piling the dirt in a berm around the edge for additional depth. Building the banks above ground level prevents ducks and geese from dragging dirt into the pond and also from bringing lots of water back out with them and causing the surrounding area to be perpetually muddy. Raised banks also clearly solve the problem of what to do with all the dirt you get out of the hole.

We dug about 6 inches (15 cm) deeper than the finished pond would be; this allowed room for the concrete, wire, reinforcement, sealing, and so on. After we had laid all pipes, we banked dirt around the edges, sloping it to an angle of about 22°, and then began installation of the bottom.

The bottom of the pond can be made of anything tough that holds water as long as it is protected from gnawing rodents by a layer of wire. We've even heard of old carpets or carpet remnants being used, hopefully not by anyone expecting a very tight seal. A trip to the dump should suggest lots of imaginative possibilities if you're not too fussy about a bit of leakage. We chose thick polyethylene construction plastic, but polyvinyl chloride (PVC) sheets are now available and are reportedly much tougher than polyethylene. Another fine alternative is roofing felt sealed with asphalt emulsion or hot pitch, which is probably sturdier and easier to clean. Hot pitch makes a good, tight, long-lasting seal but is a nuisance to apply. The asphalt emulsion is much more easily handled, since it is cold and spreads with a putty knife or paintbrush. It is sold in hardware stores as a general-purpose waterproofing material.

Before installing this sealing layer, we covered the bottom with 1-inch (2.5 cm) poultry wire mesh. This was a precaution against any attempts by gophers to chew through the bottom of the pond. A recent neighborhood incident inspired this last-minute addition: incautious gophers had chewed kamikaze-style through someone's large water-filled plastic swimming pool, and the neighbors were bailing out their basement for weeks. Coating this protective wire layer with tar or asphalt emulsion will help keep it from rapidly rusting away.

The wire was brought partway up the edges of the banks all around. It was overlapped and fastened together with baling wire where two pieces came together. Then a thin layer of dirt

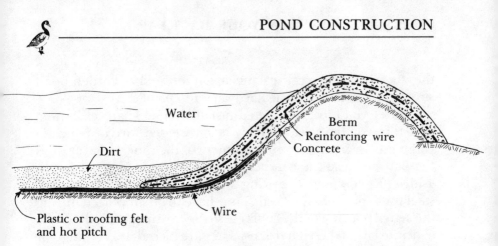

Water

Berm
Reinforcing wire
Concrete

Dirt

Plastic or roofing felt
and hot pitch

Wire

was spread over the wire to form a smooth foundation for the sealant. The construction plastic or roofing paper (or whatever) should be laid down next. If plastic is used, purchase a piece big enough to cover the pond with one sheet. Roofing felt should be overlapped well and waterproofed with hot pitch or several coats of asphalt emulsion according to directions on the label.

As an alternative to the sealing layer, a backyard pond builder may want to consider the recently developed chemical soil sealants. These compounds make it possible to use nothing but raw dirt as the bottom of a pond. The sealants are dissolved in the pond water, and over a short period of time they seek out the tiny pores in the soil and fill them in, very much the way automobile radiator sealants do. The permeability of soil may be reduced 85 to 95 percent by this technique. Such sealants should be used only on soil that has some clay or adobe content, as otherwise the results will not generally be satisfactory. If the chemical sealant option is chosen, it becomes even more critical to protect the bottom of the pond from gnawing rodents by installation of a wire barrier.

Should your pond develop leaks later on, you might want to try patching them with this type of chemical sealant. You just pour it into the pond and gradually it finds the leaks and seals them up. If you're in a hurry, it is necessary to put in a heavy dose. The birds should be removed while it's working, and the water must be drained and replenished before they are put back. If you're not in a hurry, use a light dose and it will be safe to leave

89

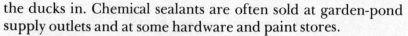

the ducks in. Chemical sealants are often sold at garden-pond supply outlets and at some hardware and paint stores.

After you have completed installation of whatever bottom structure you have selected, lay heavy welded wire of 2-inch (5 cm) mesh, or finer, for reinforcement of the concrete all around the banks where the concrete will be poured. Alternatively, a 1-inch (2.5 cm) poultry netting would do. For extra reinforcing, steel rods could also be used. They have to be supported during the actual pouring of the concrete so they are in the middle of the concrete layer when it hardens. They are placed in a rectangular grid and should be bent if necessary to fit the contour of the pond. Reinforcing rods are essential only if the concrete extends across the entire pond bottom.

Finally, you're ready for the concrete, which is the biggest part of the job. Here is where we got by only with a little help from our friends. We rented a cement mixer and had a small load of sand and gravel delivered. The top of the bank should be covered with a 2-inch (5 cm) layer tapering out to a 5-inch (12 cm) layer at the base.

As the banks are built up all around, and as the concrete work is being finished, it's important to keep testing for level edges. After the pond is filled, irregular spots will show up all too plainly, but while the pond is still under construction the eye can be fooled. In fact, it can be *very* fooled, especially if the terrain happens to be sloped. A friend who didn't know this now has 18 inches (45 cm) of high and dry bank on one side of his pond to prove our point. To keep things plumb, periodically lay a thick plank across the top of the banks with a level resting on it.

Concrete takes several days to cure completely and must be pampered a bit in the meantime so it won't crack. This involves spraying it with a fine mist several times a day until it is thoroughly dried. Also, it must be given a sealer coat to make it fully waterproof, as concrete is otherwise somewhat porous and water seepage is fairly rapid. It is easy to make up a sealant. In a pail, mix a thick paste out of water and pure cement—don't put in the sand and gravel used in making concrete. Paint this mix-

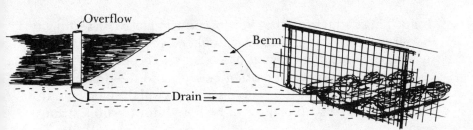

ture over the inner surface of the pond with a large paintbrush once each day for three successive days following the initial pouring.

We provided our pond with a drain by burying a 4-inch (10 cm) pipe in the ground, running it under the bank and terminating it at the deepest point in the pond with a right-angle elbow joint. This large a drainpipe is sufficient to allow muck and debris to flush through it easily. We must admit that so large a metal pipe is very expensive, and we only used it because we had it lying around. You could probably make do with a piece only half the diameter. Better yet, get a section of 4-inch (10 cm) PVC (polyvinyl chloride) pipe; it will be much cheaper and just as satisfactory.

In our pond, a 30-inch (75 cm) section of pipe is screwed into the upward-facing end of the elbow joint to serve as a combination drain plug and overflow. We used a much narrower pipe for this piece and adjoined it to the elbow by means of a reducing bushing, available at most hardware stores. The bushing is unnecessary if your overflow pipe and your drainpipe are the same size. The overflow pipe comes to 2 inches (5 cm) below the lowest edge of the pond so that when it rains the drain serves as an overflow. To drain the pond, the overflow pipe is simply unscrewed with a large pipe wrench that's extended with a piece of pipe if extra leverage is necessary.

To ensure against leakage, we took special care to seal the drain outlet when the concrete was being poured. Some people leave the overflow pipe off while finishing the pond, but then concrete or other building debris must not be allowed to plug the drain. Those who leave the overflow pipe in place risk sealing it in permanently. Professional plumbers get around this by stuffing the opening with rags or a bit of old carpeting.

If the pond is drained often enough and the drainpipe is large enough, most of the bottom sediment will flush down with the water. Any that remains can be hosed down with a strong spray.

When the sediment has been accumulating for a long time and is too thick to go through the drain, an alternative is to let it dry several days in the hot sun, until it is just thick enough to stay on a shovel; then scoop it out into a wheelbarrow and delight your vegetables with it. Bottom sediment can be used in the garden, around fruit trees, or added to compost. A flat blunt-edge shovel should be used for muck removal so that the sealing material won't be damaged during cleaning.

Landscaping

Birds need shade to loll beneath during hot summer days in warmer regions. The shade of trees or thick brush shrubs will also help keep down algae growth in the water.

Vegetation around the pond does provide a nice landscaping touch, but keeping it there can be difficult. Ducks and geese relish almost any kind of greens, though waterfowl keepers have reported success in maintaining hardy pampas grass, various types of bamboo, and low-growing juniper and yews. Even trees planted around the pond for shade are not safe from avaricious waterfowl, for they gnaw at the bark of young trees. Geese are especially villainous on this point and can completely girdle and kill a small tree in just one golden afternoon. Newly planted little ones should have wire guards around them to protect the tender and tasty bark until toughened by a few year's growth. Before we knew this, we failed to protect a pretty little apricot tree planted in the orchard where we kept our first geese. The geese were apparently critical of our meticulous pruning job and rearranged things by shredding the tiny limbs to a frazzle.

Trees should not be planted so close to the edge of the pond that in years to come they will push against the concrete and cause it to crack. Even at a reasonable distance their roots will probably find the water that inevitably seeps through the bottom. But that's okay—it's there to be drunk and they will flourish. Deciduous trees should not be planted where their branches will hang over the edges of the pond, for the leaves they drop each year will have to be cleaned out.

Decaying vegetation in the swim water may cause a serious problem. Ducks and geese are sometimes poisoned by toxins associated with decomposing animal or vegetable material. To guard against this eventuality, be sure that the pond water is kept fresh and renewed, and that any organic matter that has fallen into the water is promptly removed. We discuss this matter more fully in the section on symptoms of trouble in Chapter 14, "Disease and Other Perils."

Attempting to landscape around the pond is frustrating enough, but trying to keep aquatic vegetation growing in small ponds is even more difficult. Most of the common water plants are considered a gourmet's delight by ducks and geese. What they don't actually eat they usually manage to uproot. Water plants may grow in very large ponds with very few birds, but not many backyard pond-builders have been successful in keeping water plants and waterfowl together.

Elegant touches

To fill the pond, you can get by with as simple a system as running a hose into it from time to time. However, you may prefer something more permanent as well as fanciful. To fill the pond in an elegant manner, and to provide a plaything for the birds, we installed a fountain. It's nothing more elaborate than an old gas jet! When our water is on full force it sprays high into the air, creating a dramatic shower which helps cool overheated ducks and geese during the summer. Different spray patterns can be arranged by altering the position of the

93

stopcock. Others we know have used showerhead nozzles. They are cheaply and easily obtained, and various types create different patterns of spray. Fountain heads with an elaborate assortment of fancy sprays can be purchased for fancy prices. Several sources for these formal fountains are listed in Chapter 16, "Resources."

To ensure the the availability of drinking water, incoming water is supplied to some ponds by way of a trough that fills and overflows into the pond, providing fresh, clean, drinking water as it slowly renews the swimming water. Even with a fountain, a shallow bowl fastened beneath the nozzle will collect clean water during times when the fountain is left on slow drip rather than full force.

Of course, for a perpetually elegant-looking pond, a recirculating pump can be used to keep the fountain going constantly without drawing new water and overflowing the pond. In areas where the pond might freeze in winter, a recirculating pump additionally helps keep the swimming water ice-free. A system like this need not be expensive. We use a retired swimming pool pump with a good filter.

The recirculating pump can be installed in a box in some out-of-the-way place where it will be protected and unobtrusive, but accessible for service. Cover the intake pipe with a screen to filter debris. The pipe should be relatively low in the

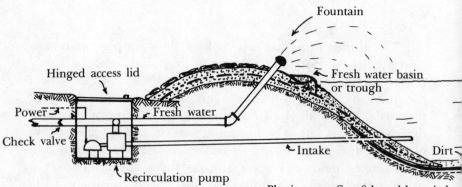

Fountain

Hinged access lid

Fresh water basin or trough

Power

Fresh water

Check valve

Intake

Dirt

Recirculation pump

Plastic or roofing felt and hot pitch

pond but not down where the muck accumulates. Bury the power cable to the pump and protect it according to code. You can install an on-off switch in this power line at some convenient point.

The recirculating system can be independent of the inlet system if you wish. In this case the recirculation should go to the fountain, and the inlet arrangement can be plain and unromantic. If you connect the two, be sure to install a check valve in the inlet pipe before it reaches the recirculating system junction so pond water is not mixed with your domestic water supply.

Whether or not a recirculating system is used, it's handy to use a float valve to admit new water when the pond level gets low. Of course, you can manually turn on the faucet when necessary and dispense with the float valve. But it's just one more thing to have to think of, and the float valve is easy to install. You can use the mechanism from a discarded toilet tank. Since ducks and geese love to pick plastic apart and otherwise ravage the works of man, it is necessary to protect the float valve by installing a cover over it. Build one if you're handy or improvise with a wooden crate.

An island is a nice addition to the pond. Placed in the center it seems to attract the waterfowl, who enjoy standing to preen or nap in the sunshine, as well as tormenting their

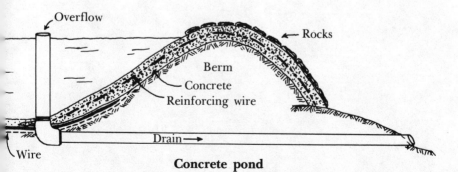

Concrete pond

nonswimming predators. An island of sorts can be created by placing a large rock in the center of the pond or by anchoring a small raft there. Wide ledges around the banks or a platform at the top of a ramp also provides favorite resting spots for ducks and geese.

If you'd like to have a pond that is some other color than cement grey, you can add a bit of stucco dye to your waterproofing mixture. We used brown in ours to give it the color of earth and preserve the illusion that the pond was constructed of natural materials. The natural look was enhanced by some large river rocks we had collected and distributed all around the perimeter of the pond. As the concrete was poured and patted into place, the Perimeter Beautiful Committee squished the rocks into the outer bank.

7

Feeding your Ducks and Geese

Elsewhere in this book we discuss young waterfowl, waterfowl for eggs, waterfowl for breeding, waterfowl for meat, and waterfowl for show. There are special feed considerations for each of these cases, but we have gathered all the information on feeding into this one place to make it clearer and more easily understood.

Unfortunately, not enough is known about the nutritional needs of ducks and geese. Most of the research has been done by two groups: the industry that produces ducklings, largely centered on Long Island, and conservation organizations interested in perpetuating wild waterfowl. The latter is of little help to us, for there is a great deal of variation in the natural diets and nutritional requirements from species to species among waterfowl. Even within one species, at the same season and within a few miles of each other, wild waterfowl have been found to be thriving on totally different diets. Thus it may not be reliable to extrapolate from wild waterfowl to domestic, and vice-versa.

We can at least get the broad perspective from nature, however. Examinations of the crop contents of wild ducks have shown that a mallard's preferred diet consists of 90 percent vegetable matter. That they are partial to wheat, barley, oats, and buckwheat can be attested to by the prairie grain farmers of the midwestern United States and Canada, on whose crops great flocks of these birds stage mass raids each fall. The remaining 10 percent of their diet is animal material, largely consisting of such tasty tidbits as mosquitoes in any stage of their life cycle, as well as occasional worms, snails, bugs, and flies.

Though the animal fraction is small, it is evident from watching them that they relish this part of their diet, for they certainly can go through a lot of trouble to get it. You may think your ducks have gone crazy the first time you see them chasing flies. With heads lowered and necks outstretched low along the ground, they dart about in an attempt to follow the erratic flight of buzzing summertime flies that your eyes can barely discern.

Muscovies are more omnivorous than mallard-derived domestic ducks and rank as the most avid eaters of slugs, snails, and other garden pests. We related in Chapter 3 the story of our grandma Muscovy, Missy, who once ate a nestful of baby gophers which our shovel had accidentally dug up. Like other types of ducks, though, Muscovies are primarily vegetarian.

One of the distinctions between ducks and geese is in the refinement of their respective bills. A duck's bill is designed for probing muddy pond banks and picking up tasty bits from the surface of the water and below, while the bills of geese are designed largely for clipping and tearing terrestrial vegetation during grazing. Geese are almost totally herbivorous and for this reason can be very inexpensive to keep as long as adequate grazing area is available. Though they will eat grains, their favorite foods are succulent grasses and greens including lettuce and other salad ingredients.

Although the information on waterfowl nutrition that has been gathered by the Long Island duckling industry will be of some help to us, it is not as relevant as one might guess. Commercial raisers of ducks and geese presumably require a feeding program that will produce fast economic growth, and consequently this is the area about which most is known.

Of course, one of the purposes of having waterfowl in your backyard is for meat, and the lessons of the Long Island duck industry will be useful. There are other purposes for raising waterfowl, however, and they mandate other types of feeding programs. Birds raised for eggs should not be grown too rapidly, and layers require a diet commensurate with the drain on their systems imposed by their egg production. Breeders have these same dietary needs but in addition require extra vitamins and minerals vital to the health and vigor of the young birds that will hatch from their eggs. Waterfowl raised specifically for show have still different needs. Some breeders have developed feeding programs that foster the proper size and shape for their breed, the finest plumage with the richest hues, and so on. No wonder there is some confusion about feeding programs for ducks and geese—there are perhaps as many different waterfowl diets as there are waterfowl owners.

Since domestic waterfowl cannot migrate in order to find the foods required to satisfy their nutritional requirements, these must be met by providing them the many vitamins and trace minerals necessary for adequate growth, for maintenance of health and vigor, for reproduction capabilities, and to prevent a host of nutritionally related ailments.

Besides the fact that research is incomplete, and that fowl raised for different purposes require different menus, there is still a third level of complication: the nature of the feeds that are available to you for purchase or that grow naturally in your yard, and the extent to which you choose to rely on them.

If you've got only a few ducks and you're not pushing them hard for production or show, it is not necessary to be fussy about what you feed them. Mixed grains would probably do if the birds are able to forage a lot of goodies in your yard. If not, and in any case to be safe, we recommend a good high-protein all-purpose lay mixture suitable for chickens as a supplement to the grains. Above all else, don't feed them a diet of stale bread!

We do urge you to read on through the whole chapter, however, just to appreciate the subtleties involved in waterfowl nutrition. Someday you might need the information, and if you intend to mix your own you'll definitely need it.

We will first discuss feeding programs under three headings: commercially prepared waterfowl feeds, if they are available; commercially prepared feeds to substitute if waterfowl feeds are not available; and grow-your-own programs in case commercial feeds of any kind are off your list. We will necessarily have to get increasingly technical as we go. We will include discussions on some specific problems relating to the diets of birds for meat and eggs, both young and mature.

Finally, we will talk about some miscellaneous considerations of interest to all raisers of waterfowl, including feed facilities, form, quantities, schedule, supplements including greens, feeding show birds, geese as weeders, grazing geese, fattening them, providing water, and winterizing your ducks and geese.

Commercially prepared waterfowl feeds

Both local and national feed processors produce complete lines of duck and goose feeds, carefully blended to meet the known requirements of these particular birds. Unfortunately, these lines are not available in all areas. Even feed stores carrying national brands do not always handle the waterfowl feeds of these manufacturers if demand for them is low among their customers. They might even be totally unaware of the existence of such feeds.

Commercial feeds are typically available in four types.

Starter feed. This is designed for very young ducklings and goslings to get them off to a secure start. It should be used from hatch till about two or three weeks. The protein content is usually around 19 to 22 percent, which is within the range recommended by various experts. It is adequate for a good sturdy development, but not so hot that it will burn them out. This particular feed is suitable for all young domestic waterfowl, regardless of the purpose for which they are raised (except for certain special classes of show birds). At the next stage, though, it is necessary to differentiate.

Grower feed. This feed is designed for started birds being readied for butchering. The protein content has been throttled back somewhat from the starter, to about 16 or 17 percent. It is still plenty high enough to promote rapid growth to a satisfactory size for table use. Commercial practice is to butcher ducklings at eight weeks and goslings at 15, but you may wish to wait longer—see Chapter 12, "Raising Ducks and Geese for Meat." In any case this feed can be used right up to the day before slaughter.

Developer feed. This feed is intended for growing birds that will be used as layers, including those specifically intended to be breeders. It's a good feed for show and pet waterfowl as well. The protein content is 12 to 14 percent. This provides a more moderate growth rate, giving the internal organs and supporting structures a chance to keep up. The birds will grow as large as they would on higher protein preparations: it will just take a bit longer and cost a little more. But their health and fitness require this extra expense.

Though birds on starter and grower diets should be provided as much feed as they want, some manufacturers—particularly those whose developer feed is on the high side in protein content—recommend that growing birds on developer be fed only 80 percent the amount they would naturally eat if given all they want, making sure there is ample room at the feeder for all birds to eat at once. This is another way to throttle back on their growth, but it is undoubtedly easier and probably pleasanter to find a slightly lower protein feed and give them all they wish.

This feed is also satisfactory as a holding feed for adult birds that are not in production. When they are actually laying, the next feed should be the one used, but in periods of dormancy, to which they will cyclically return, it is unnecessarily expensive enrichment.

Breeder-layer feed. The protein content goes back up to 17 or 18 percent here, and a smorgasbord of vitamins and minerals is provided that laying birds are known to need. This should keep them in top shape for the rather taxing business of laying. Males used for breeders will be kept in the peak of vigor so that fertility will remain high. Eggs will contain all the nutriments known to be needed by developing embryos to produce viable and vigorous hatchlings. Birds should be taken off the developer and put onto the full layer-breeder ration a week or two before they are expected to begin laying.

We should mention one other option that is sometimes provided by manufacturers of feeds—the high-protein concentrate. This is a preparation that is intended to be diluted with grains to form a complete feed. It is rich in vitamins and minerals and ordinarily has a protein content of about 34 percent. It can be used in place of any of the above feeds except starter, depending on what it's mixed with. Directions for the various combinations are on the label.

Usually these prepared feeds (except concentrates) are intended as a complete ration. The manufacturers hypothesize that birds will have access to nothing else. However, virtually all manufacturers will recommend that certain supplements be provided if at all feasible. These would include grit, oyster shell, and greens. Later in this chapter we'll discuss the place of these supplements in the feeding program.

Feed stores normally stock mixed grains, commonly known as chicken scratch. Such mixtures, normally consisting of whole corn, milo, cracked wheat, or other common grains, are useful as a supplement to certain feeding programs. We will describe them below. Mixed grains should not be used as a sole ration for confined birds.

Grains are high-calorie feeds. For the same reason that they generate body warmth and are great wintertime supplements, as we explain in "Tips for Winter" later in this chapter, they can cause extreme discomfort during hot weather. Grains should therefore be used sparingly in the summertime.

Alternative commercial feeds

If you are among the many people who cannot find regular waterfowl feeds at your local supply outlet, there are several alternative feed lines normally available that will make satisfactory if not perfect substitutes. You should in this case make certain that your birds have ample forage, as this will allow them to make up for any possible deficiency in their diet. The differences between the standard waterfowl feeds and the substitutes are not great and for the most part will have only a minor and perhaps even undetectable effect on your fowl. You and your birds can be perfectly happy on any of these substitute programs. It is only those who deal with fowl on an immense scale who have to worry about the last measure of efficiency.

It turns out that the vitamin and mineral needs of game birds and turkeys are very close to those of waterfowl. These feeds are normally rather high in protein also—say 28 percent—but if you can find a lower-protein feed—around 20 percent—this would do very nicely. It could be used as your sole ration. If you can obtain only the high-protein feed, try cutting it with some lower-protein feeds such as chicken feeds or mixed grains. Excessive protein cannot be used effectively by growing ducks and geese, and in fact its presence puts a great strain on some parts of their systems. For example, their bones and joints may be weakened by having to support excessive weights before they are sufficiently developed.

The differences between the nutritional needs of waterfowl and chickens are rather picky, so if chicken feed is what is most easily obtainable in your area, use it. Choose a chick or chicken feed that has the appropriate protein content for your birds, as described under the headings of the preceding section.

You should stay away from medicated chick feeds. Baby chicks are very susceptible to coccidiosis and other high-mortality diseases, and for this reason many chick starters contain inhibiting agents and antibiotics. There are pros and cons to using these for chicks, but that is not the issue here. Waterfowl are not nearly as susceptible to diseases and in any case are not susceptible to those the medicated chick feeds are intended to prevent. (There is some evidence that certain medications, particularly the arsenicals, will poison young waterfowl.) Fortunately, chick starters are almost always available in both medicated and nonmedicated forms so there should be no difficulty getting feed without this medication.

Mixing your own

It makes sense to mix your own only if you're going to grow your own. That takes land, special planting and harvesting equipment, storage silos, and so on, and is more trouble, we suspect, than the average backyarder would want to get into. If you mix your own from raw materials you buy, you're only assuming all the problems of supply and proper blending that the feed companies have already solved. Yet you normally won't save any money, and you don't get a product that is purer or in any way superior. Of course, if you do grow your own foodstuffs, you would presumably have both a purer and a less expensive feed source.

So, for what it's worth, we are including some charts that will be useful in blending proper feeds for ducks and geese. In Chart 1 we have listed the appropriate proportion of various ingredients to make 100 pounds of each of four different kinds of feed, one for each of the purposes we spoke of earlier. The last few items in Chart 1B are to be supplied in such small quantities that we have indicated them in grams. (A gram is 1/28 of an ounce.) In Chart 2 we have listed the chemical analysis of many of these same ingredients in case you want to do some custom blending, either because of the unavailability of certain components or just for the sheer joy of intellectual inventiveness.

The materials required in the minutest quantities are among the most important, so it is vital not to omit them. Most of these substances are found in adequate quantities in the natural foods of waterfowl. There are only four that you really need to worry about: vitamins A, D, B_2, and B_{12}. In addition, there are a few others of these substances that might be in short supply if your feed ration is mixed with little or no quantities of animal protein and high-fiber vegetables, namely vitamin E, vitamin K, niacin, choline, and pantothenic acid. Either drugstore solutions of these must be added to the ration, or foods high in them must be included in the diet (consult Chart 2).

Natural forms of vitamins A, D, and E are unstable and may decompose in the feed before it is consumed. They are, however, available in stabilized forms. If unstable forms are used, larger margins of safety must be allowed in determining appropriate quantities.

When mixing your own it is essential that your feed be thoroughly mixed; otherwise, the careful blending you have done to guarantee a balanced diet is wasted. It is even more critical that the vitamin and trace-mineral premixes be completely blended, first by themselves and then throughout the feed mix.

One other thing to keep in mind is the relative amounts of calories and protein. Your birds will grow rapidly if they are fed lots of calories, but this will be largely fatty growth unless the protein content is sufficient. On the other hand, you already know the suggested limitations on protein. About 1,200 calories per pound of feed (2,600 calories per kg) is a good compromise for growing and adult birds, and perhaps 1,300 or 1,400 calories per pound (3,000 calories per kg) is appropriate for hatchlings.

Feed Facilities

It is better to place feed in special containers from which your ducks and geese can eat than to simply toss it on the ground. For one thing, this centralizes the feed so that the birds can readily find it and thus reduces waste. For another, it is more sanitary, since the birds will not be forced to pick up the feed from among their own droppings.

Many of the feeders designed for use by chickens are equally suitable for ducks and geese. Actually, the choice of feeders for waterfowl is far more flexible than for chickens, since you don't have problems with them roosting over the feed or taking dust baths in it; nearly any type of large container that is not easily tipped will do. Many waterfowl keepers like the hanging tube type feeders that can be adjusted to the height of the birds' backs, as these feeders tend to minimize waste.

So-called self-feeders are available for those who do not or cannot feed every day. They can hold a good deal of feed and make it available gradually as the birds eat what has already fallen into the hopper. We have found these feeders to be wasteful and so don't like to use them unless absolutely necessary. We had originally thought that the outrageous amounts of feed use associated with these containers was due somehow to their stimulation of our ducks and geese to consume more than usual, but it did not take us long to discover the enormous numbers of wild birds that were stopping in for a free handout, not to mention the army of nocturnal rodents coming around for midnight snacks.

Though ducks and geese require drinking water as they eat, feeders should be placed away from the water source so your birds cannot get water in the feed or feed into the water. Soupy feed tends to go sour or moldy if not immediately consumed. On the other hand, the water and feed should be handy enough to each other that the birds do not have to expend undue energy running back and forth. A matter of six to eight feet (2 or 3 M) is about right.

Feeders should be provided some protection from rainstorms. We built a miniature lean-to over our feeder. If you have a simple four-post-and-roof shelter, you'll find it convenient to place the feeder under its protection. Feeders may be kept in an enclosed shelter but should be covered or removed when the birds are shut in at night, as explained in Chapter 5, "The Pond and Other Amenities."

For storing feed, it's a good idea to get some galvanized garbage cans with lids and keep them in your shelter or in a shed or the garage or some other place out of the weather but near your birds. Plastic containers might also be used but in the long run are not as durable, and they tip over more easily than the heavier metal ones. Storage cans keep your feed protected from the pillaging of rodents, which are inevitably attracted to feed-storage areas. The burlap and paper sacks that feed usually comes in are far too vulnerable. Even your very own birds might be tempted to bite holes in them if they get impatient for dinner.

Feeds deteriorate with time; so it's best not to purchase (or mix) too much at once. A two- to four-week supply is not unreasonable. Feeds milled locally are less likely to contain oxidation-inhibiting agents (preservatives) and will therefore go stale more quickly.

Above all, don't let feed get wet and moldy. If it does,

throw it out, as it may develop highly toxic poisons that would make your birds sick or even kill them.

Feed forms

Commercially prepared feeds are made in three forms: pellet, crumble, and mash. Mash is a finely ground powder; pellets are small nuggets of compressed mash, held together with the same type of inert binder used in vitamin pills and aspirin; and crumbles are pellets that have been smashed to bits, but not as small bits as mash. Ducks and geese find pellets easiest to eat. Moreover, there is considerably less wastage with pellets, since any they drop will probably be picked up again sooner or later. Crumbles are relatively satisfactory but are a bit harder to eat and there is some waste. Mash is a very poor choice. It will clog in their bills and throats, they will drop mouthfuls of it in the water dish, and an enormous quantity will simply fall in the dirt and be lost.

Though not every feed is available in all three forms, you should have little difficulty obtaining the pellet form. The chief problem is getting a satisfactory pellet feed for the very youngest birds. They also should have pellets, but they clearly cannot eat the same size pellets that grown birds eat. Some companies make a junior-size pellet about ⅛ inch (3 mm) in diameter, but it's relatively uncommon. Most feed companies cater to chicken growers since poultry is clearly a high-volume business, and chicken growers normally don't like to use the pellet form for their chicks. You may have to settle for a crumble form for your ducklings. Mash should definitely be avoided.

Grains also come in several forms, including ground, cracked, and whole. Whole grains are better than cracked or ground forms, since they contain the entire nutriment of the kernel. Cracked or ground grains are often separated from the germ, where most of the vitamins and minerals are located. Whole grains have the additional advantage that, being seeds, they may sprout when dropped and pressed into the earth during feeding activities and will surely be eaten by the first observant duck or goose that happens by.

WhEN ANd how much to feed

We like to feed our ducks and geese first thing each day. Strolling about the yard to greet its inhabitants each morning is a kind of meditation that helps prepare us for whatever slings and arrows the day may bring. Others like to feed their birds at night as a sort of after-work cocktail to help them unwind from their day's tensions. Feeding at night has certain other advantages. Where there is plenty of vegetation for ducks and geese to graze on, delaying feeding until late in the afternoon encourages them to forage for much of their own food during the day. Further, where it gets nippy at night, late feeding gives waterfowl extra energy that keeps them warm all night long. Feeding time, however, is generally a matter of the owner's preference, as long as the birds are fed on a regular schedule each day.

How much to feed at one time is also a matter of personal preference. We like to see that our birds have a little something at all times. Others prefer to feed only as much as the birds will clean up in 15 minutes. This latter method discourages waste, for the ducks and geese are not given a chance to play in the feeders when bored, nor is much left for wild birds and rodents to munch on while fowl are between feedings. Many of those who feed by this method feed twice a day, once in the morning and once in the evening. Those who follow the 15-minute twice-a-day plan generally have more area available for between-meal foraging than those who provide continuously filled troughs. The latter is definitely preferable for young birds being raised for meat. For a mature flock, take your choice.

Leaving the same feed in troughs for more than a day encourages it to become wet and moldy, causing spoilage and all the gruesome things that spoilage entails. It's best to see that the trough is completely cleaned out at least once a day.

The amount of feed to allot depends largely on the age of your flock, the time of year, how active the birds are, and how much they can forage for themselves. To give you some rough guidelines, a growing duckling will start out eating only an ounce or two a day (30 to 60 gm) but move up to about half a pound (250 gm) a day as he nears full size. A mature duck may eat only 5 to 7 ounces (140 to 200 gm) of feed each day when not laying but as much as 12 to 15 ounces (330 to 420 gm) per day when laying. Geese and goslings may be expected to eat about four times these respective amounts. All these quantities hypothesize an absence of any supplements and would obviously be less where natural forage is available.

Fresh greens and other supplements

Ducks and geese require and relish fresh greens. Finely chopped grass from freshly mown lawns, unsprayed by chemical poisons, is a perfect alternative to farmyard pastures (which, of course, are not always available to backyarders). Where grass is not available, some backyarders plant greens in a special section of their garden. These include kale, cabbage, lettuce, alfalfa, or clover. If nothing fresh is available, rabbit pellets will do, since they are simply made of compressed alfalfa. Or they may save leftover scraps from dinner, weeds and surplus from the garden, or collect trimmings from a local produce stand. Competition is high for the waste from produce stands, especially in rural areas, and backyard waterfowl raisers often must compete against local hog farmers for scraps from produce stand bins.

There are other supplements that add zest to your birds' diets and help you keep down your feed bill at the same time. We once made an arrangement with our neighbors to get all of their windfall apples for our geese in exchange for the service of keeping their yard cleared of the fruit. But even in this case our geese lost the competition against local hogs, for one morning as we headed across the street with our wheelbarrow, we discovered a hog farmer's truck in our neighbor's driveway, loaded with windfall apples. We upped the ante by offering our neighbors a roasting goose for the next holiday, but it seems that the prior offer of an exchange of pork chops had been too tantalizing to pass up.

When we suggest feeding leftovers or scraps, we don't mean that ducks and geese should be given garbage. Rotten vegetables, like moldy feed, may contain highly toxic poisons. And you will find out how horrible that can be when you read Chapter 14. Sort through any vegetable discards before tossing them to your birds and remove anything that has begun to rot.

It's up to you whether or not to feed continuously, but you should leave a hopper of insoluble granite grit for ducks and geese at all times. Such grit can be purchased at feed stores, or you can use coarse sand or fine gravel from clean riverbeds. If ocean sand is used, it must first be thoroughly leached to avoid salt poisoning. Grit in the gizzard acts as a bird's teeth by helping to grind up whatever passes through. Virtually any small hard objects have this function, but they aren't particularly useful if they are themselves dissolvable, for they would get ground up quickly along with everything else and have to be renewed continuously. Birds of all ages need grit. A finer grit should be provided for younger birds. Birds that roam free need less than those that are confined, since they are able to find a lot of pebbles on their own.

Calcium, often given in the form of commercially prepared ground oyster shells, should also be provided continuously during lay, for it is required by female ducks and geese to help them build thick shells around their eggs. Oyster shell is available at most feed stores in fine, medium, and coarse grades to accommodate birds of a variety of sizes. Recycled eggshells may be used but should be dried and crushed before being fed back to the birds. In themselves, recycled eggshells do not provide enough calcium, so a supplement is still required. Birds that can forage usually pick up plenty of calcium from the crawly things they consume. Calcium should be available to grown birds at all times. Growing birds do not require supplemental calcium and in fact should be kept from it, since an excess of calcium may put a burden on their internal organs.

Feeding for show

There are special feeding programs for show birds which will enhance their plumage color and brightness, keep their weights within the standard limits, and produce the proper coloration in bills and legs. Such feeding programs vary with each breed and depend on weight and body type as well as on plumage colors.

To give some examples, Call ducks raised for show must be small, and it is therefore necessary to limit their protein consumption for the first week or two to prevent overgrowth. You can provide yellow corn to increase the splendor of the iridescent greenish sheen in feathers when this is desirable. Corn also enhances the plumage color of the brown varieties but may cause browning in those varieties that should have purely black or blue plumage. Xanthophyll, the orange pigment found in corn and many green feeds, brings out the rich coloring of orange bills and feet. The fiber in feeds such as oats, lettuce, and alfalfa helps keep the feathers in good condition.

Specifics on feeding for show are best learned at poultry shows from fellow exhibitors who have worked out their own feeding programs. You'll likely still have to do a little private experimenting to determine which types of feeds produce the results you desire in your particular strain of show birds.

In addition to improving the appearance of the birds, there is one other consideration in feeding birds for show. Because birds on exhibit are often fed exclusively on grains, they should be used to eating whole grains, especially if shows are more than a day or two long; stress resulting from failure to eat, in addition to the unfamiliar surroundings, may result in the physical decline of an otherwise fine show bird.

It is important to see that a bird does not have a crop full of grains when the judges come around, for this may spoil its natural lines. Many exhibitors withhold feed on the morning their breed is to be judged, feeding only after the judge has had his look. Ascertain feeding policies from the show management when you coop in your birds.

Geese as weeders

Since geese can get along almost exclusively on succulent green pasture, it is natural that someone would come up with the idea of saving money two ways by using geese as weeders for commercial crops. At one time it was popular for large-scale farmers to be in the goose-raising business as a sideline, supplying themselves cheap labor for cultivation. In fact, it was less than cheap. A field hand expects to be fed in exchange for his labors as a weeder, but geese are fed in the very act of weeding—and, best of all, at the end of the season, they feed their keeper!

A dozen geese can take the place of one person with a hoe and can more easily get at weeds growing close to the bases of plants without damaging the crop roots. Chinese geese are most often used as weeders because they are energetic, active, and yet light enough not to do much crop damage. However, any breed of goose will do for weeding. Since ducks are not particularly active grazers, their use in this capacity is unsatisfactory.

Geese have been used to eliminate grasses, especially such bothersome varieties as crabgrass and Bermuda grass, in a number of commercially grown crops. Fields of sugar beets, sugarcane, potatoes, onions, and tobacco have been cultivated by teams of geese, but their greatest use as weeders has been in southern cotton fields. Geese are also kept in strawberry fields until the berries ripen and become more palatable to the geese than weeds, and they have been used in fields of vine-growing berries. Growers of flowers and ornamental plants use geese to keep down unwanted vegetation. In vineyards and orchards, the geese keep the land cultivated and pick up windfall fruit which may harbor harmful insect pests. Geese will keep fields free from weed growth between crops. They can keep irrigation ditches free-flowing by clearing out grass and water weeds. They can also be used to prevent weed growth along fences— and because of their long necks, they even see to it that weeds don't grow for several inches on the opposite side of the fence.

Geese are generally not allowed into the fields until after a crop has grown beyond the young succulent stage and is no longer as appetizing to the birds as newly sprouting weed shoots. In the meantime, the fields should be fairly well cultivated so that when the geese are put to work they can keep up with the weed growth. On the other hand, should succulent green feed become scarce, they will certainly attack the crops with the same energy and dedication that they had formerly reserved for weeds. In orchards the geese may even strip bark from fruit and coniferous trees if there is not enough green vegetation available, and the girdled trees may die. As long as there is growth the geese prefer, the crop is safe.

Though weeder-geese have been largely replaced by herbicides in commercial operations, those who are organically inclined still find them effective in removing unwanted vegetation. (In addition, they are efficient spreaders of organic fertilizer.) A pair of full-size geese will keep a well-kept but not overgrown acre weed-free, and for free! For most backyard gardens, even just one pair of mature geese would do more harm than good, so gardeners who wish to employ geese as weeders should use only a few small goslings.

Goslings make better weeders than full-grown geese for other reasons: they are more active than their adult counterparts, especially during warm summer months, and they have not yet become accustomed to other types of diets such as prepared feed mixtures or more succulent pastures. Goslings will begin weeding as early as one week of age. They should be

113

brought in each night for warmth until six to eight weeks old, depending on their rate of development and on the weather.

Supplemental feeding may be required if there are not enough weeds or if the weeds are not providing proper nourishment. It is important, though, not to overfeed weeder-geese so that they will continue to forage eagerly for weeds. Feed supplemental mash or grain during the late afternoon or early evening to ensure that geese weed actively throughout the day. Supplemental feeding should be of the same feeds regularly given geese of the same age.

When using geese as weeders be sure that there is always plenty of shade and water available for them. If nearby trees or shrubs don't offer adequate shade, a portable source of shade may have to be provided. For backyard use, a beach umbrella could be erected in the garden. Geese will tend to concentrate their weeding efforts near the source of shade and water. If the garden is large, it may be necessary to move the water and shade periodically so that all parts will be weeded. Locate the

source of water so that plantings aren't trampled by the frequent forays of thirsty geese for a drink.

Grazing geese

A gaggle of young geese does quite well in a large meadow with little else but succulent, newly sprouting grasses to graze on and a side dish of mixed grains and prepared feed. Goslings that are raised mostly on pasturage take longer to reach eating size than those that are pen-fed but will be much cheaper in the long run. Pasture-raised goslings may take up to 24 weeks to reach an acceptable table size, nine weeks after commercially raised goslings would have been on their way to market.

Geese should only be allowed to graze in areas where grasses and other vegetation are young and succulent: fresh young sprouts provide nutriments missing from their older, tougher counterparts, and tough, fibrous vegetation is difficult for waterfowl to digest. Fibrous plants wad up in the crop, forming a hard, tight ball. As with long-haired cats and dogs afflicted with hair balls, such wadding of fibrous material prevents foods from passing through the digestive tract and may result in the death of the bird. Called crop impaction, this condition may require a modest surgical operation which, while not entirely impossible to accomplish at home, is not really something most backyarders would want to try. Making the cuts in the right places is critical to the future of the bird, not to mention the peace of mind of its owner.

Impaction is evidenced by a general lack of enthusiasm, coupled with weight loss and an easily felt tight wad of material in the crop. If you have a duck or goose with crop impaction, consult a local veteran waterfowl breeder or bird-oriented veterinarian for advice. It would be most prudent to keep waterfowl on fresh succulent greens instead of old thorny vacant lots where they are likely to develop impaction.

Another problem may arise as a result of forcing geese to graze on dry, tough vegetation. In pulling up whole plants and eating their roots, fibrous material may lodge in the intestines

115

as a form of constipation. Other coarse, dry feeds may also clog up the alimentary canal and prevent food from passing. A mild dose of castor oil is recommended to help pass the mass, but if that doesn't work, it may be necessary to grease up your fingers with petroleum jelly and gently work the offending material out through the vent. As with all other problems related to the raising of waterfowl, it is obviously best to avoid this problem by providing satisfactory conditions from the start.

Fattening

Those who run their ducks and geese on pasturage often like to fatten them up to ready them for the butcher. Fattening is perhaps a poor choice of words, especially considering the reputation that waterfowl have gotten for overly fatty meat. We are really talking about the process of bringing a duck or goose to full plumpness for the table. A plump bird is one that is fully fleshed out and does not necessarily have to be greasy.

Fattening of ducks and geese should begin when they come into full feather, indicated by the primary wing feathers reaching the tail. They are generally fattened for the three to five weeks prior to butchering, in an area small enough that they cannot burn off a lot of energy in activity. It is counterproductive, however, to make the area so small that they cannot keep clean and relatively dry, for they may decline in vigor and actually lose weight. Ideally, a fattening pen should be located where the birds will not be disturbed or agitated in any way, for overactivity due to harassment may also result in a lower growth rate.

In this pen the birds should be fed all they can eat of a good grower feed. If necessary to stimulate their appetites, they can be coddled with some mixed grains, but these are usually lower in protein and should not comprise more than a third of the ration. Although feed should be available at all times, it helps to top off their feeders three or four times a day. The attention seems to stimulate their interest in eating.

WATER

Being naturally adapted to a water environment, ducks and geese are used to eating their food moistened, and it is extremely important to give them water with their feed. They require copious quantities of drinking water, especially in hot weather. If free-flowing water does not keep pond water fresh and clean, provide a source of uncontaminated drinking water. A water container should be designed for easy cleaning, as frequent flushings wash out the sediment that ducks and geese somehow manage to drop continuously into their water. Place wooden slats or wire guards over or around the waterer in such a way that the birds cannot get into it for a swim, but can get their heads far enough into the water for a deep and satisfying drink. Ducks and geese keep their bills free of mud and caked feed by squirting water through their nostrils. If they cannot submerge their heads in their drinking water at least up to their eyes, feed and mud may gather around the eyes and nostrils and ultimately a low-grade infection may set in. Thus, where swim water is not available and they cannot fully bathe, they should at least be able to wash their faces.

Ducks and geese like to bill water out of troughs, and often when swimming water is not available frustrated waterfowl toss drinking water over their backs in a bathing gesture. If no countermeasures are taken, unsanitary and offensive mud puddles will form in which the ducks will be tempted to swish their bills and play around. It is therefore important that the area around a waterer drain quickly. Puddles can also be discouraged by placing the waterer on a platform of wooden slats or a wire frame, with a wide layer of deep gravel underneath to drain away the overflow.

Automatic watering of some sort is a good idea. Even for the backyarder with only a few ducks and geese, it can be burdensome to check the water situation several times a day during hot weather. You could spend your whole life running out to fill up containers. Many farmers use hog waterers for geese, and some of the commercially made automatic chicken waterers are suitable for ducks. Many problems related to providing fresh drinking water for ducks and geese are eliminated by incorporating a drinking trough as part of the inlet of a pond, where the overflow simply spills into the already existing pool as described in Chapter 6, "Pond Construction."

Birds generally aren't able to store water in their bodies and may suffer a serious decline in health if deprived of adequate drinking water for even the greater part of a day. Laying birds can virtually be counted on to stop laying if this occurs. In fact, one of the standard methods of throwing a bird into a molt, which some producers like to do to renew slackened laying, is to withhold drinking water for a day.

Tips for winter

Providing water in the winter can sometimes be a problem, especially when the temperature drops below freezing for periods long enough to freeze up the normal sources. Since it is absolutely essential to provide water, something must be done to keep a supply available. A recirculating pump on the pond, as described in Chapter 6, tends to retard freezing and keeps water available on the pond.

You could buy either heating coils to wrap around your water pipes or a heating device that rests in the water trough to prevent freezing. These heaters can often be found at electrical supply outlets or poultry specialty dealers. Running the water lines into a winter shelter helps keep the water from freezing, especially if you have arranged for heat in the building. Despite our negative comments in Chapter 5 regarding watering your birds inside the shelter, this sometimes is a necessity. If all else fails, it may be necessary to leave a faucet dripping in order to keep the line open.

Don't leave vegetable scraps where they can freeze, as this makes them less palatable and diminishes the nutritional value of certain greens. Provide only as much greens as can be eaten up before freezing.

As discussed in Chapter 3, "Meet the Waterfowl Family," certain breeds of ducks and geese do well in cooler areas, but even they will be able to withstand chill better if high-energy grains are fed to produce extra warmth. Corn especially is known as a high-energy feed, and though not a balanced diet when given exclusively, does improve cold-weather comfort when increased in wintertime diets. And of course when we talk about high-energy we mean high-calorie, so expect a bird to become fatty when fed too much corn in seasons when cold weather stress is low or absent.

The feet of ducks and geese are especially susceptible to frostbite, and waterfowl commonly freeze their feet while standing around feeders on cold packed snow. Since birds generally tend to congregate in the feeding area, clear away ice and snow in that vicinity or spread sand, straw, or other litter over the frozen ground.

Some years ago when a freak snowstorm was predicted for our normally temperate area, a concerned neighbor insisted that we knit booties for all of our ducks and geese. Fortunately for us—and for the birds—the predicted storm failed to materialize.

CHART 1. SUGGESTED FEED MIXTURES FOR DUCKS AND GEESE

Several suggested diets for waterfowl. Choose on the basis of which ingredients are most easily obtained. Formulas for vitamin premix and trace-mineral premix are given in Charts 1A and 1B. Ingredients given in pounds.

Ingredient	Starter			Grower		Breeder-Developer			Layer		
Cornmeal, #2, yellow	52	63½	46	58	72½	65	33	37	58	52	46
Oats or barley, pulverized	10		10	5		10	10	20		5	10
Wheat, standard middlings			15	5			40	14½	6	9	5
Soybean oil meal (50% protein)	30½	27	12½	26	18	18½	5	14	26	7½	12½
Fish meal (60% protein)	3	3	8	1½	3	1		5	2	5	7½
Fish solubles, dried		½	½		½			½			
Meat scraps (50% protein)									5		
Stabilized vegetable oil	1			1							2½
Alfalfa meal (17% protein)	½	1	3	½	1	2½	9	4	1½	5	2½
Brewer's yeast, dried (40% protein)			1					1		2½	2½
Whey, dried		1	1		1			1		2½	2½
Grain distillers solubles, dried		1			1						2½
Trace-mineral premix	2½	2½	2½	2½	2½	2½	2½	2½	6	6	6
Vitamin premix	½	½	½	½	½	½	½	½	½	½	½

(Makes 100 pounds)

CHART 1B. VITAMIN PREMIX

Vitamin	Starter	Grower
Vitamin A, stabilized	8,000,000	6,000,000
Vitamin D^3	1,000,000	1,000,000
Vitamin E acetate	10,000	10,000
Vitamin K (menadione sodium bisulfite)	4	4
Riboflavin (Vitamin B$_2$)	8	8
Niacin (50%)	160	160
Choline Chloride (25%)	2,400	2,400
Calcium Pantothenate	16	16
Cobalamin (Vitamin B$_{12}$)	12	12

(Makes approximately 10 pounds. Use ½ pound per 100 pounds of feed.)

CHART 1A. TRACE-MINERAL PREMIX

Trace-mineral premix is available commercially. If you want to mix your own, here is a suggested formula. Since research on the trace-mineral needs of waterfowl is incomplete, these quantities provide a considerable safety factor. Ingredients given in pounds.

Mineral	Starter	Grower	Breeder-Developer	Layer
Dicalcium phosphate	17	25	29	24
Limestone	32	24	20	122
Iodized salt	7½	7½	8	7
Manganese sulfate	¾	¾	¾	¾
Zinc oxide or zinc carbonate	¼	¼	¼	¼
Copper sulfate			¾	¾
dl-methionine	2½	2½	1¼	1¼
Makes	60 lbs	60 lbs	60 lbs	156 lbs
Use per 100 lbs. feed	2½ lbs	2½ lbs	2½ lbs	6 lbs

Since research on the vitamin needs of waterfowl is incomplete, these quantities provide a considerable safety factor.

Breeder-Developer	Layer	Units
6,000,000	8,000,000	Int'l units
1,000,000	1,000,000	Int'l chick units
4,000	20,000	Int'l units
2	2	grams
2	4	grams
30	30	grams
1,200	1,600	grams
8	8	grams
2	6	milligrams = 1/1,000th gram

CHART 2. NATURAL ANALYSIS OF

A blank entry indicates that the information was unavailable. Two numbers separated by a hyphen indicate a range.

	Protein %	Fiber %	Ash %	Fat %	Carbohydrate %	Metabolizable Energy kilocal/lb	Productive Energy kilocal/lb
Alfalfa leaf meal (20%)	20.9	18–20	10.4	2.5–2.9	41.1	720	310
Alfalfa meal (17%)	17.8	24–25	9.0	2.8	37.8	620	260
Barley	9.7–12.7	5.4–6.2		1.9–2.2		1,280	800
Barley meal	11.6	6.0	2.4	1.8	66.5		
Blood meal	80.0	1.0	5.6	1.6	3.8		
Bone meal	12.1–13.4	1.7		3.2			
Brewer's grains	26.0	15.0	3.6	6.2	42.2		
Brewer's yeast	45–47	2.8		1.2	35.7	920	480
Buckwheat	10–11	9.0	1.8	2.5			
Buttermilk	32.4	0.4	9.6	5.7	43.3	1,160	520
Corn	8.9	2.0		3.9		1,530	1,100
Corn, distillers solubles	27–29	3.3–3.8	7.0	var	47.6	1,350	850
Cornmeal	13.7	11.0		6.0	68.9		
Corn germ meal	42.9	3.9		2.0	56.1		
Corn gluten meal	41–43	var		var	40.1	1,150	840
Cottonseed oil meal	41.0	10–12	6.1	var	26.3	790	
Fish meal, menhaden	61–62	1.0	19.0	7.7–9.4	4.2	1,320	900
Fish meal, sardine	65–67	0.9	16.0	4.3–5.0	5.4	1,320	900
Fish meal, whitefish	63.0	0.1		6.7	0.1		
Fish solubles	29–32	0.6	2.7	var		654	450
Hominy	11.1	4.9–5.6		6.0	63.9	1,310	860
Linseed oil	35.0	8.1		5.6	36.9		
Liver and gland meal	65.1	1.6		16.0		1,330	1,090
Meat scrap	53.0	2.4		9–10	7.3	900	720
Meat and bone meal	50.6	2.2	32.7	8.6–9.5	2.0	900	720
Milk, skimmed	34.0	0.2		0.9–1.2	50.3	1,160	520
Milo	11.3	2.2–2.5		2.5–2.9	71.1	1,500	1,110
Molasses	3.0		8.1		62.1		
Oatmeal	16.0	3.0	2.3	5.5–6.3	64.4	1,540	
Oats	9–15	var		4.5–5.4	66.1	1,210	760
Peanut oil meal	42–43	11–14		7.6–8.3	23.0	1,200	
Rice bran	12.0	13.0	16.0	11.0	41.7		
Rice polishings	11.8	3.0	8.0	13.0	56.6		
Rye meal	12.6	2.4		1.7	70.9		
Shrimp meal	40.0	11.0		2.0	6.0		
Soybean meal (high-protein)	50.9	2.8		0.8		1,140	610
Soybean meal (low-protein)	45–46	5.5–6.0	6.1	var	31.8	1,020	570
Soybean oil meal	42.0	6.0	4.6	4.0	29.9		
Wheat, hard	15.2	2.6		1.8		1,400	1,020
Wheat, soft	9.9	2.7		2.0		1,400	920
Wheat, bran	15.0–16.4	10–11	6.0	var	53.0	590	
Wheat, flour middlings	18.1						
Wheat standard middlings	17–18	5–7		4.6	58.5	860	580
Wheat, red dog	18.0	2.3		3.6		1,240	
Wheat, germ meal	24.0	3.0	4.3	7.0			
Whey	12–16	0.1–0.2		0.8–1.1	70.4	870	490

COMMON WATERFOWL FEEDSTUFFS

The symbol "var" indicates that there is a wide variation due to soil, climate, and other conditions of growth.

Calcium	Phosphorus	Iron	Copper	Manganese	Zinc	Riboflavin (Vit B12)	Niacin	Pantothenic Acid	Choline	Cobalamin (Vit. B12)	Vit A Int'l Units
				milligrams per pound						micrograms/lb	
1.7	.28	177.1	7.1	28.6		7.4	17.3	18.5	.45		105,000
1.7	.23	149.8	3.1	15.0	9.1	7.3	9.0	12.0	.40		70,000
.06–.09	var	22.7–31.8	5.0	7.8–8.3	7.8	0.8	24.1	3.7	.53		
.07	.42										
0.3	.22										
29.0	13.6–15.1	381.4	7.4	var	193.0	.04	2.0	0.8			
.27	.50								1.80		
.13	1.43	58.1	15.0	2.5	22.2	14.0	213.6	49.1			
.1	.30			36.0		1.0	8.0	6.0			
1.34	.94			1.6	2.8	15.8	2.8	13.5			
var	.3	9.1	0.9	2.3	11.8	0.5	9.8	2.6	.20		2,000
.35	1.37	250.6	37.6	33.4	45.9	7.7	52.0	9.5	2.20	1	50
.16	.4	181.1	12.8	3.3–4.4	31.3	0.7	23–25	3.8–4.7	.15		12,000
.15	1.2	119.4	8.9	9.3–12.9		2.5	13.0	4.4			
4.9–5.5	2.8–3.4	254.2	3.8	10.0–11.7	46.3	2.3	25–26	4.0	1.60	40	
3.7–4.9	2.5–2.8	135.3	9.2	10.2		2.5	26.0	1.3			
var	.7	155.3	21.9	5.4	15.4	6–10	120–160	17–18	1.40	100	
.05	.5–.7	44.9	4.4	6.9–7.3		1.1	20–22	3.7	.44		5,000
.66	1.14	222.5	44.1	3.3		18.0	73.0	48.0	4.80	230	
8–9	4.2	199.3	4.4	4.0–4.3	75.0	2.4	26–27	2.2	.90	20	
8.1–10.6	4.5	225.6	0.7	5.3–5.6	75.0	2.1	21.4	1.5–1.7	1.00	20	
1.26	1.03	23.6	5.2	1.0–1.2	2.8	9–10	5.7	15.6	.65	20	
.03	.27	22.7	7.8	5.9	7.0	0.4	13.0	5.0	.20		
.9	.05										
.05–.07	.45	26.8	1.6	18.7							
.09	.4	36.3	2.4	19.2		0.4	8.2	6.8	.43		
.16	5.6–7.6	122.6				2.4	77.5	24.1			
.06	1.4										
.05	1.4										
.26	.62			20.7	32.2						
.26	.6	76.7	8.2	14.	32.7	1.4	17.1	6.2			
.25	.63					1.5	12.0	6.6	1.25		
.05	.4	22.7	2.0	18.0	15.9	0.5	24–27	5.2–6.3	.45		
	.3	31.8	4.4	27.7		0.5	26.8	5.2–6.4	.45		
.14	1.2	78.1	5.6	52.6–56.0		1.4	63.5	13.6			
.07	.06			39.0		0.8	44.2	var	.45		
.15	.91	47.2	10.0	53.7		0.8	44.3	9.3	.49		
1.08	.51	27.7	2.0	17.1							
.05	.8										
0.9–1.7	0.8–1.0			1.1	3.4	13.0	5.1	22.4	.90	7	

8

The Golden Egg

Duck and goose eggs are delicious to eat, despite the prejudice of many Americans to the contrary. An egg is an egg, but to hear some people talk they'd sooner eat spider brains or fetal octopus than duck eggs. In many countries duck eggs are more popular than chicken eggs.

A goose egg makes a dandy omelette, though most people prefer to save them for hatching. Because the laying of geese is so seasonal, their eggs are usually considered too valuable for eating. That's why this chapter will lean heavily toward keeping ducks for eggs. Duck eggs, because they tend to be more plentiful, are more commonly eaten than goose eggs. However, should you not have to provide your gaggle much of its feed by virtue of having lots of meadow, or should you wish to indulge yourself in the luxury of eating goose eggs, be assured that you have a high-quality food item in your frying pan. We have a friend who keeps geese solely to impress his friends with huge one-egg omelettes!

If you intend to keep waterfowl specifically for eggs, then it is important to get a breed known for its egg-laying capabilities. Of the ducks, Campbells and Runners are the two most commonly kept for laying, as both lay nearly year-round. In warmer areas Muscovies can also be prolific layers. Chinese are the best known among the geese for numbers of eggs, the other breeds having shorter laying seasons. Meat breeds are generally not as prolific as those bred for laying, and most ornamental breeds are highly seasonal layers.

Among the laying breeds of ducks, you may get your first eggs from six-month-old birds regardless of what the season may be, but in most breeds of ducks and geese, laying won't commence until early in the spring following the year they hatch. Both the rate of lay and the times when the laying season begins and ends are determined by the breed, strain, and age of the bird: what it was fed; the weather; the general care; and whether artificial lighting is used. Virtually all waterfowl lay at least in the spring. The laying season may end at any time from late spring until the day before next spring. For the seasonal layers—geese and the wilder strains of ducks—eggs may be expected from early spring into summer. The best layers keep churning them out for months at a stretch and may cease laying only during the fall molt. Ducks lay an egg every day while geese lay one every two days; and almost invariably laying occurs around dawn.

Though the thoroughly domesticated breeds of ducks may lay without interruption for months on end, it is normal for geese and the wilder ducks to lay their eggs in a "clutch," a batch that would be about the right size to hatch. If you left the eggs in the nest, the duck or goose would probably go to setting and not lay any more that season. Even if you take the eggs away as they are laid, there is likely to be a natural pause at the end of a clutch. The pause may last a week or two.

The first year we had our Embden goose, Minerva, she laid 15 eggs and then quit. We had really expected somewhat more than this for putting her up a whole year. We thought maybe she was mad at us. Fortunately, a friend more experienced with the ways of geese put us in better spirits with the news that the interruption was only temporary. Sure enough, in a couple of weeks Minnie was laying again, and we eventually had three good clutches from her.

Mallard-derived ducks will normally continue to lay well for three years, with some strains stretching through to four or five years. Muscovies may lay for six or more years. Most breeds of geese will not reach their full potential as layers until their second year of laying, and though they generally peak at five years, they may lay as long as ten years.

If you're keeping a flock principally for eggs, it would be wise to replace your older birds before they lose their efficiency and while they are still useful as table fare. After you get a cycle started, it is possible to replace just a few birds with young ones each year, so you are never starting over completely. This is especially important if you are hatching your own and your flock is essentially self-perpetuating after the initial acquisition. Of course, if you're planning to buy laying ducks or ducklings to regenerate your flock, it doesn't much matter how many you replace at once.

The laying ability of any strain can be improved by selectively breeding for it. This is done by hatching eggs only from the best layers. There are two ways to tell the best layers—direct and indirect.

The direct method is most reliable but is somewhat impractical. You have to have some way of keeping track of each duck's laying record. It is possible but unlikely that you would recognize each bird's egg. You could keep your females in separate compartments, but then it is rather time-consuming to care for them. You could use "trapnests," nests the duck can get into to lay her egg but not out of until you come along to identify her and turn her loose. But trapnesting seems to work more successfully with chickens than with waterfowl. When they can't get out of the nest, ducks may panic and break their eggs. Nonetheless, some breeders have reported satisfactory results and feel they justify the hassles.

Many breeders rely on indirect methods. The laying abilities of a female are estimated by examining her physical features. The better layers can often be picked from a flock by their lack of plumage luster and their scraggly feathers. Closer examination will reveal baggy abdomens, sometimes even dragging on the ground, with pubic bones that are flexible and wide-set. By removing birds from your breeding population that do not have these features, you have a hand in upgrading your bevy.

A less scientific method, but one that works for many backyarders, is to hatch during the slower laying periods, the theory being that birds which lay fertile and hatchable eggs at that time must be good layers and should produce offspring which are better than average.

The size of egg to expect depends on what breeds you raise and even on the strain—within each breed, certain strains will lay larger eggs than others. Basically, the size of the egg depends on the size of the bird. Small, yolkless eggs commonly signal the beginning and end of each egg-laying season but are also found during very hot summer weather, especially when adequate drinking water is not available. Goose eggs weigh about five times as much as duck eggs and are fun to amaze your friends with. Even duck eggs are large, however, when compared with chicken eggs.

Geese lay white eggs, but the color to expect from your ducks depends on the breed. The chart in Chapter 3, "Meet the Waterfowl Family," lists the color laid by each breed. Incidentally, the color of the shell has nothing to do with what's inside. The only difference to you is in what color you like to look at. The difference to the duck is how well she can hide her eggs.

Providing NESTS

Covered nests facilitate collecting the eggs, as they give birds a comfortable and attractive place to lay and improve the chances that you will not have to search out new hiding places each morning. Nesting facilities discourage ducks and geese from laying on the ground or at the edge of the pond where eggs tend to get soiled or broken, or in the pond where they don't show up until they rot and come floating to the surface

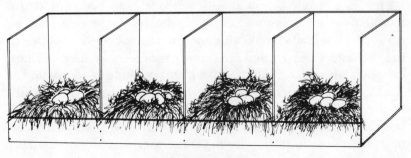

Nesting boxes

127

SIDNEY QUINN

two or three weeks later. Dirty eggs are unhealthy for eating and are more difficult to hatch. Nests protect eggs from scorching sun, from rain, and from freezing weather. They may help to hide the tasty morsels from predators, although crafty egg-eating animals and nest-robbing birds are not easily discouraged.

Nests need not be expensive and complicated and may often be assembled from something lying around the backyard. Abandoned doghouses do nicely. An old tire casing partially sunken into the ground, filled with nesting litter and provided some shade, is the delight of many a duck or goose. Another popular nest for geese is a 50-gallon barrel or oil drum turned on its side. A few bricks along each side help keep the drum from rolling when a goose enters and exits. A wooden packing crate on its side also makes a dandy nest; tack roofing paper to the top and sides to make it waterproof. An 18-inch-(45 cm) long box with a foot-square (30 sq. cm) opening is adequate for ducks, while for geese both the length of the nest and the width of the opening should be doubled. The size of the nest is not critical as long as certain factors are kept in mind. The nest must be tall enough for the birds to enter and sit comfortably without scraping their heads. It must be wide enough so that they can turn around when they want to get out. (Apparently the Manufacturer left out reverse, since for some reason ducks and geese don't like to back up.) Preferably, the nest should be just barely big enough, as birds are more likely to lay in a darkened, seemingly secluded place. Because waterfowl prefer to lay in fairly well hidden nests, we pile evergreen prunings in front of our nests to give them that feeling of seclusion. The ducks and geese have no trouble finding their way through the tangle of brush; once they're in the nest they prefer that you pretend you do not see them there.

Provide one nest for each three to five females unless they are expected to set, in which case, of course, you will need one nest for each setting female. The nests should be widely spaced and preferably evenly distributed throughout the yard, but you will find that some locations are more popular than others.

Lay down a thick layer of litter to keep the eggs clean and reduce breakage by careless birds. You can encourage the use of a nest by placing fake eggs in it. Safety seems to play a role in a bird's decision where to lay an egg, and fake eggs apparently indicate to a bird that here is a safe place to put another egg. Plastic and stone eggs manufactured expressly for the purpose can be found in feed stores or poultry supply outlets. But you can use golf balls or any other egglike objects. One manufacturer of ladies nylon hosiery gives away a free fake goose egg with each pair purchased. We frequently find birds setting on rocks, apples, and even tennis balls. If it rolls, they love it. We have a friend who lives next to a golf course and gets a lot of stray balls in his yard. Whenever he sets off to play golf he first supplies himself with golf balls from the nest one of his birds keeps. He can always count on this source. She finds every ball that comes over the fence and rolls it into her nest.

Regardless of how nice the nests are, it is practically inevitable that a duck or a goose will occasionally lay eggs somewhere else. This is partly due to the decrease in nesting instincts that comes with increasing domestication. Some birds will just drop the egg wherever they happen to be standing when the urge strikes. Novice layers who haven't caught on to what's happening may not think of finding a nest in which to deposit the egg. Eventually they'll discover what the nests are for. But even experienced layers sometimes lay eggs in places other than the nests you provide. This is sheer perversity. Typically they get a maternal urging and seek a dark, secluded spot in which they fancy to assemble and hatch a clutch, without *you* finding out about it. They will deliberately seek out a place you and the other ducks and geese in the yard don't know about—in a hollow tree trunk, *behind* the nest, even just in a clump of tall, dry grass where they can be so remarkably flat and still that you have to trip on them before you notice. No matter how many nesting boxes we provide, each year at least one of our ducks successfully hides her eggs. Sometimes she will disappear altogether and in four weeks proudly come marching back at the head of her regiment of little downy puffballs. The darker breeds, especially the Mallards, are particularly good at hiding their nests because they blend in so well with the vegetation.

Those who provide night shelters, as described in Chapter 5, "The Pond and Other Amenities," find that they have the egg-collecting problem solved, since eggs are laid in the building early in the morning before the ducks and geese are let out. Also, the eggs are likelier to be clean, as long as the building itself is clean.

An additional advantage of a shelter is that it provides the opportunity of extending laying through artificial lighting. If the natural length of the day is extended to 14 hours through a few hours of artificial lighting in the fall and winter, the females' systems will react as though it is perpetual springtime, and the irregularities in the laying of eggs from season to season will be somewhat smoothed out. You don't normally get more eggs this way—you just get them better spread out over the year. These night lights can be put on a timer by those who go in for automation.

Problems

Egg-binding. There are a few problems associated with egg laying. One is a condition called egg-binding, wherein one or more eggs get jammed up in the oviduct and are unable to pass through. This is likelier to happen in the more prolific layers. It may occur when an overly large egg attempts to pass through a small oviduct, as when a young bird tries to lay its first egg or when any bird lays unusually large eggs for its breed. Birds that tend to lay double-yolked eggs often get egg-bound. Double-yolkers occur when one yolk catches up with another in the oviduct, and both are wrapped in the same egg white on the way down. Eventually the yolks are covered by one large shell, and a double-yolker is laid. Double-yolkers are great for eating but lousy for incubating since they rarely hatch. Other causes of egg-binding are thin-shelled eggs and over-weight females. Thin shells may result from inadequate calcium in the diet, or some other mineral deficiency.

Egg-binding may be suspected if a duck or goose is inactive and listless, and stands awkwardly with ruffled feathers. Closer examination reveals a distended abdomen, and the hard eggshell can be felt through the abdominal wall. An egg-bound bird should be placed in a warm area with food and water within easy reach. Sometimes a bound egg can be eased out by applying olive oil, mineral oil, or petroleum jelly to the oviduct and then working the egg out with a finger. A particularly stubborn egg may have to be broken inside of the oviduct and then worked out by hand. Since sharp edges of the broken shell or the blow necessary to break the egg may cause injury, this method is used only as a last resort.

Blow-out. A second problem, and one that sometimes follows egg-binding, is called blow-out or prolapse of the oviduct. This happens when a bird has to strain while passing an egg, pushing part of the oviduct and cloaca through the vent. It is thought to be an inherited weakness but may be aggravated by a hormonal imbalance, overweight, the laying of

131

too-large eggs, or laying by a young duck or goose before it has fully developed the necessary equipment. The protruding organs should be gently washed and pushed back into place. Sometimes a relaxant such as a hemorrhoidal ointment must be used to relax the muscles so the bird will retain the organs. The bird should be put into a warm, secluded place to recuperate. A low-protein diet will temporarily discourage laying and hopefully allow the bird to mend properly. Since this condition is thought to be inherited, it is best not to hatch any eggs from such birds so that the characteristic will not be perpetuated.

Marauders. As we noted in Chapter 5, skunks, raccoons, stray dogs, and even blue jays can radically disrupt your carefully laid plans for harvesting duck and goose eggs—by eating the eggs or even the birds. If this problem occurs, check our suggestions on "Protection from Predators" in Chapter 5.

Eggs for eating

We are often asked to describe the differences between duck and chicken eggs. Their flavors are very similar when produced under similar feeding and management programs. We find the chief difference between them to be that duck eggs are firmer in texture, with the raw whites being more cohesive. Duck eggs have a thicker, tougher membrane and a larger yolk in proportion to the albumen (the technical term for egg white). The whites are difficult to separate, so duck eggs are not particularly suitable for meringues and angel foods. We generally save duck eggs for recipes that are compatible with their firmness, and for dishes that don't require separation of yolk and white. For baking, we prefer to use duck eggs since their larger yolks contribute a greater richness. Incidentally, people who are allergic to certain enzymes in chicken eggs often find that they are not allergic to other types of eggs in which the offending enzymes do not happen to be present. They would be deprived of their morning protein were it not for the availability of duck eggs.

Eggs should be picked up each morning to prevent them from losing their freshness, getting frozen or cooked by weather extremes, or falling prey to marauders. Duck eggs tend to dirty easily, and it is important to get the eggs cleaned (if necessary) and into the refrigerator as soon as possible to avoid spoilage. Since eggshell is porous, it is possible for contamination that is stuck to the shell to work its way inside. If only lightly soiled, eggs may be cleaned without water by scraping or brushing. If water is necessary, it should be warmer than the eggs; otherwise contamination may be sucked in as the contents contract. Very dirty eggs should be thoroughly cooked before eating to kill bacteria that may have penetrated the shell or otherwise gotten into the egg itself.

When an egg is laid, it is coated with a moist film called the bloom. This quickly dries to form a natural protective coating. Washing an egg removes its bloom and therefore reduces its keeping ability. The best plan is to keep things tidy in your yard so the eggs are always clean, as they will last longer if they don't need to be washed. It is not possible to increase the storability of a dirty egg by not washing it, though, because more harm is done by leaving the dirt on than by washing the bloom off.

Eggs with cracked shells or with holes pecked in them by marauding birds should be used neither for hatching nor for eating. We often cook such eggs into an omelette to treat our cat. Contrary to popular practice, raw eggs should not be fed to pets. Raw egg whites have the nasty knack of tying up biotin, causing a deficiency of this B vitamin in dogs and cats.

Eggs sometimes show red or brown spots on the yolk when cracked into a pan. These are called blood spots or meat spots and are usually caused by minor hemorrhaging in the oviduct of the bird. The fact that such harmless spots are rarely seen in eggs purchased in stores is a result of the commercial practice of not marketing spotted eggs in deference to finicky eaters. Commercial eggs are candled for this defect as well as for cracks in the shell and other irregularities. By thus examining each egg for its salability, commercial producers ensure uniformity. Such meticulous quality control is generally not of concern to backyard farmers.

Sometimes we are asked about eating eggs from yards in

which there are drakes or ganders along with the ducks and geese, since of course these are most likely to be fertile. There is no significant difference in palatability or nutritional value between fertile and infertile eggs. Because of the life factor within the fertile egg, its keeping quality is somewhat reduced, but this is virtually negligible at normal refrigerator temperatures. In other words, *unrefrigerated* fertile eggs can't be stored as long as infertile ones—if that matters to you. Refrigerated eggs may be kept as long as two months before eating, but are best used within two weeks, while still at the peak of freshness.

Because most breeds of waterfowl lay in seasonal patterns unless exposed to artificial lighting, it becomes important to store surplus eggs for use during a shortage. The home freezer is the ideal egg storage facility. If frozen when perfectly fresh, eggs may be kept for up to a year as long as a temperature of 0° F. (−18° C.) or less can be maintained. The eggs cannot be frozen whole, for the shells may burst and spill their contents into the interior of the freezer compartment. We break the eggs into a bowl, add a teaspoon of honey or a half-teaspoon of salt per cup, and scramble the eggs slightly. Mixing air bubbles into the eggs by overwhipping should be avoided, since air will cause the eggs to dry out during storage and they will deteriorate more rapidly. Yolks and whites can be stored separately if desired. Salt or honey is needed only in the yolk, to keep it from getting pasty. In either case, the mixture is poured into ice cube trays, frozen solid, then removed from the trays and put into plastic bags. Whenever we need an egg for baking, we simply take out a cube and let it thaw for about half an hour before using it. Such thawed eggs should be used no longer than 24 hours after being taken from the freezer and should not be refrozen.

9

The Parental Instinct

If you plan to raise young, then by the time spring arrives you should have decided how you are going to handle incubation of the eggs. The easiest way, of course, is to leave it all to the birds, although there are at least two major reasons why the easiest may not be the best. First, you'll get fewer young overall if you let them do it, since they stop laying while they're brooding. Second, you may be raising a breed that doesn't get the urge to brood, and you simply won't have that option. Domestic waterfowl exhibit varying degrees of desire to brood, depending on the strain and the purpose for which the breed was developed. Because broodiness is not compatible with heavy egg production, it has over the years been bred out of certain breeds of ducks in favor of egg laying. Those breeds known to lay the best are less likely to set their own eggs than those whose laying is more highly seasonal. But even if you know the probability that your type of duck or goose will set, there is always the chance that individuals within a normally brooding group will decline to set, or one from a breed known for egg production will decide to go broody.

Artificial incubation has its own complications, discussed in the next chapter. Before you make a decision, you might want to read through it to see what's involved. Here, we're going to talk about leaving it all to nature.

The broody

When a duck or goose gets reclusive, hides her eggs where you can't find them, or spends more and more time on her nest, then you can suspect she is developing that age-old maternal instinct. Ducks and geese are more inclined to go broody and

135

stay broody if nests are located in secluded areas. Broody ducks and geese should not be moved unless you deliberately want to break them up.

Sometimes a potential mother will steal off into the bushes to build her nest and hide her eggs to assemble a clutch that's well protected from predation. This is an important preliminary function in the process of natural incubation of eggs. One year we searched in vain for a missing Mallard hen, only to discover her, at last, nesting in some ferns beneath a water faucet that we used several times a day. This just goes to show how perfectly nature has colored the Mallard hen in order to camouflage her on the nest. The hiding instinct is not so strong in the more domestic breeds, and they are usually satisfied to lay their eggs in the semipublic nests their keeper has prepared for them.

If predators are a problem, hopefully the potential mother will choose a safe place in which to brood rather than hiding in a pile of leaves under the shrubs. Nests for brooding should be specially designed to prevent disturbance or death of the broody. Marauder-safe nests should have closable openings that can be latched at night.

Nests against the earth are best for hatching since the soil helps to retain moisture necessary for a successful hatch. But such nests are not always safe from local marauders that might find easy prey in a mother duck or goose conscientiously defending her eggs. Though a gander will do his best to defend his mate, he may not always be forewarned, as when the setting goose of one of our friends was killed by a tunneling animal that came up under the nest and chewed a hole in her belly as she quietly covered her eggs. Mother ducks do not even have the potential protection of their fickle mates. Wooden or dirt-bottomed nests, then, should be provided the protection of a layer of fine-mesh aviary netting securely fastened at the bottom. Earth may be used over the wire to line the bottom of the nest and ensure humidity retention, with nesting materials placed on top.

As we have mentioned, male Mallards and drakes of derivative breeds do not retain the same plumage pattern year-round. They acquire their nuptial plumage in early fall, which gives the females plenty of time to consider their choice of mates. Among ducks, it is the females which make the final choice, incidentally. The females also acquire a nuptial plumage, though their color pattern stays so nearly the same year-round that it is difficult to distinguish any difference. Yet the molt and renewal of special feathers is an important event for the duck, since it is at this time that she acquires on her breast the special down with which she will line her nest. This down is longer, stronger, softer, and generally more suited to nest-building than the down she wears the rest of the year. As a mallard-derived duck prepares her nest and begins to assemble a clutch in it, she gradually pulls this down, lining her nest with it until finally, when she is ready to set her clutch, a proper duck nest has been made. Actually all waterfowl, to a greater or lesser degree, use their feathers and down to line their nests, making them soft, cozy places for the eggs to spend the incubation period, and for ducklings and goslings to enter the

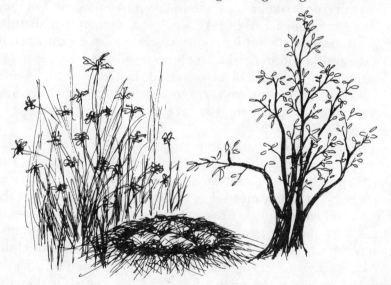

world in. Down and feathers help to keep the eggs warm and are usually pulled over the eggs for their protection whenever mother leaves her nest for short periods. When large quantities of feathers and down have appeared in a nest, you can safely suppose that one of your female ducks or geese is becoming maternally inclined. This usually occurs in spring or early summer, depending on breed, age, and weather conditions.

As feathers and down accumulate in the nest, eggs will also begin to accumulate, laid each day or two by the expectant mother until a full clutch has been gathered together. As this clutch-gathering occurs, you may wish to step in to aid your duck or goose in ensuring hatching success. While ducks and geese in nature take care of collecting their own clutches, often natural phenomena occur which prevent completion of this task. Marauders might rob the nests of their eggs, or severe extremes of weather may freeze or overheat the eggs, causing them to lose their hatchability. It is therefore often necessary to help a duck or goose by collecting the eggs and storing them in a safe place, returning them when a sufficient number has been gathered for setting.

Waterfowl usually continue to lay in the same nest as long as one or two eggs, real or fake, are left as reassurance that the eggs are still safely hidden. Since ducks and geese apparently can't count, a motherly duck or goose will not become suspicious that her eggs are being removed. In Chapter 10, "Artificial Incubation," we explain how to store eggs for hatching, and it is the same whether the eggs are to be hatched naturally or artificially.

You may wish to collect the eggs for other reasons, such as attempting to keep the ducks or geese laying so that you can hatch the eggs in an incubator, or so you will have plenty of fresh eggs for family meals. Eggs may be collected as long as the birds are laying, and it does not seem to cause psychological stress for a duck or goose to be denied the opportunity to nest and hatch a brood. But if you want your birds to hatch out little ones at some time during the season, this can often be done by simply returning a number of eggs to the nest. Whether the

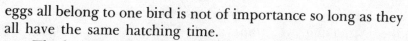

eggs all belong to one bird is not of importance so long as they all have the same hatching time.

The brooding urge develops in most breeds of waterfowl after a certain number of eggs are in the nest. Only in Muscovies have we consistently seen females persist in setting on empty nests, a fruitless practice they share with domestic chickens. Returning a dozen or so eggs to a nest thus encourages a duck or goose to go broody. The closer your waterfowl are to being wild the more likely it is that a female will want to set when she sees her nest is full of eggs. A "full nest" to a duck or goose is not necessarily the optimum number to set on. Their eyes can be bigger than their stomachs, so to speak. For best hatching success a nesting bird should have anywhere from 12 to 15 eggs. On no account should a bird's ability to cover the eggs be overextended since, as the eggs are rotated periodically, all may eventually be chilled and lost.

For whatever reason, many people who wish their ducks or geese to set and hatch a clutch of eggs will first collect a number of eggs for other purposes. As a bird begins to set, laying ceases at least temporarily, but sometimes for the remainder of the season. Though some breeds will recommence laying if their young are taken away shortly after the hatch, individuals may be disinclined to do so.

As the laying season progresses, a duck or goose has fewer vital nutrients in her body to put into her eggs, so that her offspring will not be as healthy and vigorous. Where it is desired to extend the hatching season by not letting a duck or goose hatch her first clutch, it is all the more important to see that an adequate breeder feeding program is followed, as outlined in Chapter 7, "Feeding Your Ducks and Geese."

During the actual incubation process, the mother will leave the nest occasionally to have a snack or a swim, keeping herself fit and well nourished for her important task. Most broody waterfowl pull the nesting materials over the eggs when they leave the nest to prevent the eggs from chilling and to hide them from predators. A broody duck or goose may be off the nest as long as 30 minutes to an hour, once or twice a day.

When a mother duck or goose comes back from her swim, she is soaking wet underneath. This moisture, which she inadvertently sprinkles over the eggs as she settles back into the nest, provides the essential humidity to help the shells of the developing eggs become soft and pliable so the little ones will eventually be able to open the shell when the time comes to pip. This moisture must be introduced artificially in an incubator. While settling into the nest, the mother also turns her eggs (much as they must be turned by human agency when hatched in an incubator) which prevents the yolks from sticking to the shell and killing the embryos. She does this not only on her return after an absence but also on the average every hour or so through the day, paddling the eggs about with her feet as she shifts position in the nest. The theory is that her underside gets uncomfortably hot next to the warmed eggs, so she rotates the cooler faces against her. No one really knows why she does it. She just does it. That's the main thing.

Sometimes during the process of getting on and off the nest, in rearranging the nesting material, or in frantic efforts to ward off intruders, an egg or two may accidentally be rolled from the nest. People sometimes think that the mother knows which eggs are infertile, and not wishing to waste any further effort on them, summarily rolls them out of the nest. But examinations of the contents of such eggs generally shows the

QUINN

rashness of this assumption. A good broody will roll an errant egg back into the nest with her bill, but if the egg has gotten too far, or the mother doesn't notice it, or she is simply lazy, the egg will remain out in the weather to die. This is one of the hazards of natural incubation, and we have watched eggs lost one by one in this way until there were none left in the nest to hatch.

The new family

If all goes well, the new members of the family will hatch on schedule—28 days for mallard-derived ducks, 30 days for geese, and 35 days for Muscovies. If for some reason the eggs turn out to be infertile or for other reasons do not hatch, the mother's internal calendar tells her when her time is up, and within a few days of the anticipated hatch she will leave the nest to go on about her business. Unfortunately, sometimes her clock is ticking too rapidly and she may leave the nest two or three days early. Though an infuriating experience for someone who is excitedly looking forward to a family of downy little sweethearts, this happens occasionally to the best of waterfowl breeders.

Newly hatched ducklings and goslings generally stay hidden under their mothers for the first day or two until they have rested up after the prodigious effort of getting out of their shells. It is during this period when the hatchlings are normally resting beneath their mothers that it is easiest to introduce purchased or orphaned day-old babies to a mother duck or goose whose eggs were infertile or otherwise failed to hatch. Provided the foster brood is not already too old, they and their new mom likely will accept each other. Since hatching waterfowl imprint so readily on the first moving object they see, it is best to handle a brood intended for this purpose no more than necessary, lest they attach themselves to you as their parent.

Once they leave their nest, the hatchlings will not snuggle under their mother, as baby chicks hide under mother hens, but will crowd around her for warmth. Their downy fluff helps

141

to keep their bodies at an even temperature, and they are remarkably capable of coping with most climatic situations. On particularly cold or rainy days the mother may open up her wings to form a protective umbrella. In the event of severe rains or late snowstorms, it may be necessary to help out the mother by enclosing the whole family in a shelter.

Baby waterfowl understand an extensive vocabulary immediately upon hatching. They understand their mother when she tells them to come to her from their scattered wanderings, to follow her to a new place, to get out of the pond, to run and hide, or to crouch down and be still.

The young birds themselves have pretty remarkable vocabularies for such young babies. Adult geese have a highly developed set of vocalizations, and goslings hatch with a good start in their abilities to express themselves vocally. The cheerful and contented "happy to see you" double-syllable "whit-whit" of little goslings is one of the most endearing things in the world, but they can be very vociferous in their complaints when not pleased about something. Ducklings, though not having quite the personalities of goslings, nonetheless also start out with a good working vocabulary and can let their mothers know, for instance, when they are lost or when they are warm and happy. In fact, their two-syllable "peep-peep" is the baby version of an adult duck's expression of contentment or pleasure at a happy reunion. One syllable repeated loudly and shrilly always denotes alarm or discontent.

As ducklings and goslings grow and mature, they become less dependent on their mothers and eventually wander off to find mates as the next season approaches. When the mother's young become old enough to get around on their own and her work is nearly done, she will begin her postnuptial molt. By this time her feathers have become worn and frazzled, and so nature exchanges her ragged apron-strings for fresh smooth plumage with which to begin a new year and a new cycle of mating and motherhood.

FOSTER MOTHERS

A reliable chicken hen makes a dandy foster-mother for orphaned ducklings and goslings. If she's been setting tenaciously for most of three weeks so she's psychologically prepared for motherhood, and if the hatchlings are fresh out of the egg and have not yet imprinted on their mother figures, they'll take to each other like magnets. It will never even cross their minds that they weren't really meant for each other. We had a friend whose banty hen raised three goslings one year. It was a bit unsettling to see her clucking to the babies when they were a mere three weeks old, towering over their foster mamma like three Baby Hueys. It may look unnatural to us, but it obviously isn't or how could four birds be so happy together? Of course, there may be some consternation in such arrangements, for instance on the day the young waterfowl first discover water. They'll wonder how come mom never told them water could be so wonderful, and she'll bustle up and down the bank clucking admonishments to them for their foolishness.

143

As well as giving hatchlings to a foster mother, duck or goose eggs themselves can be hatched under a female chicken or turkey. Since the bodies of landfowl do not provide the requisite humidity needed for hatching waterfowl, the eggs have a better chance of hatching if moistened daily as though they were in an incubator. The larger the egg, the more important this becomes. In addition, it may be necessary to turn goose eggs and large duck eggs by hand, since most breeds of chickens are unable to turn oversized eggs by themselves.

The number of waterfowl eggs that any particular hen can cover depends entirely on her size. A large chicken can cover about 9 to 11 duck eggs and from 4 to 6 goose eggs, while a banty will overload on any more than half this many. A turkey may safely brood 18 duck eggs or 10 to 12 goose eggs. Because the ducklings and goslings don't sleep under the hen as baby chicks would, it is not necessary that they all be able to fit under her after the hatch.

Due to the longer incubation period of waterfowl, there is a risk involved with using chickens to hatch waterfowl eggs. Chickens, like ducks and geese, have internal clocks running while they brood to tell them when to give up hope for a clutch and go do something else. Chickens may therefore not stick out the four to five weeks required to bring waterfowl eggs through their full incubation period.

Mites and lice are not the chronic problem for ducks and geese that they are for landfowl, but parasites are capable of infesting your waterfowl hatchlings that come in close contact with them. Many waterfowl breeders don't make certain that foster-mother hens are free of these pests until it's too late. An infestation of mites and lice get newly hatched ducklings and goslings off to a bad start, for these vermin will weaken them and possibly even kill them. A number of commercial preparations can be used to dust a setting hen and her nest to destroy mites and lice. Check with your local feed dealer. Be sure to follow any precautions listed against using the product too close to hatching time. Some of the dusting powders are safe to use on ducklings and goslings, while others can be more harmful to

them than mites and lice. It's a good idea to dust well ahead of hatching. It's a better idea to get your broodies from a parasite-free flock of chickens.

Sometimes baby waterfowl do not respond to a foster hen's motherly cluckings and may wander off to die from exposure or fall prey to marauders. We lost several hatches of Mallards this way, until we learned to gather up the hatchlings as they fluffed out and bring them into the house to raise ourselves. We never learned whether it was the hen's fault for failing to mother her little charges properly, or if it was the ducklings' fault for not heeding her stern commands. Perhaps it was a bit of both.

The father's role

In order to get fertile eggs from your waterfowl, it is critical to have the proper number of males and that they be of the proper ages.

Most domestic ducks can be kept in breeding pens with four to six females per male—more in the light, active breeds and fewer in the heavier, sedate breeds. If the ratio exceeds this, you must expect a certain percentage of infertile eggs, as the males will not be able to get around to all of the females frequently enough to keep them fertile. If the ratio is very low,

145

there is the danger of strife between the males. If it is merely low, they won't care but there will be a certain inefficiency for the keepers.

Mallards normally mate in pairs, or at most trios. The Chinese, being lighter and more active, can usually be penned in the same ratio as domestic ducks, four to six females per male.

A drake is fertile at the young and tender age of six months. His fertility begins to fall off after his third season. A gander's fertility builds up over his first two seasons, and he's at his best between the third and sixth years.

Those interested in hatching eggs may find themselves wishing to distinguish the fertile from the infertile eggs in advance of incubation on the excellent theory that the latter might as well be eaten. It is unfortunately not possible to tell without breaking an egg out whether it is fertile or not, and by that time obviously it's too late to think of hatching it. But there might be some value to examining an egg or two, for example to determine, prior to making some momentous decision regarding your breeding and hatching program, whether your male birds are taking care of their end of the business. In any case, when cracked into a pan, close examination will reveal to the sharp eye the presence or absence of a tiny embryo. At the top of the yolk, or perhaps just to one side, is a little white spot.

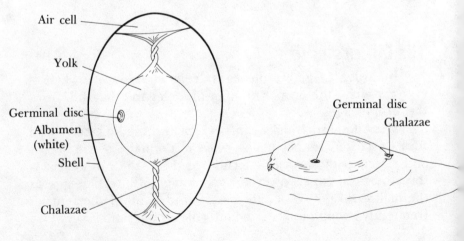

Air cell

Yolk

Germinal disc
Albumen
(white)

Shell

Chalazae

Germinal disc
Chalazae

If this spot is disorganized, mottled, and irregular in shape, then the egg is probably not fertile. But if the spot is rounded and firm like a bead of tapioca and consists of a series of shaded concentric rings, then the egg has been fertilized.

The white fertility spot on the yolk should not be confused with the two white, curly things on either side of the yolk, called the chalazae. These little cordlike connectors served to keep the yolk positioned in the center of the egg while it was in the shell, though they don't by any means work perfectly. For the safety of the embryo during incubation, the yolk must be prevented from drifting to one side and sticking to the edge. Since these whitish things are so highly visible, many people believe them to be a new little bird; because of their prominent size, they may even assume that the bird is faily far along in development. Such is not the case, however, and at any rate these "strings" are perfectly edible.

As ducks and geese begin to set, a radical difference becomes evident in the way the males act. Drakes that pair with one mate for the season generally hang around the nest for a while, but will finally give up to pal around the pond with other forsaken husbands. At this time drakes begin their eclipse molt, during which they take on the color pattern of the females. Since the female coloring makes it easier for a duck to hide, it is reasonable that the drakes would take on this more camouflaging coloration during the time when they molt their primary wing feathers and cannot fly. As a matter of fact, they'd best be camouflaged in drab colors all year long for safety's sake. But this would cut their love lives to ribbons and there would be nothing to live for! A little fling at gaudy plumage once a year is worth the risk.

The eclipse molt can be startling to those who are unaware of this peculiarity of drakes. It certainly startled us the first day we saw all of our Mallard drakes had become females. A few weeks later we were relieved to see tinges of green coming into some of the heads, and half of our Mallard population once again became drakes. As soon as the flight feathers are renewed, the males immediately begin a second, partial molt to resume once again the beautiful plumage for which they are so well known.

Other mallard-derived breeds go through this double molt each year, but the effects are not nearly so startling. Khaki Campbell drakes, for instance, lose the deep bronzeness in their heads and take on the overall tan hue of their mates. These other breeds take even less interest in the homemaking efforts of their many wives than their mallard forefathers, for they have been busy socializing with the rest of the bevy all season. Muscovy drakes, which molt only once a year, take scandalously little interest in the process of hatching their own young, for the two sexes tend to remain segregated most of the year anyway, socializing only when a drake decides to step out for a little fun.

In geese, as the maternal instinct becomes strong in the female, her mate becomes very paternal and protective. He will stand by as his wife pads the throne on which she will be spending the next four weeks. After she has assembled the clutch and begun to set, he will become even more adamant in his insistence that intruders keep their distance. It is the gander's attitude at this time of year that has given geese their reputation for meanness.

By the time ducklings hatch, even those drakes which had taken some modest amount of interest in the occupation of their spouses have long since turned their attentions elsewhere, but the gander seems just as delighted with fatherhood as his mate is with motherhood, and he may care for the early hatchers himself while his Mrs. busily works at getting out the rest of the family. When all the goslings have finally hatched, he will shepherd the little ones around and see that no harm comes to them.

Mr. and Mrs. Lautrec, our Toulouse pair whose sad demise we have related, once had a very poor hatching season and that year managed to produce only one baby. As a matter of fact, we hatched it for them in our incubator. But they knew it was theirs the minute we put the little fellow outside. That gosling was their pride and joy, always safely sandwiched between its two parents. In fact, it was quite some time before we actually

148

saw their little son again, for they kept him well hidden, always shielding him whenever we approached for a peek.

Though at times geese can be ornery toward the young of other species, geese with parental urgings have been known to adopt baby ducks. One year we had a brood of ducklings that had outgrown our living room duck-rearing facilities. Much concerned that they were still too young to be left on their own, we put them in the yard with the larger waterfowl, keeping a wary eye on them to be sure that they were getting along all right. We had no cause for concern, as it turned out, because our big gander King Tut, who was usually very tyrannical toward the ducks, decided to adopt the babies. He watched over them while they slept, took them for walks, made sure they got their share at the feeder, and told them in no uncertain terms when he felt that they had played long enough in the pond.

10

Artificial Incubation

Ducks and geese have had literally millions of generations to perfect their main line of business—hatching eggs—and it's certainly lots easier for keepers to leave all details of propagation to the birds. Among the decided advantages of leaving the hatching up to the ducks and geese are the following which may not be obvious. First, the natural mother usually has a nearly 100 percent success rate. Second, she takes care of the babies. Third, her sanitation is superb and difficult to match in an incubator. But sooner or later many waterfowl breeders find it necessary to make the acquaintance of an incubator and to acquire a knowledge of at least the rudiments of how it operates. There are many reasons to resort to artificial incubation: the breeds of waterfowl raised may not be a type inclined to set—some breeds, especially those developed for egg production, have been selectively bred against brooding instincts; the waterfowl may for some reason be disinclined to set in the area in which they are kept; you may wish to hatch more eggs than the females can hatch themselves, or you may wish to keep the birds laying and therefore deliberately want to keep them off the nest; wild birds and other marauders may not allow the females to collect clutches; and finally, a setting female is a likely victim for local predators once she has made the decision to stick with the nest at all costs, and you may opt not to expose her to this risk. A good look at the particular breeds you have chosen to raise, at your goals, and at your backyard situation may tell you whether artificial incubation would be necessary or desirable.

If by chance you should find that you need some eggs incubated but don't care to organize your own hatching program, you may wish to locate a custom hatcher. This is someone who will hatch your eggs for a small fee or for a percentage of the hatch. Sometimes small commercial hatcheries do custom hatching, but most hatcheries won't bother with it. More often it is individual poultry or waterfowl fanciers that provide this service for their fellow breeders. Custom hatchers can generally be located through poultry-oriented organizations and often advertise on feed-store bulletin boards or in the want-ad sections of newspapers under "poultry."

Of course, if you raise chickens, you may have your own little custom hatchers to help you. Consult the section on foster mothers in Chapter 9.

The incubator

Assuming that you wish to get an incubator, you must first decide what size you want. The capacity of an incubator is conventionally given by the number of chicken eggs it will hold (more exactly, Leghorn chicken eggs). To calculate how many waterfowl eggs an incubator will accommodate, figure roughly that for each 100 eggs of rated capacity it will take the same number of Call eggs, 75 Mallard eggs, 60 Muscovy eggs, or 30 to 40 goose eggs. Since eggs vary substantially in size, these figures are very rough estimates but should give you some idea what to plan for.

Having settled on a size, you must next decide whether you want a still-air or a forced-air incubator. Still-air incubators come in various smallish sizes, including models for just a few eggs, and are handy to have if space and funds are limited. Still-air incubators are extremely sensitive to conditions in the surrounding environment and should be kept where the temperature is not likely to fluctuate. A constant room temperature of 70° F. (21° C.) is ideal. The incubator should be kept where sunlight is unlikely to fall on it, and away from drafty windows and any nearby heaters. Very large eggs such as those of a goose cannot be hatched successfully in some still-air in-

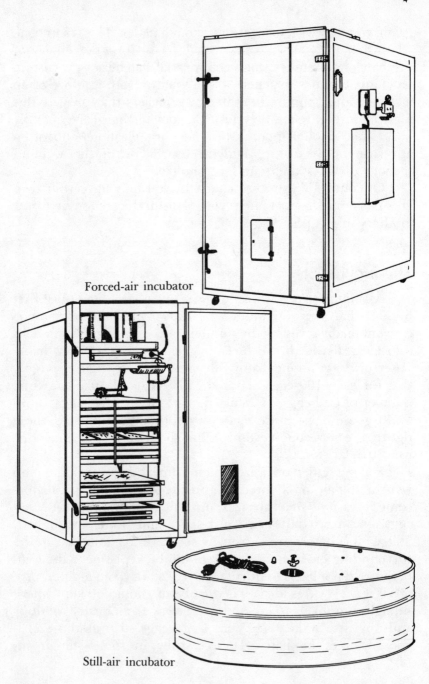

Forced-air incubator

Still-air incubator

cubators, for one part of the egg will be much closer to the heating coil than another part, and the uneven heating that results will upset the development of the embryo.

In a forced-air incubator, a fan forces the air to circulate, ensuring an even temperature throughout. Forced-air incubators tend, on the whole, to be larger than still-air incubators, ranging in capacities from several dozen to thousands of eggs. Although there are fairly small forced-air incubators, comparable in outer dimensions to some still-air incubators, the more complicated machinery involved in forcing air is obviously much more suitable for large incubators. It is difficult to construct a small forced-air incubator that is economical. You must be prepared to pay a premium for the luxury of forced air on a small scale.

Forced-air incubators are less sensitive to the surrounding conditions, but for best results should nonetheless be kept where the temperature is not likely to fluctuate much. Subterranean storage spaces are ideal spots to store and operate incubators, because they are usually well insulated and experience little daily or seasonal temperature variation. Additionally, family members and guests are unlikely to visit these areas, and the chances are reduced that the incubator will be tinkered with or the electric cord tripped over and unplugged.

Once the choice is made between a still-air and a forced-air incubator, a wide assortment of additional features must be decided upon. The temperature should be automatically regulated, and all but makeshift homemade models will have this feature. The humidity will have to be regulated, and this can be done either manually or automatically. The automatic feature is, of course, an added expense and requires special plumbing to connect water pipes to the incubator. Some models have adjustable vents for regulation of the humidity and oxygen supply.

Really fancy incubators have warning devices that sound an alarm or turn on an alert-light to indicate that the temperature or humidity is out of the desirable range. This warning signal is designed to summon the operator, who is supposed to rush immediately to the scene, determine what's wrong, and correct the situation right away. With most home models, especially those used by small backyard fanciers, unusual temperature and humidity conditions are discovered by chance—either the operator casually checks the conditions on a trip past the incubator, or else the critical condition is not discovered until time to turn the eggs. There is rarely any way to tell how long the condition has prevailed and whether the hatch can still be saved. Because there is always the chance something might go wrong, it's a good idea to locate the incubator where it can be conveniently checked at periodic intervals throughout the day.

The necessity of turning the eggs requires another decision on whether to increase the complexity of the machine. In most smaller incubators, the eggs must be turned individually by hand. For models with trays containing egg-positioning racks, wire turning devices are often available. To turn the eggs, the wire device is pulled out of one tray and pushed into another, so it is necessary to have one wire per two trays. This goes very rapidly. Sometimes there are special kinds of turning wires for duck and goose eggs. Some models have devices to turn all of the eggs with a flip of a crank on the outside. Some incubators even have time-set turning devices that automatically turn the eggs on schedule, so you don't even have to be home to take care of it.

There is no question that it is highly desirable to be able to place hatching eggs in a location apart from other eggs still developing, as this permits giving them slightly more favorable conditions and keeps the mess of hatching confined to one place and away from succeeding hatches. The more elaborate incubators provide a separate hatching compartment.

Models are available which incorporate varying combinations of these features. In general, still-air incubators are less complex than forced-air models and therefore usually provide fewer extra features. Some models, especially among forced-air incubators, provide all of the features we have discussed.

It is possible to make your own incubator, but unless you have both a thorough understanding of the workings of an incubator and some skill at cabinetmaking, the results may be most disappointing. Then again, you could be lucky. Our neighbor has successfully hatched eggs in a Styrofoam picnic basket! The free circulars "From Egg to Chick" and "The Avian Embryo," listed in Chapter 16, "Resources," provide detailed instructions for making rudimentary home-built units. Kits can be purchased which allow you to create an incubator out of easily obtained materials. Simple homemade models are great educational projects for classrooms and are fun for a let's-see-what-happens family undertaking, but can prove exasperating for the serious breeder unless some of the more sophisticated features developed by the commercial manufacturers can be duplicated.

For classroom projects, special glass-topped incubators have been designed through which the entire four- or five-week performance of a clutch of eggs can be observed. Of course, the most exciting part of the show occurs during the final act. These models are also recommended for home hatchers who simply must see every detail of the hatch, since constantly opening the incubator to peek inside causes temperature and moisture to be lost and jeopardizes the hatch.

Incubators and kits can be purchased at local feed stores or through farm catalogs and are retailed by several of the many incubator manufacturing companies, some of which are listed in Chapter 16. Used incubators may, of course, occasionally be offered for sale through classified ads or feed-store bulletin boards. Used incubators tend to hold their value well, and moreover, there is always a greater demand than supply. Consequently, you should be prepared to have difficulty locating a used incubator and to pay a high fraction of the initial price if you do find one. If you need some consolation, think ahead to the day when you may be the seller.

Every incubator, new or used, has its own individual personality, and until you are used to its quirks and peculiarities, it may not function well for you. It may turn out in the end that you are totally incompatible, and divorce will be the only civilized solution. We mention this now because it's

155

hard to say objectively that an incubator is no good just because one person couldn't hatch with it. More than once we've heard of a party selling a lemon to a sucker only to discover later, to his great consternation, that the buyer got along fine with the machine and had excellent success with it.

The eggs

Following the example of the ducks and geese themselves, we prefer to hatch eggs in spring and early summer. This allows adequate warm-weather growing time for the little ones to fatten up and feather out before chilling winter weather sets in. Late-season hatches tend to be unhardy due to the depletion of resources in the female's chemistry, as mentioned in the preceding chapter.

The eggs should be collected at least once a day, or possibly more often if the weather is extreme, or if wild birds and other egg-eaters are likely to damage eggs left lying around. Once you recognize the laying patterns of your birds, you should be able to tell whether you have picked up most of the eggs that are likely to be laid each day. Since waterfowl generally lay in the early morning, more than one daily collection is normally unnecessary.

Sort eggs as they are collected for uniform size, shape, and color normal for the breed and for solid, thick, even-textured shells with no cracks. Naturally, you will want to hatch eggs from only healthy, vigorous stock and from parents free of defects and deformities. Those eggs that don't measure up for hatching can be reserved for consumption.

Of course, you will want optimum fertility in the eggs you set to hatch. There is some important information on the subtleties of fertility in "The Father's Role," the last section of the preceding chapter.

Operating an incubator is much simplified if eggs are saved and set in clutches, rather than being put into the incubator a few at a time as they are collected. Those who think that an egg must be set immediately upon being laid should stop to consider that female waterfowl don't lay their entire clutch at once but assemble it over a period of time before setting commences. The reasons for not putting them right into the incubator will become obvious as we explain what is involved in operating an incubator. Basically, the problem is that it is practically impossible and at best unreasonably time-consuming to monitor the progress of eggs which have been haphazardly stuck into the incubator. Even mother ducks and geese would find it impossible to keep track of their babies if they hatched at different times. On the other hand, eggs do deteriorate when stored for too long, and hatchability is generally reduced greatly during the second week of storage. A reasonable and convenient compromise is to set once a week. Seven days is not an excessive time for eggs to be stored under the proper conditions, and when settings are made at one-week intervals, the successive hatches will be reaching their respective stages of development on the same day of the week.

It is helpful to mark the eggs as they are picked up each day when you're saving them for hatching. If the date is placed on the eggs, length of storage can be traced as a factor should the eggs not hatch as well as expected. If more than one breed is raised and the eggs look alike, the breed could be indicated on the eggs as they are gathered.

Use a grease pen, wax pencil, or crayon to mark eggs, rather than a spirit pen or others containing substances that might soak into the shell and harm the embryo. Pencils and fountain pens are difficult to use because their sharp points so easily pierce the shell. Moreover, such a mark may well be worn off by continual wetting before it has served out its usefulness.

Eggs stored for hatching should be kept pointed-end-downward in a place where proper temperature and humidity are maintained. A constant temperature of 50 to 60°F. (10 to 15° C.) will ensure that the eggs are neither so warm that they begin to hatch nor so cool that the embryos die. A relative humidity of around 75 percent allows the eggs to retain sufficient moisture to keep the embryos viable. The best storage places are in cellars, as the temperature there is uniformly cool and the air is moderately humid. Hatching-eggs, wine, and potatoes have about the same preferences in storage conditions. If the storage place tends to be a bit drafty, keep the eggs in an egg carton, or in flats in a cabinet to help decrease moisture loss.

Some authorities say that the eggs should be turned twice a day during the storage period so that the yolks will not stick to the inside membranes and prevent the eggs from hatching. A female duck or goose does this when she settles on her nest to deposit her next egg. You can do it by placing the eggs in an egg carton or flat and elevating one edge somewhat so that it is sloped. To shift the eggs, merely elevate the opposite edge of the flat; thus you avoid the necessity of handling each egg individually every day.

We ourselves have found no significant difference in the hatchability of eggs that have not been turned during the first week. Should it become necessary to store the eggs for longer than a week, hatchability will decrease if the eggs are not shifted daily. If for some reason the eggs must be kept for longer than a week before being set, remember that the hatchability begins to decrease, and that after about two weeks it will rarely be worth attempting to hatch them.

Duck and goose eggs are often very dirty when collected, particularly in wet weather or when laid near the pond. It's a good idea to clean them before putting them into the incubator. If any bacteria are present in the dirt, they will flourish in the ideal conditions inside the incubator unless previously removed by cleaning. Also, the pores of the shell are unblocked by cleaning, and the oxygen and moisture exchange with the surrounding atmosphere will be allowed to occur at the proper rate.

Should you decide to enclose your birds in a shelter at night as described in Chapter 5, and keep the litter fresh, you will find that eggs tend to remain cleaner than those laid outside.

While there are commercial preparations for cleaning dirty eggs, most backyard waterfowl raisers do not have sufficient quantities of eggs to follow mass-production procedures. We simply rinse our dirty eggs in lukewarm water and dry them right away. Washing in this manner does not seem to affect the hatch adversely. Those with only superficial soil and debris clinging to them can be given just a dry brushing. A quick dip of all eggs in a solution of Clorox and warm water, mixed in the proportions listed on the label for household cleaning, helps further to reduce the chances of bacterial growth. The wash water or Clorox dip should always be warmer than the eggs; otherwise, as the contents contract in cooling, harmful materials may be drawn inside.

The length of time eggs can be saved before setting may depend on whether the incubator is operated on a single-clutch basis, or whether continuous hatching is practiced as explained below. Each method presents problems and limitations for the small-time hatcher. The best possible hatching results are obtained by saving up a clutch of eggs, setting them all at once, and not adding any eggs to the incubator until the hatch is finished. This way the temperature and humidity can be regulated according to the stage of the hatch, and the best possible conditions can be provided throughout the hatching period. Most authorities and all incubator manufacturers recommend this single-clutch method because it results in the highest hatch rate. On the other hand, there is an obvious disadvantage to this system: since you really shouldn't wait more than a week between settings due to the decrease in hatchability we have noted, you would have to own four or five separate incubators in which to set your consecutive hatches until finally the first machine is free again for another round. Not wishing to make such an immense capital investment in incubators in order to hatch one clutch in each, single-clutch practitioners are often tempted to stretch the maximum storage time to its limits in order to have the largest possible collection of eggs, thus after all negating the advantages of single-clutch hatching.

Many of us compromise and practice continuous hatching, which involves the setting of eggs in an incubator at periodic intervals so that settings overlap: some are freshly set while others have been developing for a while, and still others are about to hatch. Most practicers of continuous hatching set their eggs once a week, for reasons noted earlier. For continuous hatching, it is impractical to regulate the conditions within the incubator according to the stage of development of the embryo, since the eggs are scheduled to hatch at different times and so do not all have the same requirements. If the optimum conditions necessary during the major part of the hatching time are maintained throughout, then, all other things being equal, continuous hatching need not unduly reduce hatchability despite its compromise nature. Success with the continuous hatching method can be increased by using either an incubator with a separate hatching unit or a second, smaller incubator as a hatcher. Each clutch of eggs is transferred to the hatcher just before the eggs are expected to pip, and can be provided the most favorable conditions for hatching. At the same time, succeeding hatches are protected from the general filth and debris associated with a hatch.

In any case, after a clutch has been readied, the eggs are put into the incubator with the pointed end slightly downward. Incubators with trays provide a handy way to keep track of each week's hatch—simply tape the date of hatch on the front of the shelf for easy reference. That way, as soon as the incubator door is opened you can tell at a glance which trays are scheduled to hatch when. In a small incubator all eggs may have to be on the same shelf. In order that the different hatches don't get mixed up, it is helpful to be able to readily identify which setting they belong with. Thus, each egg in one week's hatch might have a longitudinal ring drawn around it, the eggs of the second week's hatch might have a transverse ring, those of the third week's might have both, while the fourth week's might be left without any such mark. Unless Muscovies are being hatched (which take a week longer than other domestic waterfowl), after the fourth week the eggs from the first week will no longer be in the incubator, and the cycle of marks can begin over again from the first week.

If there are positioning racks in the incubator, the slots which hold the eggs in place should be of the proper size. Manufacturers of these models usually make several different-sized racks. Those designed for chicken eggs are too small for most duck eggs and are certainly too small for goose eggs. The function of these racks is to keep the eggs evenly spaced and to ensure that no more than a specified number of eggs is placed on each tray.

An incubator should not be crowded with more eggs than it was designed to hold. Overcrowding makes turning more difficult and also makes it more likely that eggs will not be kept in the proper position with the pointy end down.

As we shall shortly explain, there is a barrage of turning, dunking, and miscellaneous to-do that follows a certain schedule as the hatch progresses. We find it helpful to have a calendar handy on which we make copious notes regarding each clutch as it is set. This reminds us of the various tasks that will be appropriate to each stage of the incubation period, which is essential in keeping things straight when practicing continuous hatching.

TEMPERATURE

Because proper incubator temperature varies with the type of incubator and the type of eggs being hatched, we have provided a chart listing the appropriate temperature for each given condition. The difference between the still-air and the forced-air temperatures merely reflects different operating principles and does not mean that the eggs themselves are actually hatching at different temperatures. Obviously, a mother goose or duck does not have different still-air and forced-air operating temperatures. This temperature difference among incubators is due to the peculiarities of the machines themselves, associated with the fact that developing eggs generate their own heat.

The temperature is monitored by viewing a special incubator thermometer through the peek-window of the incubator. It is important that the thermometer be the specially designed incubator type, since it allows a reading within ¼ °F. (⅛° C.) A proper thermometer should be supplied with the incubator; if not, one can be purchased at some feed stores or through mail-order poultry outlets.

It is also important to follow the manufacturer's instructions on where to place the thermometer in the incubator in order to ensure an accurate reading, since the temperature varies slightly from place to place within the apparatus.

The temperature is regulated by a thermostatic device called a wafer, which is an ether-filled disc that expands as it heats up and contracts as it cools. The wafer in turn presses a button as it expands, and releases the button as it contracts, causing the heat to go off and on. This button is called a thermal switch. The distance between the wafer and the switch is usually adjustable by turning an adjustment screw on the outside of the incubator. Bringing the wafer closer to the switch decreases the temperature, and moving it farther away makes the temperature rise.

The temperature may fluctuate ever so slightly as the thermostat allows the heating coils to heat up and cool off, but this variation should be within about ½° F. (.25° C.) on either side of the proper temperature. Fortunately, the egg temperature stays more even than the air temperature. Poorly designed incubators allow the temperature fluctuation to be greater, resulting in poor hatches.

We have found that the temperature in the incubator sometimes inexplicably varies for short periods of time, usually during changes in the weather, but soon stabilizes itself. Since changes in pressure as well as temperature cause the wafer to

	Operating temperature	
	Forced-air	Still-air
Mallard-derived duck	99½°F. (37.5°C.)	102°F. (38.9°C.)
Muscovy	99½°F. (37.5°C.)	102°F. (38.9°C.)
Goose	99¼°F. (37.4°C.)	101½°F. (38.3°C.)

expand and contract, it acts effectively as a barometer, and there will inevitably be minor variations in the temperature maintained by the wafer as the barometric pressure changes. Unless absolutely necessary, do not readjust the screw. Playing with it may cause the temperature to fluctuate so wildly that an otherwise beautiful hatch may be ruined.

The incubator temperature should be regulated well ahead of setting the first clutch of eggs so the walls get warmed up and the heat flow reaches a steady state. A small incubator should be operated 12 to 24 hours before eggs are put in, while a larger incubator requires two or three days to be sure that the temperature has stabilized before eggs are set. Removable trays should be left in whenever the incubator is in operation, including when initially attempting to stabilize the temperature. The temperature will often drop when eggs are first placed in the incubator, especially when large numbers of eggs are put in or when the eggs are large. The thermometer reading will return to normal as the eggs warm and reach the temperature of the interior of the incubator. Do not tempted to fiddle with the thermostat during the first few hours after a setting is made. You will spoil the accomplishment of the many hours or days you spent in making the initial adjustments.

Authorities recommend that the temperature be readjusted during the last days of incubation as indicated on our chart at the end of the chapter. While this slight variation improves the hatch when setting a single clutch at a time, those of us who practice continuous hatching find it impractical and actually harmful to subsequent hatches to readjust the thermostat. Leaving the temperature set at one level throughout the hatching season has provided us with adequate results for our hatching efforts, and we recommend this for others who wish to hatch continuously.

Contingency plans should definitely be made for emergencies such as malfunctioning of the wafer or the thermal switch, or a power outage. The power can go out at any time, especially during storms, and we all know that the power company can appear exasperatingly slow in doing something about it—

especially for someone watching the temperature drop in an incubator full of valuable eggs. Be ready by having quilts or down sleeping bags in which to wrap the incubator, or by providing an alternate source of heat such as a gas or oil heater or fireplace to warm the immediate area around the incubator. (If it's summertime, you should still do all this, but keep your vigil with a glass of lemonade out on the porch.) Check periodically that it isn't getting *too* hot. If the incubator has closable vents, shut them to keep warm air from escaping. Do not open the incubator during this time even to turn the eggs: it would be better to miss a turning than to cause the temperature to drop even further.

Since a wafer may lose its ether—gradually or suddenly— keep an extra wafer or two around the house in case of emergency. Different incubators use different kinds and sizes of wafers, so be sure you are purchasing the right one for your model. Thermal switches sometimes malfunction if clogged with dust and down from the newly hatched birds, so keep a spare thermal switch handy also. Become familiar ahead of time with the process required to change it, since when the time comes there will be a great deal of urgency in getting the incubator functioning again. In addition, have on hand an extra indicator light bulb or two in case the little light indicating that the heat is going on and off burns out. These spare parts should be available at feed stores, through incubator manufacturers, or through mail-order poultry supply outlets.

When the wafer goes out, the temperature begins to rise steadily because there is nothing to turn off the heat. This may even cause the mercury column of the thermometer to break if the temperature goes higher than the thermometer is designed to register. If the wafer goes out, the incubator should be opened to allow the eggs to cool while the wafer is being replaced. When the incubator is started back up, closely monitor the temperature until it has been properly adjusted to accommodate the new wafer. Depending on how long the temperature has been rising, the eggs may or may not have been affected, so it's reasonable to proceed as normal until you've definitely determined that the hatch was ruined. (This is done by candling, as described later in this chapter.)

A malfunctioning switch may cause the temperature to go either way, depending on whether it gets stuck on or off, so this problem can be confused with the wafer going out. Proceed as for replacing the wafer, and keep your fingers crossed that you were in time to save the hatch. Wafer and switch problems are occupational hazards of operating an incubator, so it's best to be philosophical about them. Rather than allowing yourself to seethe at the imperfections of the system, marvel instead that mankind has been able to duplicate so accurately the natural process of hatching an egg. And remember that even a mother duck or goose blows it now and then.

Humidity

The eggs of ducks and geese need a fairly high amount of moisture in order to hatch. Unless the humidity is adequate, a duckling or gosling will be unable to break out of its shell when the time comes to hatch, and it may die fully formed while attempting to pip.

Female waterfowl retain a certain amount of moisture in their feathers and replenish it periodically by taking quick swims, thus providing proper humidity for the eggs. In an incubator, humidity is provided by evaporation of water from a pan usually located near the floor but sometimes held by a special rack at the top. The pan is often divided into sections; filling more sections provides a greater evaporating surface and thus higher humidity in the incubator, and vice-versa. To aid in maintaining adequate humidity, moisten your hands with warm water before turning, and spray the eggs with a mist of tepid water during turning. Extra-fancy incubators have automatic sprayers that periodically spray a fine shower of warm water onto the eggs. Many models come with vents that may be opened and closed to provide additional control over the humidity. Exact directions for use of the vents should be found in the instruction manual.

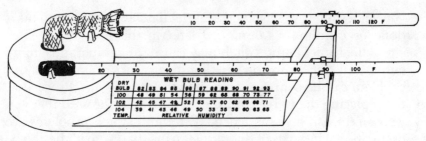

Thermometer and hygrometer

Only warm, clean water should be used in the water pan to increase humidity. Cool water will cause the incubator to take longer to regain operating temperature. The water must be clean since debris floating on its surface prevents adequate evaporation. For this reason, it is also important to clean the water pan after each hatch to remove the loose down that ducklings and goslings shed during their hatching activities. Many beginners have been fooled into thinking that they were providing proper moisture for their hatch, only to find that, though the water pan was adequately filled, down was coating the surface of the water and preventing it from evaporating.

Humidity is measured by a device called a hygrometer and is expressed in either of two different ways. The basic principle of a hygrometer is that the evaporation of water causes cooling. The drier the air, the faster the water evaporates and the greater the decrease in temperature. An incubator hygrometer is simply a thermometer whose bulb is wrapped in a wick immersed in a supply of water. The reading on this thermometer is called the wet-bulb reading, and it reflects the rate of evaporation from the wick. The lower this reading is, the drier the air is in the incubator.

	Operating humidity		
	Wet bulb		Relative
Mallard-derived duck	84°–86°F.	(29°–30°C.)	65%
Muscovy	84°–86°F.	(29°–30°C.)	65%
Goose	86°–88°F.	(30°–31°C.)	75%

At each temperature the air has some maximum possible capacity for water vapor. Another way to express humidity is in terms of the percentage of moisture actually in the air compared to the maximum possible. This is the so-called relative humidity. At the standard operating temperature of an incubator, there is a precise conversion between relative humidity and the wet-bulb reading. Some hygrometers are calibrated in one set of terms, some in the other. In our charts we have given proper humidity readings both ways.

The proper operating humidity for duck and goose eggs can be found in the accompanying chart. Like the thermometer, a hygrometer should come with the incubator, but if not, one can be purchased where incubator supplies are sold.

To get an accurate humidity reading, it is necessary to keep the hygrometer supplied with water for evaporation. This should be checked each time the eggs are turned. It is also important that the wick be kept soft and absorbent, using soft water and rinsing the wick in soapy water periodically. For accurate readings, replace the wick if it gets encrusted with mineral deposits. It's a good idea to have some spare wicking handy.

It is often impractical to take up precious hatching space in smaller still-air incubators with the rather bulky hygrometer, so the air cell within the eggs may be used as an indicator of adequate moisture. This technique is described in the section on candling later in this chapter.

You should soak goose eggs in a bucket of warm water (100°F. or 38°C.) to help soften the tough shell and increase the chances the goslings will be able to get out. Goose eggs should be dipped in clean, warm water once every other day after the first week of incubation and once every day after the 18th day until pipping starts. Soaking in cold water may chill or even shock the embryo, and dipping in dirty water may coat the eggs with foreign matter. As hatch time nears, watch for signs of pipping so that you do not drown a young gosling by filling its shell with water. Do, however, continue to moisten the eggs by sprinkling them until the goslings have gotten all the way out of the shells.

167

As indicated in the chart at the end of this chapter, the humidity should be raised at a certain point near the end of incubation. We'll discuss the specific procedures in the section below on "The Hatch."

When first starting up an incubator, before any eggs are placed in it and while the temperature is being regulated, it's essential to bring the empty incubator to the proper humidity level. This is especially important in wooden incubators, as they tend to dry out during storage and therefore will absorb a good deal of moisture at the beginning of the hatching season. Better this moisture should be drawn from a water-filled pan than from your newly set eggs.

Turning

When incubating a single clutch at a time, you should place the eggs in the incubator and leave them alone for the first 24 hours while they adjust to the conditions within the incubator. For continuous hatching, the incubator must be opened to turn eggs in preceding hatches, but the newly set eggs should be left untouched. After the first day, the eggs must be turned several times each day until shortly before the hatch. At this time the new ducklings or goslings are planning where to crack the shell in order to make their entry into the world and would appreciate your desisting from spinning them round and round. The day on which turning should cease for each kind of egg is indicated on our chart.

	Turn through
Mallard-derived duck	25th day
Muscovy	31st day
Goose	25th day

Turn your eggs at least three times a day and preferably more often. The mother duck or goose settles in her nest quite often during the day, and so, although she doesn't count how many times each egg was turned, they all get moved around enough to keep the embryo floating in the center of the egg. We like to time the turning to coincide with our regularly scheduled daily events in order to help us remember this important operation, so we turn the eggs when we first get up in the morning, just after getting home from work, and at night before we go to bed. Some people turn their eggs five times a day, and others seven. Turning a large number of times per day not only cuts into the day, but also does not allow the incubator sufficient time to heat up before it's time to turn again if done manually. With an external lever it's more practical to turn the eggs often. If you are blessed with an external turning lever, remember to check the hygrometer for proper humidity when you turn the eggs, and to soak the goose eggs periodically as mentioned below. In any case, turn at regularly spaced intervals, an odd number of times each day so that alternate sides of the egg are up during the long overnight period. Wash your hands before turning to ensure that no grease or grime will clog up the pores in the shells.

We keep a bucket of warm (100°F. or 38°C.) water handy during turning and dip our hands into it periodically as we proceed. This not only helps to increase the humidity, but also provides a little friction which makes the eggs less slippery and thus easier to turn. Goose eggs are dunked into the bucket according to the schedule described in the section on humidity. Finally, we use the warm water to replace any water that has evaporated from the pan since the last turning.

In order to facilitate turning by hand, some people like to mark an X on one side of each egg and an 0 on the other side: the eggs all show the X side up after one turning, and the 0 side after the alternate turning. Before closing the incubator, be sure to check that the eggs are still pointy end down to ensure that the duckling or gosling will pip at the large end of the egg. Otherwise, the young bird may not be able to get out at all.

Before opening a forced-air incubator, turn off the motor and wait until it is completely stopped so that the fan doesn't blast the warm air out and bring in an unpleasant cold draft. Always remember to turn the motor back on again when finished. Still-air incubators should be left on during turning; since they have no fan, there is no danger of producing a gusty draft.

Candling

While there is no known way to tell if any particular fresh egg is fertile or infertile without first breaking it, you can check for fertility after about seven days in the incubator. Special candling devices are made specifically for checking the development within an egg. Since we are always pleased to place idle machinery to novel uses, we've found that our slide projector with its bright beam makes a dandy candling device. A simple and inexpensive homemade candling device can be assembled from a small wooden or corrugated cardboard box with holes cut into the sides and a light bulb placed within. The holes should be just a little smaller than the diameter of the smallest eggs to be candled. Those who raise

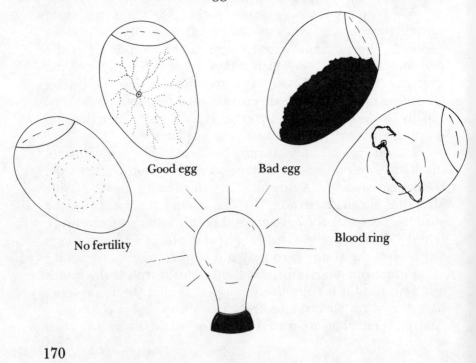

Good egg   Bad egg

No fertility   Blood ring

both ducks and geese should cut a smaller hole in one face of the box for duck eggs and a larger hole in the opposite face for goose eggs. With the light on inside the box and an egg held against the hole, it is easy to see what is going on inside of the egg. Candling is best done in a darkened room.

If an egg is fertile and is developing properly, candling should reveal blood vessels running out in all directions from a central spot, looking somewhat like a reddish spider web. You may have to rotate the egg a bit to bring this network into view. If you see nothing, it probably means that the egg is infertile, or the embryo was weak, indicating that perhaps the parent stock was unhealthy or there were too many females per male. Such eggs are aptly called clears. A thin dark ring around the egg means the embryo was once developing but has since died. If you see murky clouds floating about inside the egg, it has begun to rot. Eggs rot for a number of reasons: partial development, perhaps caused by a duck or a goose on the nest prior to incubation; improper conditions or storing time before setting the eggs; and improper conditions within the incubator. A handy color poster called "How to Identify Infertile Eggs and Early-Dead Embryos" is available from the University of California Division of Agricultural Sciences; for details see Chapter 16, "Resources."

All of the eggs should be candled after one week of incubation in order to identify those that aren't developing properly. This not only saves the operator of an incubator time otherwise spent handling eggs that will not hatch, but also provides more space in the incubator for other eggs. Further, rotting eggs use up oxygen in the incubator that is needed by the properly developing eggs, and sometimes bad eggs smell or even explode, quite forcefully, spewing millions of bacteria into the incubator and making an awful stinking mess for someone to clean up.

In addition to candling, use your eyes and nose to monitor the development of incubating eggs. Watch for changes in shell color or cracks caused by pressures from within; check for the source whenever you notice off-odors.

171

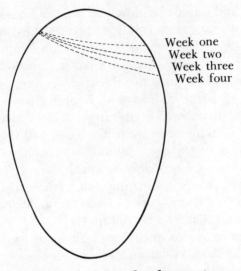

Week one
Week two
Week three
Week four

Air cell during development

Some people like to candle their eggs again after two weeks of incubation to monitor the conditions and see that the embryos are still on the right track toward hatching. Looking at the eggs each week also provides an opportunity for checking to see that the air cell is enlarging at the proper rate, as shown in the accompanying sketch. If it is enlarging too rapidly, increase humidity; if it is remaining too small, the humidity should be reduced.

Be sure to candle eggs fairly quickly so that they are back into the incubator before overly cooled. Work with rapid, efficient motions, but not so frantically that the eggs are likely to get broken. When the incubator has removable trays, take them out one at a time for candling; the incubator can then be closed and turned on to prevent the rest of the eggs from cooling during a long period of candling. The contents of a small still-air incubator, on the other hand, can be candled in a fairly short time, so it's usually all right to leave the incubator open while candling. If there are eggs in the incubator which are about to hatch, you might either postpone candling until the hatch is finished or cover them with a warm, dampened hand towel to prevent them from cooling and drying out while the other eggs are candled.

There is a fairly inexpensive hand-held candler that greatly increases the efficiency of candling. It's like a plug-in flashlight with an intense narrow beam. To use it, pull out a tray of eggs and run the candler along the rows of eggs from underneath. You will be able to see most of what's going on inside the eggs. This method is quick and efficient since it does not require handling each egg separately. This type of candler is available at many of the common poultry supply outlets.

The Hatch

Incubation periods and length of hatching time vary slightly, depending on the exact temperature of incubation, on the strain, and on the vigor of the parents. Babies from healthy, hardy stock often pop out of their shells a day or two early. Eggs that have managed to snuggle under a broody female for a time before being collected may likewise hatch ahead of schedule.

	Incubation period	Hatching time
Mallard-derived duck	28 days	24 to 48 hours
Muscovy	35 days	24 to 48 hours
Goose	30 days	48 to 72 hours

Toward the end of incubation, turning of the eggs should cease and, as indicated on our chart, the temperature and humidity should be changed.

When practicing single-clutch hatching, it is practical to readjust the conditions after turning stops, leaving the incubator alone until the eggs begin to hatch. Aside from occasional checks on the temperature and humidity, and adding more water if moisture loss is great, you are free to await the

173

	Hatching temperature		Hatching humidity	
	Forced-air	Still-air	Forced-air	Still-air
Mallard-derived duck	98¾°F. (37.1°C.)	103°F. (39.4°C.)	90°–92°F. (32°–33°C.)	75% relative
Muscovy	98¾°F. (37.1°C.)	103°F. (39.4°C.)	90°–92°F. (32°–33°C.)	75% relative
Goose	98½°F. (36.9°C.)	102½°F. (39.2°C.)	92°–94°F. (33°–34°C.)	80% relative

outcome with whatever mixture of anxiety and impatience is your personal custom.

Even if you practice continuous hatching, it may still be possible to provide the conditions appropriate to the final days of hatching if you are lucky enough to have a separate hatching unit. Some incubators are equipped with a special compartment in which the conditions can be adjusted to differ from those in the main unit. Alternatively, a second incubator may be used as a hatcher. The humidity in the incubator is raised by filling more sections of the water pan, or by providing an additional pan of water if necessary, and by closing some of the vents if possible. In addition to raising the general humidity within the incubator, increasing the "local" humidity right next to the eggs results in better hatches: place wet sponges on the shelves with the eggs that are about to hatch.

When continuously hatching in a single incubator not equipped with a hatching unit, it is less simple to readjust conditions during the hatch. Some incubator manufacturers recommend increasing the humidity in the entire incubator even when continuous hatching is going on, and then removing all moisture for a short period after the hatch is finished to allow the remainder of the eggs still in the incubating process to dry down properly. If done carefully, this will improve the hatch, but it is pretty tricky. Our own method, which has proven successful, is to fill the empty sections of the water pan once when most of the eggs in the current hatch have pipped. We then allow the water in the extra sections to evaporate without further additions, while at the same time keeping full the sections that normally contain water. If the water pan has only one section, you can increase hatching humidity by adding a second water container such as a pie tin, or placing moistened sponges on the hatching trays.

For a variety of reasons, goslings and even ducklings may not be able to get out of their shells by themselves. Generally it is unwise to attempt to help a baby bird that is too weak to get out of the shell by itself. This tends to weaken the general stock, should the baby succeed in living after being helped out. However, if you suspect the cause is improper humidity during incubation or some other factor rather than genetic weakness, then you may want to help your little waterfowl out of their shells. Let their struggle encourage you to improve incubation conditions instead of relying on instrument deliveries at each hatch.

Some eggs may never show signs of pipping. Perhaps the little bird had its head at the small end of the shell and thus did not have the necessary room for pipping activity, a result of failure to keep the pointed end of the egg downward during incubation. Or it could be weak due to disease or poor nutrition in the parent stock. Or the incubator could have been improperly regulated during the hatch. There are any number of reasons why eggs fail to hatch. If you get 60 to 75 percent of your fertile eggs to hatch, then you are keeping right up with the average backyard incubator operator.

The most exciting moment comes when the eggs first begin to peep. Shortly thereafter the hatchlings will pip, or break through the shell. After pipping, a little duckling or gosling turns itself 360° around in the shell, cracking the egg all around with its egg tooth as it goes. The egg tooth is a little pointed dot at the front of the bill that looks like a miniature rhinoceros horn. Soon after the little bird hatches and the tooth is no longer needed, it falls off. Some people never even notice that it was there at all. The tooth is perfectly positioned for poking a ring of holes around the girth of the shell, since the bird inside the egg has its head tucked under one wing just far enough to

175

expose the tooth at the other side. After the egg has been cracked all around, the new baby gives a mighty thrust to break free from the shell and then lies quietly on the incubator tray. After its prodigious effort to free itself from its tiny prison, it is now tired and much in need of rest. It is still wet and must remain in the warm interior of the incubator until its down is completely dried and fluffed out, for otherwise it might chill and die.

As soon as the hatchlings fluff out they should be removed from the incubator and placed in a warmed and ready brooder. For instructions on what to do with them after this, consult the next chapter on the care of ducklings and goslings.

Clean-up

Goslings and ducklings can make a frightful mess of an incubator in a very short time. Gooey wastes left inside the shells stick to the hatching tray and sometimes drip beneath the racks onto anything that happens to be below, such as other eggs or the water pan or heating coils. Not only is this material unpleasant and messy—it is very dirty stuff in a clinical sense, too, crawling with millions of nasty disease-causing organisms that have flourished in the warm and favorable environment of the incubator. For this reason, we always use our lowest tray for hatching so that there will be no eggs below onto which the goo can spill. Waterfowl hatchlings also shed a lot of fluff, which is in actuality a collection of little sheaths that cover each piece of down. These fall free of the down as the hatchling dries and fluffs out, getting into the water pan and blowing into the cracks and crevices of a forced-air incubator. Ease in cleaning out this mess is one of the advantages of having a separate hatcher.

After the babies have been removed from the incubator or hatcher, thoroughly clean out this hatching mess. Dispose of eggs that did not hatch, and thoroughly sponge refuse from the hatching trays and anything below that it fell onto. Vacuum loose down from inside the incubator. Remove the water pan, clean it, and fill it with fresh water. A weekly scrubbing of the incubator with warm, soapy water, or a special incubator disinfectant, is part of good hatching practice.

Not only is a clean incubator a pleasure to work with, but it is also essential to minimizing disease in later hatches and combating duckling and gosling diseases. Bacteria and molds may breed if organic material is allowed to build up, and a thorough cleanup here is the single most important point at which to break into the disease propagation cycle in your flock.

One of the most common results of continuing to hatch in a dirty incubator is a bacterial infection technically known as omphalitis. This infection, which is common to all species of day-old birds, shows up as rough, red navels in ducklings and goslings and causes an alarming mortality as the hatching season progresses. Deaths may continue for as long as two weeks after the hatch, yet the illness is noncontagious and is due solely to contamination in the incubator. There is no cure for the illness, so prevention is a necessity.

Other diseases affecting hatchlings are also controlled by eliminating incubator contamination. There are all sorts of chemical preparations for fumigating incubators after each hatch, but these are often harmful in the small confined quarters of backyard bird raisers, especially those who keep their incubators inside their homes. Quaternary ammonia compounds are among the best disinfectants. They are sold in many places for all sorts of uses, from cleaning dog kennels to sterilizing surgeons' hands, and can be found under a variety of brand names. They leave no stain and have no odor, yet are strong and effective when used according to directions. Quats, as they are affectionately called in the trade, work well only if there is no organic material left in the incubator in which bacteria can hide. An incubator should be thoroughly scrubbed and disinfected before it is stored away at the end of each season.

Mixed Hatching

We are often asked if it is possible to hatch waterfowl and landfowl eggs together. The answer is a qualified yes. Incubator manufacturers and other autorities seldom recommend it because the conditions for optimum hatch are different for land birds and for waterfowl. It is therefore necessary to compromise by providing conditions somewhere between, reducing the percentage of hatch for both types of eggs.

We hatch mixed eggs in our incubator at the temperature required for landfowl eggs, but keep the humidity a little high and increase it slightly for the first day of each hatch. Too much humidity results in mushy chicks among the landfowl, and too little humidity decreases hatchability among the waterfowl. It's a little tricky to hit the right combination for greatest possible hatch of both. Many of our breeder acquaintances try it, with varying degrees of success. A little experimentation will help you find the right combination of conditions for your incubator.

Summary

To give you a quick reference for maximum hatching success with a minimum of hassle, we have prepared this chart for the hatching of domestic waterfowl eggs in both still-air and forced-air incubators.

HATCHING CHART FOR DOMESTIC WATERFOWL*

Type of egg	Incubation period	Operating temperature	Operating humidity	Cool daily	Moisten	Turn	Hatching temperature	Hatching humidity	Hatching time
DUCK (Mallard-derived)									
Forced-air	28 days	99½°F. 37.5°C.	84°–86°F. 29°–30°C. wet bulb 65% relative	7th to 21st day	daily	2nd to 25th day	98¾°F. 37.1°C.	90°–92°F. 32°–33°C. wet bulb 75% relative	24–48 hours
Still-air		102°F. 38.9°C.					103°F. 39.4°C.		
MUSCOVY									
Forced-air	35 days	99½°F. 37.5°C.	84°–86°F. 29°–30°C. wet bulb 65% relative	7th to 21st day	daily	2nd to 31st day	98¾°F. 37.1°C.	90°–92°F. 32°–33°C. wet bulb 75% relative	24–48 hours
Still-air		102°F. 38.9°C.					103°F. 39.4°C.		
GOOSE									
Forced-air	30 days	99¼°F. 37.4°C.	86°–88°F. 30°–31°C. wet bulb 70% relative	after 10th day	Soak every other day, 7th–17th day, every day after 18th day	2nd to 25th day	98½°F. 36.9°C.	92°–94°F. 33°–34°C. wet bulb 80% relative	48–72 hours
Still-air		101½°F. 38.3°C.					102½°F. 39.2°C.		

*The manufacturer's instructions for any particular model of incubator supercede this chart.

11

Bringing Up Ducklings and Goslings

Aviculturists appropriately describe down-covered birds that run about soon after hatching as "precocial" in contrast to those young birds that are naked and helpless in the nest for days or even months. Nothing could be cuter than the irresistible combination of downiness and precocity in ducklings and goslings. They are amazingly well coordinated and can immediately pick up things to eat with their bills. As soon as they gain their strength after hatching they are able to see, for their eyes are open from the moment they hatch (though this doesn't always prevent them from running into things). Their downy coats help keep them warm as they busily pursue their first exploratory activities. And from the moment they hatch they can recognize and emit sounds having specific meanings such as "danger is near," or "I am hungry and cold."

Despite their precocial nature, waterfowl hatchlings must be provided certain comforts in order to ensure that they grow and thrive. Parent ducks and geese instinctively know how to care for their babies and usually manage to provide all of their needs; but humans who take it upon themselves to raise ducklings and goslings must first educate themselves in the nature of baby waterfowl and their uncompromising requirements.

It should not be assumed that because you have hatched young waterfowl in an incubator, you are irrevocably committed to raising them. If the quantity is small and the hassles seem large, it may be possible to dupe a gullible duck, goose, or even chicken into adopting them. A hen that has been setting for nearly her full term (the natural period of incubation for eggs

180

of her species), even on an empty nest, will normally be psychologically prepared to mother anything that appears under her in the night. (If you opt to use a chicken, see the "Foster Mothers" section in Chapter 9.) Since the whole process of hatching, which they do by rote, is clearly a total mystery to them, it is not necessary to furnish broken eggshells with the hatchlings just because you think their sudden appearance would otherwise strike her as too puzzling. She'll never suspect a thing.

The brooder

The first requirement in the care of young waterfowl is an adequate brooder. A brooder is the place in which a brood of birds is kept, and can range from the elaborate tenement-house arrangements sold by poultry supply outlets to a simple cardboard box with a light bulb providing the heat. Maintain-

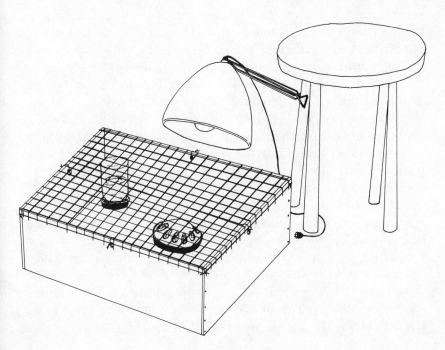

ing an adequate supply of cardboard boxes on hand can be a major chore. On the other hand, keeping the brooder clean is much simplified when all that is required is to provide a new box with fresh litter. Open-topped boxes should be outfitted with a partial roof consisting of a few sheets of newspaper to keep out drafts. If cats or children might bother the hatchlings, a piece of small-gauge wire mesh may be fastened over the opening to provide protection. Muscovy ducklings, being by nature arboreal, have amazingly sharp toenails and can climb right out of open-topped boxes. Besides, they have a perverse sense of adventure and, on succeeding in so escaping from their brooder prison, are frequently to be found marching around the neighborhood, with totally unwarranted confidence, as if they owned the place and knew right where they were going.

If you expect to hatch waterfowl as a regular procedure, a permanent brooder is more satisfactory in the long run. All-metal brooders with small-mesh (½ inch or 1 cm) wire floors and removable droppings trays beneath are easy to keep clean, for the trays can be pulled out for cleaning without disturbing the birds. A layer of rice hulls or other litter can be spread on the tray after each cleaning to facilitate the next.

If you have a concrete-floored outbuilding that can be made varmint-proof, it could provide the basis for a dandy brooder. An enclosed cold-weather shelter for adult ducks and geese, described in Chapter 5, could easily be converted into a spring brooder house if provided with an electrical outlet for a heater. Low, movable plywood partitions could be used to confine the young birds close to the heated region.

An apparatus commonly used to provide brooding warmth is a hover, a large aluminum dome or pyramid with an infrared bulb in the center. The heat can be reduced by means of a rheostat or by raising the whole hover. This device is especially suitable for brooding on a concrete floor. Hovers can be purchased ready-made at poultry supply outlets. To determine the waterfowl capacity of a commercially made hover, divide the rated baby chick capacity in half for ducklings and in thirds for goslings. Because baby geese and ducks are taller than baby chicks, place the hover a few inches higher than the instructions state for poultry.

Heat must be provided until the young birds have had a chance to grow heat-retaining plumage. Manuals for waterfowl raisers generally state that the brooder temperature should start at 90°F. (32°C.) and be decreased about 5°F. (3°C.) per week until 70°F. (21°C.) is reached around the fifth week, when heat is usually no longer required.

While a thermometer can be used to monitor such changes, the appropriate brooder temperature can actually be obtained very accurately without one—the little birds themselves will tell you how they feel. Their behavior indicates the correctness of the temperature they are provided: if vigorously pursuing their routine activities, they are perfectly comfortable; if huddled under the light and peeping distressfully, they are too cold; if pressed as far as possible from the source of heat and panting, they are too hot.

As the birds grow and their level of activity increases, their bodies generate more heat so that less artificially provided heat is required. The larger a batch of young birds that is kept together, the less is their need for artificial heat, for in greater numbers they keep each other warm.

Within comfortable limits for the ducklings and goslings, the more rapidly the heat is reduced, the more rapidly they will grow and feather-out. Also, they will do better against inclemencies in the weather when they are eventually put out to fend for themselves. When they go, it will be less of a shock if they have been "hardened off" a bit (to borrow a nurseryman's term). Nature reacts to a gentle stimulus by providing defenses, and whatever doesn't kill an organism makes it tougher.

Some brooders are heated by electric coils which are regulated thermostatically by a device very similar to that used to regulate heat in an incubator. Heat may also be provided by a simple light bulb, which should be placed in a protective reflector consisting of an aluminum bowl with a clamp by which it may be attached to the brooder. (Such reflectors are usually available in hardware stores.) Start the wattage at 100 and reduce the temperature by decreasing the wattage or increasing the distance of the lamp from the brooder floor, or both.

We like to start our hatchlings in a cardboard box in our house so that we can watch them a few days to be sure they are getting along all right. As soon as they become active, they are put into readied brooders, providing approximately ¼ square foot (250 sq. cm) of space per duckling and twice as much per gosling. Of course, as they grow they require more and more space—about double by the third or fourth week, and double again from the fifth or sixth week until they are put outside.

As older birds are moved to larger quarters, their former residence may be thoroughly cleaned and used for younger broods. The quats (quaternary ammonia compounds described in the preceding chapter) are also recommended for disinfecting brooder equipment. Because of the differences in feed requirements, as well as the differences in levels of activity, different ages and sizes should not be kept in the same brooder. It is unwise as well to mix waterfowl hatchlings with chicks or other young landfowl due to the significant differences between the species in their relationship to water.

Whatever type of brooder is chosen, it should be designed with the comfort of the little birds in mind, as well as to accommodate the propensity of young waterfowl toward messiness. Brooder sanitation requires some way of dealing with moisture and with the copious amount of fluid droppings ducklings and goslings generate. Periodic cleaning is facilitated by a layer of litter on the removable droppings trays of commercial brooders, as deep as space permits.

As the birds get older they tend to wet the droppings trays faster. To cope with this, many waterfowl breeders remove the trays and elevate the brooder over a very thick layer of litter that can easily be added to or replaced as needed. Because of the large amount of moisture generated by young waterfowl, multileveled brooders (known as batteries) are not suitable unless only the bottom section is used for them, reserving upper sections for young landfowl.

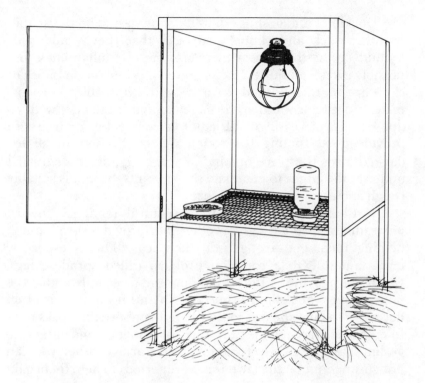

A thick layer of litter on the floor of a brooder house provides insulation against cold floors and also makes them easier to clean. Sawdust, shavings, and peat moss are all excellent for this purpose. Wet spots can be removed easily and replaced with clean litter. Gather up the young birds periodically so that the entire floor can be scraped off and hosed down and strewn with fresh litter when dry. Clean, dry litter is important to their health: lameness may occur in young waterfowl if bacterial growth from moist litter infects tiny cracks in their foot pads.

Newly hatched ducklings or goslings should not be placed directly on fine litter until they learn to distinguish it from their food, for they will fill up on the litter and could possibly choke on it. After they have begun to eat heartily, the brooder floor may be strewn with three or four inches of absorbent litter.

185

Ducklings and goslings should not be started on newspaper or other slick and slippery surfaces that they would slide around on, as this causes them not merely unhappiness but possibly even leg injuries. Paper towel or other rough paper or cloth are more solid and yet as readily disposable. Keep the material well anchored at the edges so that it can't get wadded up. Though increasingly difficult to come by, burlap bags also provide good footing for young waterfowl. Best of all for day-old birds is a piece of window screening, taped or turned under at the edges to eliminate sharp points. Screen is suitably rough and easily cleaned for reuse.

Just-hatched goslings have a natural tendency toward unsteadiness, and a rough brooder floor provides sure footing, helping them get stronger on their legs. This is especially important due to a common problem called spraddle legs, which is a splaying of the legs in opposite directions so that the poor gosling can't stand properly. When this occurs it is often necessary to bind the legs loosely together above the hocks for a few days, removing the soft cord or rubber band after the gosling has gained surefootedness. In warm weather you can put goslings out on the lawn for short periods to help them gain full use of their legs, as they have excellent footing on clipped grass.

WATER

Though water is essential to virtually all birds, it is exceptionally important to waterfowl. They don't merely drink it, they live in it, they play in it, they breed in it, they thrive in it—it is their element. They love to play in water, and even if they cannot actually swim in it, they will toss it around with their heads or dribble it from their bills. It is important that water be provided them in a way they can't abuse. Left to themselves, they will sport and wallow in it until they have at least made a mess and, at worst, literally loved it to death.

Well-designed water containers for brooding of young waterfowl are therefore a necessity. Baby ducks and geese will attempt to swim in even the smallest amount of water, so in order to keep their water clean and uncontaminated with droppings, choose a watering device that will accommodate their peculiarities. For young waterfowl to about a week old, use a chick waterer consisting of a circular dish over which is placed an inverted water-filled jar. Older birds cannot submerge their entire heads into the shallow dish to clean their faces, and a trough with a wire grate separating them from the water is more suitable. Many brooders are constructed with an adjustable barrier consisting of two sets of parallel bars placed in front of the water trough. The bars are evenly spaced at first so that small birds cannot slip through to take a swim but can still reach between for a drink. The bars are pushed closer together as the birds grow so that they can get their bigger heads through but still not their whole bodies. The setting of the bars must be conscientiously checked and readjusted daily, for birds that can get their heads between them in the morning may by evening be frantically trying to reach the water through openings that have become too small—or, having succeeded, frantically trying to extricate their heads!

In choosing a watering arrangement, look for several important characteristics. It should be stable, for if it tips the

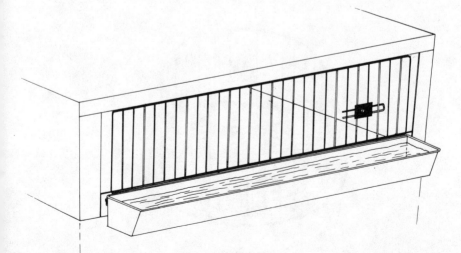

water will be lost and the litter will become a slimy, wet mess. Place waterers over drains to remove spillage from the brooding area. Ideally, ducklings and goslings should not be able to walk in their drinking water, for by doing so they contaminate it with droppings and other brooder debris. In addition, in their frenzy of delight over water, hatchlings sometimes trample each other into the container, causing death by drowning or by excessive chilling.

If it should become necessary to give them an open dish for their water supply, a circular piece of wood, cut just slightly smaller than the container, will keep things tidy; the wood floats on the surface and rides it down. There's always a little water around the edge for the babies to drink, but never enough to revel in. Another idea is to place a short cylinder of fine-mesh wire in a circular dish so there's just enough water between the cylinder and the dish rim for a satisfying drink.

Unless baby waterfowl are raised by their natural mothers, it is unwise to allow them full access to swimming water. Though baby ducks and geese are often seen swimming in ponds alongside the big guys when only a few days old, their mothers normally have the sense to bring them out of the water

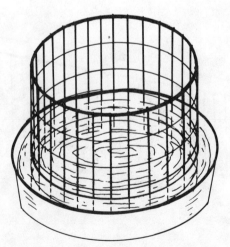

when they've had enough. Like naughty children, ducklings and goslings left on their own will stay in the water long after they should have come out, and the results will be overly wet, chilled little birds that will suffer from exposure and perhaps die. If you wish to allow your little waterfowl the pleasures of a swim now and then, and yourself the joy of watching their antics, make sure that they are under close supervision. The water should be in a warm, draft-free place. Do not let the little birds swim in it for more than a few minutes, and remove them to their warm, dry, draft-free brooder before they get wet and chilled clear through.

Feeding

As messy as ducklings and goslings can be with their water, they can be even messier with water and feed in combination. Because they need water to help them swallow dry feed, they fill their mouths with feed and then scurry to the waterer to wash it down, dropping large quantities of feed along the way. If the waterer is too close to the feeder, they'll get feed in the water and water in the feed. But if the water is too far away they may drop all the feed along the way, causing incredible waste; or they may choke on it before they can get to the water to wash it down.

Some people wet the feed with a little water or skim milk to help solve some of these problems. But it creates others. Wet mash tends to dry out, creating a sticky mass that the young birds cannot or will not consume, and it is more likely to sour or mold, resulting in unpleasant consequences for the young birds. Wet mash must therefore be provided in smaller quantities and at more frequent intervals than dry feed.

Young waterfowl that manage to get their feed wet and sloppy often smear this porridge all over themselves if especially crowded or frantically hungry at feeding time. Feed encrustation on the downy birds is not just unaesthetic—it may lead to a real problem. While waterfowl are not known to be cannibalistic, as some breeds of landfowl can be, by eating the feed from each other's backs the young birds may develop the habit of feather picking. This not only results in ugly bare patches on the birds' backs, but also can cause them to grow less rapidly. Protein needed by the body for growth is being diverted to perpetual renewal of the missing feathers. Feather picking can also in some circumstances lead to death. Commercial operations sometimes deal with this problem by debilling their day-old waterfowl, but you can simply make sure your young birds have plenty of room and plenty to eat.

Many of the problems of feeding waterfowl hatchlings are eliminated if the feed can be provided in pellet form. Pellets are harder to wet and harder to waste. But as noted in Chapter 7, pelleted feed is not always available, especially in the small size required by young birds.

Feed can be placed in containers similar to baby chick feeders for very young ducklings and goslings. When their heads get too big to fit through the little openings, troughs with wire guards (like those we recommended as waterers) are equally suitable as feeders and prevent the birds from walking in their feed.

Throughout their early weeks of life, young waterfowl should have access to feed at all times. Among other things, this ensures that the shy birds will have plenty to eat after the more aggressive ones have had their fill. On the other hand, the heat and moisture in the brooder work together to cause the feed to go sour or moldy, so provide just enough feed twice a day to last until the next feeding. Be sure to remove old stale feed periodically so that it doesn't molder away in the corners of the feeders. For their very small size, young waterfowl can really pack the feed away, especially during their "teenage" period. Naturally, you can keep the feed bill down by supplementing their diet with tasty treats you have on hand. Since the natural diet of goslings consists almost solely of grass, they will be delighted when forage time is allotted them. Ducklings also enjoy fresh air and exercise, though in nature they are not as dependent on grassy meadows as geese. Grass that has been sprayed with pesticides might be harmful to the little waterfowl.

Enclose the babies or keep an eye on them so that they do not wander off to become snacks for neighborhood dogs or other marauders. And do not leave them out on cold or windy days. Of the special treats you can give baby waterfowl, one of their favorites is finely diced hard-boiled egg. Since it's the very stuff they're made of, it's no surprise that it's as good for them as it is good-tasting to them.

It is difficult to find specially prepared feed for young waterfowl, and even those companies that do make it formulate the feed for fast-growth broilers. These feeds, and those made for young landfowl, are usually higher in protein than the normal waterfowl hatchling would obtain in nature. You can add lettuce, alfalfa, or succulent young grass clippings to their diets to supplement commercially available feeds; this provides needed minerals and extra fiber and reduces the protein content of the diet. If they are reluctant to try these at first, try enticing them by floating little bits of greens in the water dish.

This extra source of fiber also helps prevent a problem common to growing waterfowl in captivity—twisted wing

Twisted wing

191

(sometimes called angel wing), in which the flight feathers of one or both wings bend away from the body. Though poorly understood, this problem evidently results from overly rapid development of the heavy flight feathers before the wing structure is developed sufficiently to support them. Perhaps there is a genetic propensity for this condition, or perhaps it is caused by a deficiency of an important but as yet undetermined trace mineral in the diet. Interestingly, the condition is unknown among wild waterfowl but is fairly common in domestically raised flocks. It has been observed that reduction of the protein content of the diet helps prevent the problem; the reduced growth rate of the birds may prevent overdevelopment of wing feathers so that the body's needs for the various trace elements is decreased. Until researchers can discover which mineral deficiency, if any, is the cause of twisted wing, waterfowl breeders can add fibrous greens to their birds' diet to minimize occurrence. In addition, feeding chopped greens helps keep young waterfowl busy, active, and out of mischief.

Of course, if you are raising your birds for fancy dinners, then you would presumably want them to grow as rapidly as possible and wouldn't much care whether they have twisted wings or not. But ducks and geese kept for ornamental reasons are not very attractive with this condition, and show birds are useless with it. Breeders must recognize that there may well be a genetic basis for twisted wing, although no one really knows at this time. Clearly you should not breed from a strain showing any tendency toward twisted wing in case genetics is at the root of the problem.

Should wings twist despite your precautions, you might try pulling out the offending flight feathers at the earliest opportunity to help them to grow back correctly. Some people recommend putting the wing in a sling to help correct it, but it is our opinion that they do not fully appreciate the problems of trying to put a sling on a bird's wing! Having tried it ourselves, we vigorously recommend another solution. In case you'd like to read up on how other people have dealt with twisted wing, we've listed further sources of information in Chapter 16, "Resources."

Sexing

From all the various and fanciful stories we've heard over the years on sexing ducklings and goslings, the only certain information we've obtained is that Pilgrim geese can be color-sexed from the day they hatch. In this breed, the down of the ganderling is yellow while the young female is greyish. Normally, though, it is not possible to tell the sex of the young geese or ducks by their coloring or other external features. With the exception of Pilgrim goslings (and possibly to a lesser extent young Embdens), all the hatchlings of one breed of duck or goose look alike. White varieties will be yellow, brown-toned varieties brown, black types black, grey or grey-and-white varieties will be grey or greenish, and Mallards, Rouens, and Grey Calls will be black with yellow spots on the back and cheek and yellow stripes across the eyes.

If it becomes necessary for any reason to sex waterfowl at an early age, they must be vent-sexed. Rarely are young waterfowl vent-sexed by backyard breeders, because of the amount of practice necessary to attain any degree of accuracy. Furthermore, it is possible to injure or kill a baby duck or goose by rough handling. Nonetheless, if for some reason you find it necessary to sex your ducklings or goslings, be assured that it is entirely possible. This is done pretty much the same as vent-sexing of adult waterfowl, described in Chapter 4, "Understanding Your Ducks and Geese." The only difference is that in the younger birds you are looking for something a good deal smaller than in the adult birds.

Ducklings and goslings can be easily injured if mishandled, and so should be vent-sexed only after you receive advice from an experienced person. If you wish to try it anyway, by all means handle the little birds with extreme care in order to prevent possible rupture. Hold the bird in one hand while

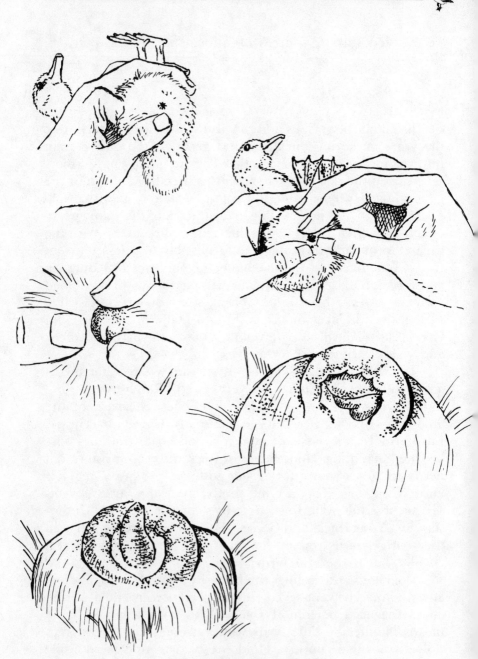

Sexing young waterfowl

manipulating the vent with the other. The breast should be upward with the vent toward you, index finger placed against the base of the tail at the back for support from below, the remaining three fingers across the breast to keep you in control. With the thumb of the hand which is holding the bird, stretch the vent downward. Using the thumb and forefinger of the other hand, stretch the vent sideways in an effort to invert the vent and cause the little penis, if present, to pop out. It helps to have a bright overhead light and a strong magnifying glass for accurate sexing. If you are unsure in a particular case, put the young bird aside and recheck later after allowing it a respite from handling.

As the birds grow and mature, they will develop the external features differentiating the sexes outlined in Chapter 4.

Identification

You may find it desirable to keep track of where your young birds came from, how old they are, what their parentage is, what sex they are (if a breed that is difficult to determine at a glance), and so forth. This can be done by any of several means. For keeping track on a short-term basis, a little vegetable dye on the birds' backs or heads will do. However, they do exchange their down for feathers quite rapidly, and in any case as soon as they have access to swimming water the dye will wash off, so this method is not effective for long.

A second method of keeping track of birds is to band them with colored, numbered bands or leg spirals. Numbered bands are required at shows for proper identification. Bands and spirals come in a variety of uniformly designated sizes. Make sure that the right size is used, as waterfowl have a way of closing up their feet by folding the webbing so that the band can slip right off if too large. Check against excessive looseness by trying to get the band off with the bird's foot folded. Of course, a bird can always bite or otherwise break off the band, so its disappearance is not necessarily a clear sign that the band

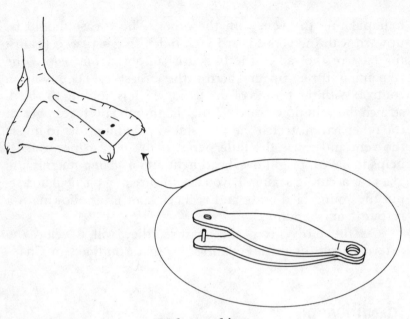

Web punching

had been too loose. But by all means, don't make the band too tight, as it will eventually cut into the leg and may cause infection. This may happen to growing birds if their owner fails to keep track of the bands and increase the size as necessary. This is the primary reason that identification of young waterfowl by leg banding is unsatisfactory.

A third method, and by far the most permanent, is called toe punching, though technically, we suppose, it ought to be called web punching. This is done by means of a miniature punch that works something like a hand-held paper punch. Day-old birds are punched on the web between their toes, and the number of punches on each web can be interpreted by means of a code devised by the breeder. Even using at most one punch to a web there are already sixteen possible combinations, since each bird has four webs.

Bands (also called bandettes) and toe-punches are available at most poultry supply outlets and firms that specialize in banding and tagging birds and other animals. Some are listed in Chapter 16, "Resources."

Diseases of young waterfowl

Fortunately, ducks and geese are not particularly susceptible to diseases if properly cared for, especially compared to landfowl. This is as true of ducklings and goslings as it is of adult waterfowl. Diseases are easily prevented in the brooder by providing a clean, dry environment, sufficient heat and ventilation, adequate nutrition, and fresh rather than stale or sour feed and water. But to impress upon you the importance of these points, we will vividly describe the most common of the diseases to which young waterfowl infrequently fall prey, and hope that the horror of it all will impress doubters of the wisdom of providing young waterfowl with the proper conditions. The gruesome diseases awaiting them in maturity are described in Chapter 14, "Disease and Other Perils." Actually, there is very little chance you'll ever need this material. But if someday you do, you'll be glad it's here, because otherwise you'd have to go a long way to find it (as we did).

Keel. There are eight known classifications of salmonella, and six of these may affect ducks. Of these, the only one of real significance to waterfowl breeders causes a disease known as paratyphoid, also called keel because affected birds may keel over and die (that's no joke—we got it from a medical manual!). This disease is fairly common among domestic fowl, and all birds are susceptible. One indication is a high death rate in young birds within a few weeks after hatching. Symptoms include trembling, gasping, rapid breathing, clicking accompanying breathing, coughing, sneezing, poor growth, weakness, diarrhea, dehydration, and sometimes watery or pasty eyelids and wet, runny nostrils. This disease is often confused with respiratory infections, other bacterial diseases, and poisoning. Stresses due to shipping, irregular feeding, chilling, or overheating may increase mortality. The disease is spread through human sewage and bird droppings by means of

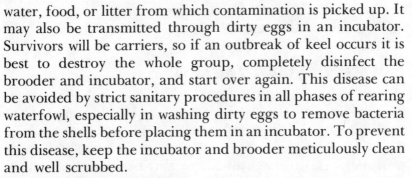

water, food, or litter from which contamination is picked up. It may also be transmitted through dirty eggs in an incubator. Survivors will be carriers, so if an outbreak of keel occurs it is best to destroy the whole group, completely disinfect the brooder and incubator, and start over again. This disease can be avoided by strict sanitary procedures in all phases of rearing waterfowl, especially in washing dirty eggs to remove bacteria from the shells before placing them in an incubator. To prevent this disease, keep the incubator and brooder meticulously clean and well scrubbed.

Brooder pneumonia. A second disease of young waterfowl is often called brooder pneumonia but is listed in technical manuals as aspergillosis. It is an infectious disease which affects birds that inhale a fungus which flourishes in food and litter, especially wet hay or sawdust. It may spread rapidly. The symptoms include gasping, inflamed eyes, bad breath, nervous activities, loss of appetite but increased thirst, and emaciation. Obviously, avoidance of this problem is the best solution: do not allow wet spots in the litter or wet feed in the brooder for any period of time. The brooder should be kept warm and dry but well ventilated without being drafty, and waterers should be placed over drains to remove spillage. Remove any sick birds from the brooder and clean and thoroughly disinfect the facilities. Destroy moldy feed and litter by burning.

Coccidiosis. Coccidiosis is not the scourge of waterfowl breeders that it is for raisers of baby chickens, but it does occur occasionally. "Cocci," as it is popularly known, is universally present, but outbreaks occur only after the ingestion of large numbers of oocysts, the organisms that cause the disease. Infected carriers shed these oocysts in their droppings, contaminating the feed, water, litter, soil, and even the dust. Though infrequent, outbreaks can be rather dramatic, with many or most of the brood affected and mortality running high. Cocci is transmitted in equipment and clothing and by insects and animals. Immunity develops through mild infections. All ages of waterfowl are susceptible to cocci, but young

198

birds more often fall victim. Symptoms include loss of appetite and weight, weakness and inability to stand, and continual distressed peeping. Bloody droppings may also be found. Coccidiosis outbreaks can be avoided by following sanitary procedures as discussed throughout this book. Young waterfowl will not be helped by the medicated feeds intended to prevent cocci in baby chicks because a different organism is involved; in fact, such feeds may prove harmful to ducklings and goslings. Sulfa compounds are effective in the treatment of this disease.

New duck syndrome. "New duck syndrome" is the common name of a disease listed in veterinary manuals as anatipestifer. It is a contagious respiratory disease that is fairly infrequent among young waterfowl and not as destructive as other diseases can be. Mortality is highest between five and ten weeks of age. Symptoms include general depression, ruffled feathers, greenish white diarrhea, inability to stand, bobbing or jerking of the head, and eye discharge. In advanced cases, look for prostration and inability to lift the head, along with mild coughing, incoordination, and head tremors. A bird may lie on its back and paddle the air with its feet. Death usually results from inability to get to water. For a positive diagnosis, laboratory testing is necessary in order to isolate the offending organism in the blood and organs. The lab will indicate the correct sulfa treatment for this disease.

Hepatitis. Baby ducks and geese may contract hepatitis, sometimes called duck virus hepatitis even though geese also get it. This highly contagious virus is common worldwide and is transmitted from parent to offspring as well as from bird to bird. It should be suspected where large numbers of deaths occur suddenly. When first struck, young birds slow down in their activities. As the disease progresses, they stop moving entirely and squat with their eyes shut, or they may fall on their sides. Death occurs within one to two hours of the first symptoms and may follow spasmodic kicking and drawing back of the head, a characteristic position in which corpses are found. Sanitation is of utmost importance in preventing this

199

disease. Feeders and waterers should be meticulously sterilized and the brooder religiously disinfected before litter is renewed. There is an antibody treatment available and a vaccine for breeders through which their offspring may be immunized. Preventive inoculations may be necessary in areas where outbreaks are known.

We hope that these brief descriptions of the most common of the infrequent diseases of ducklings and goslings have convinced you that it's lots more fun to have *healthy* little ducklings and goslings at your house and that this can be accomplished through the relatively minor hassle of keeping their environment clean and seeing that they are properly nourished.

GROWING UP

Assuming they live through the previous section, ducklings must be kept under the protection of a brooder until they are about four weeks of age and goslings to about six weeks, after which they may be put outside if the weather is nice. Provide them with some sort of shelter from wind and especially rain, as well as shade from hot sun. If the weather turns stormy during their first few weeks outside, they should be gathered up and put inside. By the time their full complement of waterproof feathering has developed, you can leave both ducklings and goslings outside at all times without fear of losing them, as long as they are provided the simple facilities outlined in Chapter 5. Mallard-derived ducklings take approximately 12 weeks to feather fully, while Muscovies and goslings require around 16 weeks.

When young birds are placed outside, keep an eye on them for the first few days to make sure that they don't get themselves into any trouble. They may, for instance, escape through holes in the fence that you didn't even know were there. Or your yard may pose dangers you hadn't thought of, such as places where they may get trapped and not be able to get out to eat and drink.

Unless the young birds are enjoying the protection of a mother, older ducks and geese might harass them. If the yard is large and the other birds few, such harassment is generally minimal, and the birds will all soon get nicely acquainted. But in some cases, especially if the birds are overcrowded, the young ones may be unmercifully harassed by their older cousins. We have seen a gaggle of geese terrorize young ducks literally to death, and have seen older ducks jab at ducklings with their bills to keep them away. It is hard to make any predictions as to how the birds will react to one another, so keep a wary eye on them until you are certain that they are getting along. Be especially sure that the younger birds are allowed near food and water.

We have already mentioned the imprinting of baby ducks and geese, through which they tend to identify as Mom the first moving thing they see upon hatching. Imprinting is developed to a very high degree in goslings, and they become strongly attached to the person who tends the brooder. While this is lots of fun as long as they are in the brooder, it becomes a pain in

the neck when trying to convince the overgrown babies that it's time to go out into the world and be geese. The first time we had the dubious honor of being imprinted, we had to resort to sneaking around our own yard and communicating everything in whispers for several days to prevent our newly independent goslings from chasing after us. Lowering their heads and calling *whit-whit, whit-whit,* they did not understand why they had been so suddenly and ruthlessly orphaned. A friend with a similar experience once made the mistake of leaving her kitchen door open, only to have her four half-grown goslings parade right up the back steps and into the living room in search of their human mumsy.

12

Raising Ducks and Geese for Meat

For many people duck or goose dinners are exotic, expensive, and all-too-rare occasions. But with a flock in your own backyard, you could have that gourmet meal any time you wish. While not being entirely economical as a backyard endeavor, raising waterfowl for the table can be one of the important side benefits of owning ducks or geese. You will have the satisfaction of knowing exactly what your meat birds have been eating and at what age they were butchered. You will probably find, as we do, that the final product of your endeavors is much superior to anything you could purchase. And while duck and goose are inherently expensive meats compared with other common fowl, chicken and turkey especially, you will undoubtedly find your homegrown meat a bargain compared to waterfowl sold in stores—that is, if you can even find it. Your meat will also compare favorably in price to many cuts of beef, pork, and mutton.

We are often asked if domestic waterfowl tastes like the kind hunters bring home. We're never quite sure whether the person who asks is hoping the answer will be yes, or *afraid* the answer will be yes! The flavor of a bird depends to a great extent on its diet, so as long as you do not feed your ducks and geese fish scraps and other strong-flavored tidbits to excess, your table-ready product is not likely to have the off-flavors of some wild varieties of waterfowl. Further, a hunter is rarely able to determine the age of his game before putting it into his pouch, and as with other types of meat, the so-called strong or even objectionable flavor of wild waterfowl increases with age.

203

Actually, a major reason for the increasing interest in raising domestic waterfowl for meat is that wild waterfowl are having trouble coping with the sprawling urbanization of their natural habitats, and consequently hunters are finding fewer and fewer places open to them for bagging waterfowl.

As time approaches for that much anticipated gourmet meal, you may want to "finish" your birds by fattening them a little. Remember that in this context fattened just means plump—a fattened bird is a fuller-bodied bird. Details of feeding meat birds, including the special finishing diet, can be found in Chapter 7, "Feeding Your Ducks and Geese."

While weight gain is clearly an important factor in determining when a duck or goose is ready for butchering, we have found that the stage of the molt is equally important. This has nothing to do with the quality of the meat per se—it's just that a duck or goose that is heavily into a molt will be nearly impossible to pluck and, without an unimaginable investment in time spent picking pinfeathers, will produce rather unaesthetic table fare. A plucker can do his most elegant work just after the first feathering. The terms "green" or "junior" are in vogue on Long Island to designate young birds at this stage. Depending a good deal on the breed and other factors, a duck is green at about 8 to 10 weeks, while a goose is green between 13 and 14 weeks. Since waterfowl achieve their maximum growth during the early period, it goes without saying that it is most economical to fatten and butcher a bird during the first prime time.

Shortly after first feathering, the birds begin molting into their adult plumage. The first optimum plucking time has passed when feathers begin to fall from around the neck, and it is best to wait until the bird comes into full plumage before thinking again of butchering it. This is the second optimal plucking time. The growth rate does drop off, however, and the bird does not gain weight as rapidly in proportion to the amount it will eat. So the second optimal time for plucking is not quite as optimal as the first. Once you've raised a horde of ducks that eats you out of house and home before you finally get them into the freezer, you will undoubtedly appreciate the benefits of keeping a constant eye on the stage of the molt as the birds near meal size.

Though ducks and geese are generally free of pinfeathers throughout the late fall and winter months, it's most economical to schedule butcher day to coincide with the completion of feathering-out. To determine whether the molt is completed, check the wing primaries for full length, pet the plumage to test for smoothness, and run your fingers lightly backwards against the feathers so you can peek underneath for pinfeathers. The plumage should be bright and hard looking, with no downy patches along the breastbone or near the vent. Should you miss your first opportunity for that tasty dinner, you may have to wait many weeks for your ducks or geese to come to full feather. Mallard-derivatives should not be kept longer than 17 weeks and geese 10 months if they are intended for table use, as they tend to get a little tough after that. Muscovies mature less rapidly than geese or other ducks, and will be ready for butchering at from 12 to 18 weeks. After about 20 weeks of age, Muscovy drakes tend to get a bit "staggy" or musky in flavor.

Commercially raised birds usually mature at a younger age than homegrown. Environmentally controlled housing promotes growth in hot or cold weather when it would otherwise be depressed. Faster growth is also induced by specially prepared feeds. You should allow for this acceleration in maturity whenever you read publications intended for the commercial waterfowl raiser and attempt to extrapolate to your own situation.

All breeds of geese are suited for table use, the chief difference being that the larger, fuller bodies of Embden and Toulouse are more suitable to those who have lots of company or just enjoy leftovers, while the lightweight breeds appeal more to those who have smaller appetites or fewer mouths to feed.

Pekin ducks are the kind found in grocery stores and restaurants, but other types of large ducks dress out very nicely. In England, Aylesburies are commonly raised for meat, but stock is not so easily located in the United States. White Muscovies are excellent table fare. In our experience, they are by far the easiest waterfowl to pick, and they dress out nicely because their feathering is less complex than others. A Muscovy drake can weigh nearly as much as a young goose, and possibly more. Muscovy meat is a little different in flavor from other waterfowl, so you may want to grow a few of each for variety.

Crossbred ducks or geese are usually fine as meat birds and, due to something called hybrid vigor, crossing sometimes produces birds of larger size than either parent. Pekin-Muscovy crosses, for instance, are currently enjoying popularity as meat birds, and moreover are reportedly lower in fat than typical Long Island ducklings. In general, stick with the white or lighter-colored breeds for meat purposes. Lacking unsightly, dark pinfeathers, they will dress out a little nicer and look better when served at the table. This is an aesthetic matter only, however. White pinfeathers are no tastier than others—they just aren't noticed. There's no harm in eating them.

Ducks and geese lose about 25 to 30 percent of their live weight in the dressing out, so when choosing a breed it is well to take this into consideration. Heavier breeds lose a smaller fraction in the dressing process than do the lighter breeds. Remember too that most available strains of waterfowl, especially those grown for meat purposes rather than for show, tend to be a little below the weights listed for them in the *Standard*.

Anyone who has experience plucking chickens and other landfowl is in for a nasty surprise the first time they tackle waterfowl. There is a remarkable increase in difficulty, for which experience in plucking chickens is hardly adequate preparation. The problem results from two basic differences: there are extra layers of feathers, and the feathers are stuck in much more firmly.

While we've heard that a good professional plucker can prepare 75 ducks a day, we must admit that we have never been able to get our plucking time down to less than an hour per bird. When we have more than one or two to pluck, we look up our friendly local custom plucker, who has an expensive machine with rubber fingers that whirl on a big drum to help him with the plucking. We may bring him as many as three dozen birds, which he manages to clean in one day, though how he does it is beyond understanding. (He has often stated that, living here in wine country, he could make more money picking grapes than picking ducks. But maybe that's because he's Italian.) If you are able to find a local custom plucker who will tackle waterfowl, consider yourself lucky. Many pluckers will do all the chickens and turkeys you can bring them but will not touch waterfowl. This is undoubtedly because waterfowl do take longer than other birds to pick, and pluckers know that many people are not willing to pay for the time. In attempting to locate a custom plucker look not only for poultry processors, but also for someone who cleans birds for hunters. The latter will sometimes take on the job but may ask that you kill the birds yourself.

In any case, it is our considered opinion that anyone who eats ducks or geese ought to try butchering them at least once themselves—it helps you develop an appreciation for the fine art of waterfowl plucking should you decide to seek professional help in the future.

Killing

So let's suppose that you have one or two choice birds fattened up and ready for that special dinner, and you are ready to tackle your own butchering. After you have scheduled an auspicious day for the ceremonials, you will want to catch the birds whose times have come and confine them at least overnight without feed. This is done so that the digestive tract has time to clear itself, making the butchering process less messy. The birds should be confined where they will not be wallowing in and ingesting mud or feedstuffs, but they should have drinking water available if confinement lasts longer than just overnight; otherwise the quality of the meat can deteriorate due to dehydration, and the skin might become blotchy and unsightly.

By now you should be giving some thought to how you're

going to kill the bird. For someone who does not intend to make a career of killing waterfowl, but simply wants to get the job done in the most expedient manner possible with the least amount of expense, we suggest simply laying the bird's head against a chopping block—an old stump will do—and chopping it off with a sharpened hatchet. Normally birds will lie very quietly and cooperatively for you up to this point, but as soon as the bird has been relieved of its head it suddenly remembers its amazing strength and begins to fight with all its might. This does not apply to Muscovy drakes, which never forget their strength and never go anywhere quietly and cooperatively. It's a good idea in any case to have a strong grip on the wings. A

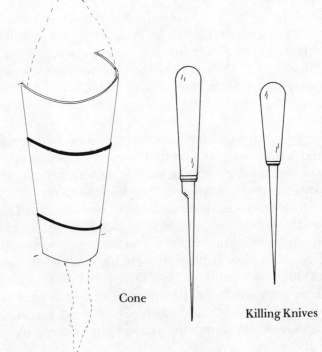

Cone

Killing Knives

highly recommended technique is to pull the wings and feet back along the tail so that one hand holds all five appendages together. This gives you superb control over the bird and complete freedom to the other hand as well. If you find this maneuver difficult, you might wish to have someone help you—one holding the bird while the other acts as executioner.

As soon as the head has been severed, tie the legs with a piece of rope and quickly hang the bird from the limb of a tree. Should you attempt to hold on to the bird, its thrashings may soon tire you out, especially if you're doing in a strong Muscovy or goose. If you choose instead to release the bird, be sure it is some distance from your favorite flower bed, as the dying bird will have its revenge in mutilated and bloody flowers. But preventing damage to nearby vegetation is not the only reason for restraining recently deceased fowl. If it is hung, it cannot bruise itself. Geese especially tend to bruise easily during butchering, creating a blotchy appearance of the skin, and an unprofessional-looking final product. The blood will drain away in a fairly controlled manner, providing you with a valuable additive for your compost, as well as preventing the unsightly spread of blood around the backyard.

Too short a bleeding time will also result in unsightly blotches on the skin. On the other hand, the bird should not be left hanging for too long, as it will become stiff and difficult to pick. The proper bleeding time depends on the size of the bird, so watch the flow of blood and take the bird down when the flow ceases, usually in less than five minutes.

There are certain technical objections to decapitation as a method of killing. An alternative to decapitation is to hang the live bird by its feet and cut the throat at the base of the bill. This severs the jugular vein and allows proper bleeding. A blow to the back of the skull with a board or heavy stick, in addition, is said to loosen the feathers and facilitate picking.

So much for farmers' methods. Professional methods may better suit your personality: a special short, narrow, very sharp knife is made for sticking into the mouth and piercing the brain. This results in instant death—if the thrust is well placed and this does take some practice. A misplaced stab may result in an unpleasant scene for all concerned.

The jugular vein is cut inside the mouth, just below the base of the skull. If the knife is then thrust through the groove in the roof of the mouth, into the rear lobe of the brain at the base of the skull, and given a twist, for some reason the feathers will be loosened and picking will be a little easier. To facilitate the use of this knife, there are cone-shaped collars in which a bird is placed to keep it still during killing. Some cones are adjustable while others come in different sizes to fit specific breeds. In these modern times, cones and killing knives are sometimes hard to come by. Check with your local feed store for sources of new or used equipment.

Removing the feathers

Now that the bird has been properly dispatched and is awaiting further last rites, you must consider how you will accomplish the actual plucking. You have another choice to make here—whether to dry-pick or wet-pick. The dry method is simply to pull out the feathers as soon as the bird has been killed. They don't come out very easily, but there are some advantages to dry-picking. One is that it can be done nearly anywhere, thereby avoiding a mess of blood and feathers in an inappropriate place. On occasion we have had a bird unexpectedly commit suicide at a time when we were ill-prepared for wet-picking. When found while still fresh we have quickly gotten to the business of cleaning off the feathers and hustling the bird into the refrigerator while there was still time to salvage at least the meat part of the deal.

Another advantage to dry-picking is that the down does not get wet and is therefore easy to see and grasp between the fingers. Wet down tends to flatten against the skin and become semitransparent, making it very difficult to pull out. Because the down and feathers do not become wet from bloody, muddy water, they are easier to salvage for pillow-making or a nice warm vest.

You'll find dry-picking is easier if you store and chill the bird before it's plucked and eviscerated. A temperature of 33°F. (1°C.) helps firm up the skin so that the feathers come out cleanly, and you'll head off the legendary rampant bacterial growth in uncooled fowl. Before placing the unplucked bird in the refrigerator, remove any about-to-be-expelled droppings by pressing the abdomen near the vent.

If only one bird is being done, and either it is very small or there are several people willing to help, you may wish to dry-pick it. Dry-picking is not as difficult when working with Muscovies: unlike other types of waterfowl they don't have numerous layers of feathers, and for some reason their feathers come out easier. When it comes to a goose, we highly recommend convening a committee if dry-picking seems in order.

Those of us who trained as chicken-pluckers before we went on to picking waterfowl tend to prefer the wet method of plucking, called scalding. While the killing is taking place, a very large pot of water is heated to about 140°F. (60°C.) for ducks and 150°F. (65°C.) for geese. Too high a temperature discolors the skin or causes it to tear. You should be sure the bird has completed its death throes before scalding begins, or it may decide to take one final swim as it is plunged into the boiling water, and won't mind a bit if you get a scalding shower in consequence.

Assuming then that the bird is completely dead, take it by the legs and dunk it headfirst into the water. You will now discover one of the first principles of physics: because of all the air trapped in the waterproof feathers of ducks and geese, they float. Floating was great for the duck or goose when it was alive, but it won't do you a bit of good at this stage. It is a good idea to have a wooden stick or a long-handled spoon handy with which to push the bird into the water.

Once the bird is completely submerged, you may discover another principle of physics: water is displaced to the extent of the volume of the submerged object. In other words, if you have not allowed room at the top of the pot, pushing the large bird into the hot water may cause the pot to overflow. This is one reason we suggested using a *very* large pot.

Let's assume you have been smart and thought about this in advance, and the water level was just right, and the bird has been submerged successfully. Move the bird about in the water to ensure complete penetration of the water through all layers of plumage: sometimes it happens that dunking and cooling have accomplished nothing, if neither water nor steam has penetrated the outer layer of feathers. A drop of liquid dish detergent in the pot reduces the surface tension of the water and allows the water to penetrate the feathers more readily. If the pot is large enough, draw the bird backwards through the water while it is submerged; this tends to bring water through the feathers, making the hot water bath more effective. Since feathering is densest on the breast, go for maximum penetration of the hot water on that part.

Keep a duck submerged for about a minute and a half, a goose for about three minutes. The exact time required depends on the temperature of the water, on the age of the bird, and on the density of the feathers. At lower scalding temperatures, it takes longer for the water to penetrate the plumage, but the hot water is more likely to penetrate all parts uniformly. You will soon be able to judge whether you guessed too long or too short, depending on what happens at the next stage.

The next step is a matter of debate among plucking perfectionists. Some immediately remove the bird from the hot water and plunge it into cold water. The purpose of this maneuver is to prevent the skin of the bird from beginning to steam from the hot water, which makes it more likely that it will tear during picking. This, of course, results in a somewhat patchy final product—not aesthetically pleasing for gourmet eaters but nonetheless just as delicious for those not concerned with superficialities. Others claim that plucking the bird hot is the only way to go, and some even wrap it in burlap for a few minutes to steam. In this case the container of cold water need not go to waste. It comes in handy for cooling off scalded fingers.

You are now ready to start plucking. The feathers should be pulled out in the direction that they grow. This ensures that the whole feather will come out without breaking, and in the end both meat and feathers will be much neater in appearance. Start plucking with the wings. They tend to be the hardest part of the bird from which to pull the feathers, so we like to get them done first. They become less pliable very rapidly. If you're saving the feathers, it's a good idea to pluck the large wing and tail feathers first anyway so that they may be kept separate. Some pluckers simply cut off the wing at the first joint after the bird has been dressed. If you can accept a roast that has been disfigured and if you don't intend to keep the wing primaries, there's no point in wasting time pulling them out. Besides, you get yourself a handy duster. In former times, goose wings were used to clean house. Older Eskimos still use them as whisk brooms.

After the wings are done, pluck the feathers from the neck, down the bird's back, and then down its front. Doing the back first gives the breast a chance to firm up as it cools, and the feathers will come out more easily without tearing the skin.

It is often possible to pull the feathers out in small clumps, rather than one at a time. If you pull too big a clump at once, however, large patches of skin may cling to the feathers, making the job somewhat messier as well as producing a patchy appearance on the table bird. You may eventually want to obscure such blemishes with orange sauce, which few realize was invented for this purpose!

Easily torn skin may mean that the bird was left in the hot water for too long. Next time, don't dunk it for quite so long. Should the feathers be extremely difficult to remove, then possibly the bird was not held in the water long enough. In that case, it may be returned to the hot water bath for a second dunking.

After the bird has been picked over once, there will be a fluffy coating of down over most of the body. Down is simpler to remove when the duck or goose is dry, so presuming that the down has gotten wet somewhere along the way, you may want to dry the bird's skin with a towel and attempt to fluff out the down and make it visible again and thereby easier to grasp. A technique we've developed for removing down, after many years of attempting to nip it out little by little between thumb and forefinger, is to rub it off with the side of the thumb against the first two joints of the forefinger into the palm of the hand. Begin up around the neck and start scraping away with the side of the thumb, and amazing amounts of down will gather into the palm of your hand. Down can also be removed by shaving it off with a sharp knife. If you're collecting the down you'll want to avoid getting pinfeathers into it, so pick with a light touch, and don't worry if you miss a little of it. There's no way known to man (or woman) to get *all* of the down and *none* of the pinfeathers at the same time.

At this point you may wish to get a paper bag and attempt to fill it with down. We say "attempt" for two reasons: first, it takes a great number of birds to fill anything with down; second, down simply does not like paper bags and so is very perverse about going into one. Generally, it will stick to your hand, especially if your hand is the least bit damp, and sometimes even clings partway up your arm or manages to get into your hair. If you try to put your hand deep into the bag and shake the down off, you may pull your hand out to find even more down clinging to it. And when you've finally managed to get the down off of your hand and miraculously into the bag, one tiny accidental joggle of the bag will start a blizzard. Or the down may suddenly of its very own accord decide to come floating complacently out of the bag. It is important to note that down is exempt from the Law of Gravity. Playing with down is a lot of fun, and we're sure that those of you who are dedicated to filling your own three-pound sleeping bag with your very own homegrown down will find hours of amusement in your hobby—and come away with a new appreciation for the hefty prices of down-filled sleeping bags.

Once the down has been dispatched, hopefully with your sanity still intact, you are ready to do the final dressing. If the bird is not in any stage of molt, your job will be easy, with maybe just a few pinfeathers remaining to pull here and there. This is best done by tweezing the feathers between a paring knife and your thumb. Occasionally we use cosmetic tweezers for this operation, or even a pair of jeweler's pliers for really stubborn feathers. Sometimes pinfeathers on the back are impossible to remove, and you may tire of the whole thing before all of them are out. This is especially true if the bird is in a state of molt. If the little feathers are white, then you've nothing to worry about: when the bird is roasted breast-up, as is usually done, the few remaining pinfeathers won't be noticeable. If the feathers are brown or black, and you were hoping to serve this bird as a special treat for special people, then you have three alternatives. 1. Use a dark glaze with a soy-sauce base. 2. Cite the Truth-in-Packaging Law; explain to your friends that if the pinfeathers were white they would probably be eaten without notice, so it's just simple honesty that the feathers are dark and we all know what we're eating. 3. Or save that particular duck for a nice intimate family meal and try plucking another bird for company, one that's not molting or that has light-colored feathers.

If at some point while picking the feathers you decide that the bird just isn't going to come clean no matter what you do, you might wish to skin the whole thing and be done with it. This, of course, may require you to alter your recipe, since there will be no protective outer coating to prevent the meat from drying out during cooking.

There may be hairs remaining on the plucked bird after all the feathers and pinfeathers are gone. If the bird is at all moist, the hairs may be lying flat but will pop up when the skin is dried. We leave the feet on the bird up to this point to use as a handle while singeing off the hairs. The feet are used by some to add flavor and color to soup, though being thoroughly familiar with where our birds have been walking, we have so far

215

declined to try it. A gas burner is best for singeing, but if one is not available it's possible to singe the hairs with a candle. Sometimes we're asked if a match can be used to singe the hairs—sure, if you have a month or two to singe them off one by one. The hairs should be singed rapidly to prevent break-down in the fatty tissues under the skin, as this hastens deterioration during storage. If you intend to freeze the bird, you may wish to postpone singeing the hairs until after thawing.

Some inventive soul has come up with a special plucking wax to remove pinfeathers and other impossible-to-remove residues of plucking. Actually, if wax is used, a bird only needs to be "rough-picked" enough to open up spaces in the plumage, and it is not necessary to pick it down to the hairs and "pins." Quite a large amount of wax is needed, since the bird must be completely immersed in it. But then, this wax can be reused many times if cleaned as described below. The wax should be melted in a large pot that has been made into a double-boiler by putting it inside a larger pot of water. The double-boiler ploy prevents the wax from catching fire, which happens rather easily as you may know if you've ever heard of candles. Heat the wax to 160 to 165° F. (71 to 74° C.), measuring the temperature with a candy-making or dairy thermometer. Plunge the bird into the wax and immediately move it to a container of ice water for about a minute to harden the wax. A second dipping into the wax may be necessary for sufficient build-up. Again cool the waxed bird in cold water. After the wax is cool, but before it gets brittle, peel it off, and the down and hairs will miraculously come off with it. After each use, clean the wax so that it will retain its drawing power longer. First evaporate any water the wax may contain by heating the wax to 215° F. (102° C.) for a time. Then strain out the feathers and debris by pouring the liquid wax through a piece of cheesecloth. Finally, let the wax cool, and separate out any sludge that has settled at the bottom.

Working with wax can be somewhat messy and frustrating at first, but if you intend to pick waterfowl regularly you might want at least to give it a try. A source for plucking wax is listed in Chapter 16, "Resources."

Eviscerating

By now the bird should be nice and smooth and featherless, exhibiting a yellow or pinkish skin cross-hatched with rows of pores that formerly contained feathers. The bird has been transformed into something recognizable as the sort of thing that might be found at the local butcher shop. After removing the feet, get out the oil sacs at the base of the tail, where the yellowish oily residue was visible during plucking. Begin cutting a little in front of the sacs, working toward the tip of the tail, and sliding the knife deeper as you go along. Bring the knife back to the surface on the other side of the sacs. If you see some oily, yellowish substance left in the cut area, dig it out with a paring knife. The oil doesn't taste very good, and by cutting out the sacs you are doing a favor to any unwary diners who consider the deacon's nose to be the best part of the bird.

Now the bird is ready for evisceration, which you may wish to do at once or put off until the next day to gather your wits while the bird cools in the refrigerator overnight. We like to get it all over with in the same day, so we continue immediately. But some people feel that the job is easier after the viscera have cooled inside the body. In either case, when you are ready to eviscerate the bird, place it on its back with the tail toward you and make a slit from just above the vent to the termination of the breastbone. Make a second, smaller, crosswise cut to create a large opening that will facilitate removal of the viscera. Restrict your paring knife to just under the skin so that it doesn't pierce the intestines and make a mess.

Stretch the opening with both hands; then, reaching inside with one hand, work around between the inner wall of the body cavity and the bundle of viscera to loosen the organs. When you have reached as far as you can, grasp the bundle of viscera in the palm of your hand and gently pull toward you. Hopefully

217

the entire package will come out together, although some of the organs may remain inside the cavity and have to be taken out individually. Cut around the vent to detach the bundle. You may wish to pull out the lungs, which are deep inside against the back. We prefer to leave them there, as they roast up nicely with the bird and some people like to eat them. The testicles or a cluster of egg yolks, according to the sex of the bird, may be clinging to the cavity wall at mid-back and should be removed.

There is often a deposit of fat on either side of the opening near the vent. If the bird is to be stuffed, the fat may be removed and rendered for later baking. Fat is rendered by liquefying it in a saucepan over low heat. Any solid particles can be removed before it hardens. If the bird will be roasted without stuffing, you can leave the fat to render as the bird cooks, and collect it from the bottom of the roasting pan.

There are three things in the bundle of viscera that you may want to salvage for gravy, soup, or dogfood: the heart, the liver, and the gizzard. The heart is usually easily detached. Remove the outer membrane and the blood vessels inside, and rinse off the heart with cold water. The liver is nearly as simple: remove the little green bile sac nestled in among its folds. It's better to lose a little of the liver by cutting some meat away with the gall sac than to risk contaminating the whole liver should the sac break and spill its contents of bitter-tasting green liquid. The gizzard must be detached in two places, scraped of its coating of fat, and sliced halfway round to the depth of the inner wrinkled lining. If you managed not to cut the inner lining, it will come away intact with its contents of pebbles, bits of glass, pop tops, and other assorted items that seem to be the gastronomic delight of waterfowl.

Since some people feel these delicacies are fit only for the dogs, we'd best remind you that it's a good idea to cook any scraps fed to pets so as not to give them a taste for fresh duck or goose meat and thus spawn evil ideas.

Though the giblets can be cooked up with a roast or chopped and added to the stuffing, there are imaginative recipes for them alone. Livers are great in omelettes for instance, super with gravy over rice, and, of course, delicious fried in onions or bacon bits. Goose-liver pâté is very chic; and we doubt anyone would notice if you were to make your favorite chopped liver recipe with the kind of liver most immediately at hand. As for the other giblets, we've discovered an entirely novel method for their use. Since most of the animals we raise are birds of one sort or another, the meat we eat is almost entirely fowl. Once in a while we get a hankering for hamburger, but rarely can we justify indulging ourselves in such frivolities with a freezer full of our own homegrown birds. At the same time, we collect large quantities of gizzards and hearts, and not being the sort to waste any resources, we came up with a natural solution: ground in a meat chopper, gizzards and hearts make dandy "hamburger" for use in pizza, tacos, spaghetti sauce, or whatever. When we share such meals with friends, we tell them what they are eating only after they have finished the meal and begun their exclamations over the tastiness of the food and the proficiency of the cook. Then we let them in on our little secret and delight in their wide-eyed "Really?!" that ensues. Try it.

After the viscera have been removed, it is time to turn your attention to the neck. If the head is still attached, now is the appropriate moment to remove it. With a sharp knife, preferably serrated, cut through the neck at the throat. The head can be used for cooking, but we are not well versed in that culinary art, so you will have to look elsewhere for instructions.

If the head was already removed at the butchering step, there will be a bloody and probably dirty stub where it used to be. Cut the neck back to clean meat and discard the tip. Turning the bird onto its breast, slit the neck skin along the back side, starting from the junction of the neck with the body. This will leave a piece about 3 to 4 inches (8 to 10 cm) long for a duck and 4 to 6 inches (10 to 15 cm) for a goose or Muscovy. Peel the skin back from the neck, and with a sharp serrated knife cut the neck off at the body. The flap of skin can be folded over the opening and skewered into place to hold stuffing in the body cavity when you're ready to start roasting.

219

Meanwhile, you should remove bits of the windpipe, crop, and other things adhering to the neck skin.

After rinsing the bird inside and out in cold running water, it will finally be ready for that fantastic recipe you never thought you could afford to fix. A duck or goose will look more professional if a little roasting rack is formed by bending the wings around to the back and crossing them. For a goose, the wings may be tied around the breast with a string to keep them from flopping about.

Despite our many digressions, or maybe because of them, we should point out that it is extremely important to work as rapidly as possible to get the freshly killed bird into the refrigerator before harmful bacterial growth sets in. It should take less time to do than it took to read it, not to mention write it. Once in the refrigerator, your duck or goose needs 12 to 24 hours after its ordeal to relax and develop some tenderness. Rigor mortis must run its course or your teeth will have the devil to pay. Even if you wish to freeze the bird for later consumption, let it stand in the refrigerator for this same period before going into deep freeze.

Storing the meat

Any duck or goose you intend to store in the freezer should be enclosed in a plastic bag made especially for freezing food. The keeping quality of the meat is enhanced by using the airtight bags, and oxidation or freezer burn will be less likely to occur during the storage period. These bags are usually sold where canning supplies can be purchased. Make sure you get bags that are large enough. For most whole ducks, the one-gallon bag is sufficient; for female Muscovies you might need the two-gallon size; for geese and male Muscovies, a five-gallon bag is usually necessary. To save freezer space, you can halve or quarter birds for storage, in which case smaller bags may be used.

Before sealing the bag with a twist tie, expel the air by sucking it out: place an ordinary drinking straw in the opening, close the bag around the straw, and suck on it until the bag collapses. Then, tightly squeezing the bag opening, remove the straw and tie the bag before air can get back in. By removing much of the oxygen, you create a partial vacuum which helps preserve the meat. If you do not have a straw handy, the same thing can be accomplished by applying reverse mouth-to-mouth resuscitation directly to the squeezed-together opening. But don't tell anyone we suggested this, as it is considered unsanitary (by the same people who consider kissing unsanitary).

If you leave the bird whole and wish to include the giblets with the bird, slip them into a separate little plastic bag and place it in the cavity. This makes it easier to remove them if the bird is still slightly frozen when you are ready to prepare it. It also makes it less likely that the giblets will slither to the floor and get dirty as you are preparing the bird for stuffing weeks later, having forgotten you tucked them away inside.

We like to separate the giblets for storage. Besides the culinary considerations, there are the practical realities of storage. At the proper temperature of 0° F. (-18° C.) or below, giblets store well for only about three months, while duck or goose meat itself can be kept frozen twice that long without loss of quality.

When thawing a frozen goose or duck to prepare for dinner, allow about two hours per pound in the refrigerator or half that long at room temperature. Very large birds should always be thawed in the refrigerator because they take so long to thaw all the way through that bacterial growth could develop on the warmed-up outside while the inside is still frozen.

The Feathers

We like to save the feathers and down from our ducks and geese because they have so many uses. The stiff primary wing feathers, or quills, were formerly used as fountain pens, and some people still pursue the arts of quill writing and quill drawing. The people of the Middle East play a stringed musical instrument called the oud, using a stiff goose quill as a pick. At one time, gold miners used the hollow shafts of such feathers as storage vials for the gold dust they collected. Feathers also

221

make dandy pipe cleaners. Those from colorful breeds (which unfortunately are not always the most desirable for table use) can be quite attractive when artfully worked into weavings and other objets d'art. Children like to glue feathers to bird pictures. The smaller feathers, those that don't have stiff piercing quills, can be saved for stuffing pillows and feather beds, though it takes a lot of plucking to make a decent size pillow, let alone a feather bed. One goose will yield about a third of a pound (150 gm) of feathers, while one-seventh to one-fifth of a pound (65 to 90 gm) can be gotten from a duck.

The down, which is the innermost layer of feathers and a characteristic of waterfowl, is extremely soft and light, and justly well known for its insulating quality. Goose down has greater loft (ability to fluff up) than does duck down, so it's the kind used for Arctic parkas and sleeping bags. But if saving feathers for a pillow takes time, try saving down for a parka or sleeping bag! You might want to start small by stuffing a hunting vest or a pair of toasty boot liners. In any case, down is one of the side products of plucking, and if you're like us and shun waste, you might want to consider saving it even though you'll need a lifetime to gather enough to make something. Perhaps you could get together with a group of friends who raise waterfowl and form a down pool, each taking a turn at making something with the accumulated down. Just be sure you make these arrangements with long-term friends!

It is usually best to discard feathers that have gotten soiled and those that are "young." When a feather is growing in, it will have gooey stuff inside the quill. This dries up when the feather is mature. Young feathers are difficult to clean and may get smelly after a while, not to mention that they may draw insects. If you like insects and can wait a couple of weeks, you could, of course, let the insects do the job. Leave the feathers near any convenient ant trail and the ants will be happy to scour out the hollows for you.

Even if the feathers are pretty clean, you may still want to wash them. To facilitate washing, place them inside a small-mesh laundry bag and submerge in lukewarm water to which you've added a little detergent or borax, and washing soda. Slosh them around ever so slightly, then rinse in clean lukewarm water. After removing the dirt and soap, gently squeeze the feathers and spread them out on a screen or rack to dry, or hang on a line in the laundry bag or a burlap sack. They may also be dried on a towel or paper, but you'll have to turn them occasionally to fluff them out and dry them evenly, preventing matting and molding. Don't dry feathers where a draft is likely to blow them all over the house.

If you do not wish to save the feathers, you may instead want to add them to your compost pile. Feathers are around 15 percent nitrogen, so they are a desirable component of compost. They decompose quite readily, especially if kept properly moistened. We have found, though, that feathers tend to mat like grass clippings do, so it is best to spread them around or mix them with other matter when adding to compost.

The meal

People often assume that duck and goose meat has light and dark portions like chicken and turkey, and are surprised to learn that it's all dark. The color of the meat is determined by the amount of activity of the corresponding muscle. The more activity, the darker the meat. Chickens hardly ever fly, so their breast meat—the wing muscles—is white. But they do run around a lot so their leg meat is dark. Farm chickens get more activity than commercial ones and their meat is overall a darker color than store-bought chicken. Wild ducks have very dark meat all over because they fly so much. Domestic waterfowl may not fly much or at all, but they do use their wings enough to darken the breast muscles somewhat.

The skin color of waterfowl is also often a source of puzzlement for first-timers. On some birds it's pinkish and on some it's yellow. This difference has to do with the breed as well as what the bird has been eating. Feeds high in chlorophyll, xanthophyll, or carotene tend to produce yellowish skin tones. There's no difference in flavor or nutrition, though—it's all in appearance. Some people like to serve pink-skinned meat while others prefer yellow-skinned.

Butchers usually classify fowl by terms such as broiler and roaster, referring to methods of cooking. They are really telling you the age of the bird, because the most suitable method of cooking a bird depends on its tenderness, which in turn depends on its age. Fast dry-heat methods such as broiling, frying, and barbecuing are generally preferred by cooks for young ducks and geese, which are the most tender. A bird just reaching maturity is best roasted. When a bird is butchered after the optimum time and is tending toward toughness, it is still perfectly edible but slow moist-heat cooking methods are required, including fricassee, soup, stew, and pressure cooking. These are not hard and fast rules of course, but generally speaking it is less disastrous to cook a tender bird by moist heat methods than to try to cook a tough bird by quick dry-heat methods. Because of this, it is best to hedge your bets on any bird of uncertain age and cook it by the slower moist methods. But before conceding to the stew pot, you may want to try sleuthing out the bird's maturity. If its upper bill, windpipe, and breastbone are soft and pliable, you are reasonably safe in presuming the bird is tender enough for dry-heat cooking.

There are many recipes available for duck or goose, and most cookbooks have at least one, so we don't feel it's necessary to fill the rest of this book with our favorite recipes. We'll simply note that since duck and goose, like pork, is a rather rich and filling meat, it's reasonable to figure only about a pound (500 gm) of carcass weight per serving. But we would like to point out that duck and goose, if properly prepared, need not be the greasy meal some people expect. First of all, waterfowl should be cooked on a rack. This keeps it up out of the drippings as they accumulate in the bottom of the roasting pan. Secondly, the bird should be pierced all over with a meat fork before it is cooked. This allows subcutaneous fat to ooze out as it cooks off, a sort of self-basting process.

We have a friend who takes advantage of the dripping fat of roasting waterfowl by placing a rack of duck over a roast of game. As the duck cooks, the fat drips over the game roast, which, without larding, would cook up a little dry and tough. When the cooking time is up he has a feast of roast duck and game meat. He has neither to baste the bird nor lard the roast, and for his ingenuity eats neither dry roast nor greasy duck.

The fat from a roasting duck or goose can be saved and used as shortening in other cooking. Spoon it out of the bottom of the pan about every half-hour so it doesn't turn brown. We have a canister in the refrigerator in which we keep fat from roasted waterfowl. The fat comes in handy for greasing the skillet when frying such foods as onions, mushrooms, and eggs, and can be used in many recipes that call for hardened oil or lard. It's delicious in breads, and we draw many favorable comments on our duck-fat oatmeal cookies. The only baking in which the fat has not been successful for us is piecrusts. Goose fat was once used as a skin lotion and as a remedy for colds and was also considered an excellent leather polish, but unfortunately it is not too good for making candles or soap.

We are often asked if the stuffing gets greasy inside a duck or a goose. As long as the fat has been removed from inside the cavity, the only thing that happens to the stuffing is that it gathers up the meat juices of the bird as it cooks and thus becomes thoroughly tasty. If you're concerned about greasy stuffing, you could precook the bird in a 400° F. (200° C.) oven for 15 minutes before stuffing it. This may help cook off some fat, and will at least make you feel better.

Domestic waterfowl should not be covered with foil when roasting. Instead, rub the skin with the cut face of a fresh lemon and then sprinkle with a coating of salt. This helps the skin to roast up brown and crisp, creating one of the very best parts of the meal.

A famous gourmet likes to tell the story of his visit to a tiny restaurant in the south of France, where he was challenged by the maitre d' to try the specialty of the house, a dish he guaranteed the gourmet had never had and would not be able to identify. The gourmet, feeling very cosmopolitan, accepted the challenge and was shortly served a platter of fatless, evenly

grained, delicious red meat which indeed he could not identify. He was absolutely confounded as well as a bit chagrined when he finally conceded to the maitre d' and was informed "Monsieur has just eaten fillet of duck breast!"

Although the story doesn't identify the breed of duck, it is our experience that Muscovy is the duck whose breasts make the most exceptional fillets. Their delicious meat is quite different from that of other ducks—drier and different in texture and flavor, almost like veal. It is a delicacy not to be rivaled by any other single cut of meat anywhere. Nothing on a cow approaches it. We commonly use Muscovy breast as a superb substitute for steak, or as the framework for a Wiener schnitzel or a "veal" parmigiana. This meat virtually demands to be accompanied by a fine, full-bodied, red Bordeaux wine. Any recipe for veal can be adapted nicely to Muscovy breasts. A big advantage to using Muscovies this way is that they take much less storage space in the freezer. Storing a large bird with a big empty hole in the middle of it does tend to take up lots of unnecessary room.

After filleting the Muscovy breasts, there is still an impressive amount of meat remaining on the duck. The legs can be separated, to be roasted or barbecued for one meal, and the rest of the meat boiled off the bones for soup. Our favorite use of the Muscovy meat that remains after the breasts have been filleted is to make sausage. All it takes is a meat grinder and a few spices to make a most excellent patty sausage. Add a sausage stuffer and some casing, and you can have link sausage.

If you raise more than enough ducks or geese for immediate table use, you'll find the booklet *Home Freezing of Poultry* can come in handy. There is a modest charge for this USDA publication, which can be obtained through your local cooperative extension office. Another USDA publication, called *Home Canning of Meat and Poultry*, will be helpful if you don't have access to a freezer. However, if our experience is any indication, canning is not the kind of thing that waterfowl was meant for and should be resorted to only if absolutely necessary. We had a copious quantity of duck soup one year and decided to save freezer space by canning it. Now we have a copious quantity of cardboardy-tasting soup in our pantry!

13

Exhibiting Your Ducks and Geese

Not until fairly recently has the exhibiting of ducks and geese begun to come into its own. Waterfowl sections at poultry shows get larger each year, and in some places waterfowl breeders have organized their own exclusive all-waterfowl shows.

If you are interested in keeping waterfowl for show, or in showing the waterfowl you keep, you should first be sure you have show-quality stock. "Show quality" is somewhat difficult to define and sometimes just as difficult to come by. Once you have chosen a particular breed, you must find a breeder who has conscientiously bred for conformation to the standard so that features not entirely characteristic of the breed have not developed. Small breeds, for instance, if left to reproduce on their own, often become larger than the standard size. Large breeds, on the other hand, may decrease in size through the generations. Off-colors may begin to creep in until plumage is no longer of a characteristic color. Unless breeding birds are selected each year according to standard requirements, individual populations may eventually depart drastically from the standard.

So obviously you will want to become thoroughly familiar with the standard for the breed you have chosen. This can be accomplished several ways. A good start is to consult the American Poultry Association's *Standard of Perfection* or, if it's small ducks you desire, the American Bantam Association's *Bantam Standard*. Though both are basically given to descriptions of standard breeds of poultry, each contains a waterfowl section at the back. The *Standards* give specifications for shape and color of every part of the bird from the bill, eyes, head and neck, down to the shanks and feet, and list a scale of points by which the birds are to be judged, weighted according to the importance placed on each particular characteristic.

Of the many fine breeds and varieties of waterfowl, only those listed in the *Standards* compete at shows, since otherwise there are no criteria by which to judge.

Unfortunately, the *Standards* are deficient in pictures of accepted breeds of waterfowl, so in addition you might consult Oscar Grow's *Modern Waterfowl Management and Breeding Guide,* often called the waterfowl standard. Although Grow's descriptions and illustrations are not strictly speaking official, they are nonetheless a very good and accurate guide to standardized waterfowl characteristics. Additional information can be found in Darrel Sheraw's book *Successful Duck and Goose Raising,* which contains not only photos and descriptions, but also excellent guidelines on selecting stock for show and breeding. Information on obtaining all of these books can be found in Chapter 16, "Resources."

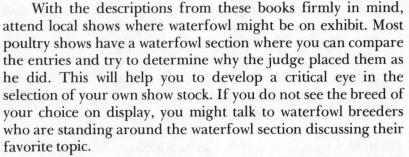

With the descriptions from these books firmly in mind, attend local shows where waterfowl might be on exhibit. Most poultry shows have a waterfowl section where you can compare the entries and try to determine why the judge placed them as he did. This will help you to develop a critical eye in the selection of your own show stock. If you do not see the breed of your choice on display, you might talk to waterfowl breeders who are standing around the waterfowl section discussing their favorite topic.

Another good way to meet waterfowl breeders is through the various poultry and waterfowl organizations. Unfortunately, specialty clubs for waterfowl are less numerous than those for poultry, but evidence is that this may be rapidly changing—Campbell breeders not long ago organized a national association, and rumor has it that a Call club is not far behind. Local organizations of poultry fanciers and exhibitors often include waterfowl breeders as well. Addresses of national as well as local organizations can be found by looking through the national monthly newspaper *Poultry Press,* whose address in turn can be found in Chapter 16.

It is best to try to locate a bona fide breeder from whom to purchase your initial stock, rather than a dealer, so that you can ask lots of questions about breeding, feeding, and conditioning programs. Every breed has its own peculiarities, and every breeder has developed an individualized program. You'll need all the help you can get here, for you'll never find this type of information in farm journals or agricultural bulletins.

By going to a local breeder you will be able to select the birds you wish to work with, whereas if you send away for birds you must be willing to take potluck.

In selecting your founding strain, don't be dazzled by the stunning colors or pearly whiteness of the birds under consideration. According to the scale of points given in the *Standard,* a duck or goose is judged only about 25 percent on color and the remaining 75 percent on shape or "type." If a bird isn't right in type, it is certainly hard to make a case for it on the basis of color. As the saying goes, "You can't paint your house until you've built it."

You might wish to keep in mind in selecting a breed for show that exhibition and utility are not necessarily incompatible. They can be combined very nicely by careful selection of breed and strain. After selecting a breed that suits your needs, attempt to locate a strain that has been developed for both utility and show purposes. If the available strains are a little deficient on either side, you can always make your own improvements by selective breeding.

We are often asked if it is better to get birds from two different strains to avoid an inbred population, or whether it is all right to acquire related birds as founding stock. Well, despite its sullied reputation, inbreeding is actually an art to be cultivated rather than a temptation to be shunned. Should you be lucky enough to find a strain of your desired breed which has been kept by a loving and selective breeder, you would be doing that breeder, yourself, and the birds a great disservice by mixing in new blood and destroying years of careful and calculated work. On the other hand, if the only birds you can find are somewhat less than perfect, you may wish to put together a breeding population from different strains that have complementary features.

Once you have selected your founding stock and have bred some birds of your own which you feel are ready for the showroom, plunge in and enter a show. If you have any doubts as to which of your birds is the best, enter more than one so that you can have the benefit of the judge's opinions on which most closely conforms to the *Standard*. Don't be disappointed if you walk off without a trophy on the first try. The best showroom attitude to take, at least initially, is that exhibiting your birds is a learning experience. Birds that look great at home, especially to a beginner, invariably look less stunning at the show. For a time the shows will merely persuade you that more work is necessary to compete favorably with experienced exhibitors.

Examine the competition carefully to ascertain why your

birds were beaten. Talk with other breeders to see if they will share any of their tricks. Most breeders are happy to talk about their birds and glad to welcome a novice to their hobby. It may be difficult to break into the circle of old-timers, but if your sincerity and interest are obvious, it won't be long before you're accepted as one of them.

Many shows set aside a special time for exhibitors to confer with the judge about how he placed the birds as he did. This is an excellent time to ask questions. If you are careful not to put the judge on the defensive, you can learn an enormous amount during these sessions. Unfortunately, too many exhibitors use this time to rail at the judge for his incompetence in not selecting their bird as the winner. Make it clear to the judge from the start that you are not questioning his judgment but merely trying to tap into his wisdom.

Once you have a good idea of your birds' faults and shortcomings, you can pursue a breeding program that will bring them into greater conformity with the *Standard*. By judicious selection, you'll soon provide competition for the best of breeders. Of course, it is almost mandatory to learn something about elementary genetics.

It helps, too, to obtain good stock from the start. But even if it turns out that your birds are only mediocre, the challenge will be there to make something better of them. Of course, if your initial selection was not as good as you had at first thought, it may be wiser to seek a new strain that conforms more closely to the *Standard*. Sadly, there are breeders who have allowed their stock to depart so drastically from the *Standard* that only the stouthearted with grim determination and angelic vision would tackle the years-long job of breeding them back up to standard.

It is interesting and significant to note that in recent times it has become more common to find waterfowl taking top honors at poultry shows. No longer are waterfowl exhibitors taking a backseat to the breeders of standard chickens, for through judicious selective breeding they have brought various strains of waterfowl as nearly to the point of perfection (as defined by the *Standard*) as the best of the poultry strains.

Exhibiting ducks and geese is especially fun for those who are inclined to make pets of their waterfowl. The constant handling required for selecting, conditioning, and training the birds to respond well under the stress and strain of the showroom will result in the development of a special rapport between bird and owner.

There is far more to say about showing waterfowl than we could possibly include in this introductory chapter. We mainly want you to know that there is such a thing, that it is a rewarding though challenging hobby, and that sources exist for further information on breeding and showing techniques if you're interested in pursuing them.

14

Disease and Other Perils

One of the felicities of raising waterfowl is the knowledge that, given proper care and sufficient space, they are extremely unlikely to contract some dread disease. In contrast with chickens and other landfowl, they are subject to very few diseases and have an excellent chance of living right through to "old age." Diseases become a real threat only where waterfowl are kept in such large numbers that proper management becomes unrealistic. Most diseases are preventable through feeding a balanced diet, ensuring plenty of clean, fresh water for drinking and bathing, and providing adequate facilities for comfort and sanitation. In some areas it is necessary to vaccinate waterfowl against diseases prevalent locally. Check with your nearest cooperative extension service agent, listed in your phone book, to find out if this is necessary in your area.

An excellent veterinary guide with information on waterfowl problems is the *Merck Veterinary Manual*. Many animal owners find it a handy reference. In fact, for most waterfowl owners, books such as this are the only source of veterinary advice available to them, since there are very few vets who can deal knowledgeably with sick birds of any sort. Unfortunately, most veterinarians find it more rewarding to devote their attentions to the common pets or the larger animals, and so have never really studied bird diseases professionally. If you are lucky, you may find a bird-oriented vet in your area who can be relied on, should you need his assistance. Your state poultry pathology laboratory, located through your local cooperative extension service office, can help in a crisis. Most waterfowl keepers, though, must acquire for themselves the information to deal with sicknesses as they occur, and frequently such information is gained through costly personal experience.

Because it falls largely on you to learn to recognize and deal with problems as they occur, this chapter will give you a starting place. Problems specific to young waterfowl are dealt with in Chapter 11, "Bringing up Ducklings and Goslings."

Symptoms of trouble, and possible causes

Signs that something is out of the ordinary in your flock include weak and listless behavior, ruffled feathers, unusual motor activities, loss of appetite or increased consumption of water, change in the droppings, and inexplicable deaths. Disease is not the only possible cause of these conditions, however, and so you should first ascertain that the birds are not over-crowded and are receiving the proper nourishment. You should also consider the possibility of egg-binding and oviduct inversion (Chapter 8), crop impaction and constipation (Chapter 7), and depression or death due to shock or nervous breakdown (Chapter 4). Extreme heat or sunstroke can also cause depression, as can frostbitten feet (or knobs on Chinese geese). Suspect frostbite if the affected area first turns pale and then becomes bright red rimmed with white. It is prevented by following the cold-weather precautions listed in Chapter 5. Given time, knobs discolored by frostbite may return to normal.

Waterfowl like to eat unusual things such as nails, pop tops, and bits of glass or wire, and this may cause depression. Such items may simply prove an irritation to the bird, but can cause blockage or tear holes in a bird's delicate interior, causing infection. In any case, once the object has been eaten, there is very little that you can do about it. Prevent such possibilities by meticulously removing any small, sharp objects about the yard and suggest to your visitors they not toss such things casually on the ground.

One symptom of disease—crusty, sticky eyes—could indicate the presence of a low-grade infection, which sometimes results when a duck or goose cannot submerge its head in water periodically to flush out its eyes. An unbalanced diet may increase a bird's susceptibility to this type of infection. When swimming water is not available, it is especially important to see that water containers are deep enough to allow ducks and geese to get their whole heads in. Isolate an infected bird, clean its eyes with an eyewash from a vet, and provide it a nutritiously balanced diet. Add a tiny bit of household bleach to its drinking water to sterilize it and help eliminate the infection. And, as described in Chapter 5, it is also important to keep their water clean and debris-free.

Finally, there is always the chance that predators are involved. We have suggested some ways of dealing with this problem in Chapter 5. We recently had a frantic call from a friend who was finding her ducks dead one by one each morning. Though there were no obvious symptoms of disease, and the ducks were dying at too slow a rate for an epidemic, she was nonetheless certain that some dread disease was going through her bevy. The more she described what was happening, the more certain we became that she had a predator problem, despite her insistence that she had found no indication of any violent deaths. We suggested watching for possible predators anyway, and several days later she called to say that having arisen earlier than usual, she had seen some dogs teasing her ducks. Each morning they apparently singled out a duck and teased it until the bird had been worried to death and was no longer fun to play with. The assassin dogs left before our friend normally got up, leaving no clues of their murderous cavortings but a mute corpse.

Another of our friends went so far as to accuse his ducklings of killing and eating each other—a barbaric practice popular among chickens but rarely ever among ducks. His theory became somewhat more difficult to defend when the last one disappeared. He finally determined the culprit to be a marauding weasel.

Poison. General problem symptoms may also be traced to poisoning. Rock salt on icy paths, or the briny slush it creates, may lead to poisoning. Birds may be poisoned by lunching on vegetation that has been sprayed with insecticides. Spray may even drift into their water from a neighbor's garden. Bait meant for slugs, snails, and other garden pests could also be the culprit—a duck of our acquaintance chowed down on some earwig bait and was dead in 15 minutes.

Ducks and geese can also be poisoned from spoiled food or kitchen refuse, which can develop a type of botulism toxin. Most people associate botulism poisoning with improper home canning techniques, but the organism causing this highly toxic poisoning may develop and thrive in any kind of decaying matter. So it is important to sort out anything that has begun to rot from scraps and tidbits you use to supplement their feed.

The botulism organism is widespread and ever-present in many areas, but it requires certain conditions in which to develop and flourish. These conditions are too frequently met in decaying matter, including rotting garbage as well as anaerobic (oxygenless) alkaline environments created in shallow bodies of water. The organism itself is harmless, but certain excretions manufactured by it as a by-product of its metabolism are among the most deadly known poisons. Maggots which have fed on botulism-affected carrion are not sensitive to this poison, but ducks and geese eating such maggots may become gravely ill or even die.

Since wild ducks and geese are accustomed to feeding and cavorting in swamps and marshes where water tends to be foul and stagnant, it is not uncommon for such birds to die of poisoning. Through the years there have been major outbreaks of botulism poisoning in marshes where wild waterfowl feed on the bottom of shallow stagnant pools, especially in the western states where the soils tend to be alkaline. In fact, in a few instances during this century millions of ducks have died in a single outbreak. It was only recently discovered that these disasters were caused by botulism toxins. Before that the mysterious condition that causes such unexpected and widespread mortality was known simply as Western Duck Sickness. For more information on the interesting history of this problem and its control, see the California Fish and Game leaflet called "Waterfowl Botulism Management," listed in Chapter 16.

Outbreaks of botulism can also occur among flocks of domestic waterfowl if their swim water becomes fouled. Don't let droppings build up in it, and clean out decaying organic material regularly. Also remove any carrion from the pond or the area where the birds are kept.

Symptoms of botulism poisoning occur within 8 to 48 hours after eating the poison. Where only small amounts have been eaten, recovery is likely, but larger amounts may result in death. In mild cases the only symptom may be a brief bout with weak legs before the birds return to normal. But in more severe cases they may take on a sleepy appearance and become unable to hold their heads erect due to paralysis of the neck muscles. The wings and legs may become paralyzed, too, causing the birds to lie on their sides. Waterfowl stricken while swimming in water may drown as a result of muscle paralysis, but most suffocate from paralysis of the respiratory system.

Treatment includes removal of contamination and disposal of any dead birds to prevent further spread of the sickness. If the poisoning is not severe and the birds are still able to drink, it may help to replace all other water with a solution of dissolved Epsom salts in the proportion one pound per 15 gallons (.7 gm per liter) of water.

In most cases, though, by the time botulism has been noticed, the birds are beyond help. Rather than watching ducks and geese go through the agonies of botulism poisoning, it would seem prudent to avoid giving them any spoiled foods that may result in sickness or death, and to keep their swim water clean.

There are toxins other than botulism that can be produced by molds, bacteria, and staphylococci when they are encouraged to multiply in warm, wet, fecund environments. Since there is always a chance these will affect your flocks adversely, it is prudent not to allow such conditions to develop in any source to which they have access.

Penis paralysis. Drakes sometimes experience a condition known as penis paralysis which is popularly thought to be the result of the overexertion a drake experiences in trying to keep all his women happy. However romantic this notion may be, the evidence is that this condition has other causes than the drake's fancied altruism. Since inability to protract the penis does sometimes occur, it should be watched for in any bevy.

Rather than resulting from overuse of the sex organ, penis paralysis is probably a genetically inherited weakness of the muscles controlling this organ. The condition may possibly be aggravated by a dietary deficiency, and some evidence suggests it may result from lack of swimming water in which to breed. In any case, an affected drake is not able to retract his protruding penis, which as a result bounces around in the dirt and mud, eventually drying out, becoming dirty and scabby, and perhaps even falling off altogether. The drake may lose weight or die. If this condition is noticed before the organ becomes very soiled or infected, the drake should be placed in a quiet, secluded pen with plenty of clean litter and ample bathing water. It may be necessary to wash the organ with a mild disinfectant and gently push it into place. After a month or two of seclusion, the drake should be back in fine shape. For the sake of the drake himself, as well as any offspring which might inherit the trait, it is wise to retire such birds permanently from the breeding pen.

Lameness. By far the most common ailment among waterfowl is lameness in some form. The basic structure of their legs is just not very strong. Leg weaknesses are especially common to geese, and goslings are particularly prone to spraddle leg, as described in Chapter 11.

Lameness in adult waterfowl may be caused by thorns or slivers of glass lodged in the foot pad. The foreign material should be removed and the foot thoroughly cleaned. Sometimes a hard, warty callus will be found on the bottom of the foot pad that causes the bird to limp. This condition is listed as "bumblefoot" in veterinary manuals and seems to occur when waterfowl are forced to walk on dry, hard-packed ground, especially if they do not have swimming water. Apparently, the dryness and hardness causes cracks in the feet through which bacteria enter, resulting in the formation of an abscess. It is likelier to occur in older and heavier birds and may appear on one or both feet. Treatment includes thoroughly washing the feet, cleaning with a bactericide, and removing any hard core or pus. Keep the bird in a quiet, secluded place with deep, clean litter or in a grassy area with plenty of fresh swimming water. To prevent this problem, keep feed and watering areas clean and cover hard surfaces such as concrete, gravel, or hard-packed earth with clean litter.

Contagious diseases

In the event you detect disease symptoms among your birds, the wisest course is to remain calm and go through all of the possibilities in this book and in your vet manual one by one, considering the simplest explanations first. One sure sign of a contagious disease is a combination of symptoms in conjunction with the sudden occurrence of a number of deaths. If you think that there is a possibility that your flock is experiencing an epidemic, unlikely as that is, consult your nearest pathology laboratory for advice. Treatment is tricky if the symptoms are all nearly alike, and a bacteriological examination would be the most effective means of determining the proper remedy. The pathology lab may require several samples of recently dead birds and may also ask for a live one (which will not be returned to you) that is exhibiting symptoms. Lab diagnosis is desirable for a number of reasons in addition to knowing what treatment to give the remainder of the flock. You will be able to find out how to clean your area to make it safe for new birds. By knowing what is affecting the birds, you can find out whether the seemingly unaffected ones could be carriers, thus presenting a threat to any new waterfowl brought in, or to newly hatched young. You can determine if it would be possible to vaccinate new birds so that they will not contract the disease. You may also be told, incidentally, to destroy your entire flock and start over again with new birds. If the disease is reportable you may have no choice. Otherwise, it is up to you to weigh all the factors and decide whether to accept this recommendation. Backyarders are normally more reluctant to follow this advice, since emotional as well as economic considerations may play a role.

It's a passing good thing that disease is highly uncommon among backyard ducks and geese, for the two most likely diseases that adult ducks and geese contract have the formidable names of cholera and plague.

The proper name for cholera is fowl cholera, and it affects not only ducks and geese, but many other species of birds, both domestic and wild. Cholera is highly contagious, and in areas where outbreaks are prevalent, vaccination against this disease may be desirable. While cholera is not very common in domestic birds in this country, the disease is still the most likely for waterfowl to contract. There are different strains of cholera which produce different degrees of severity, from acute to chronic. Sometimes a change in the droppings to a greenish, watery diarrhea provides an early warning. Other signs in addition to those already listed as general symptoms of disease are nervous twitching and jerking, walking in small circles, watery encrustment around the eyes and nostrils, swollen legs and feet, and respiratory problems. These symptoms are easily mistaken for those of both poisoning and blood parasites.

The disease is spread through contaminated feed, air, water, and soil. It is carried by rodents and other scavengers, and possibly by flies. Outbreaks may follow cold, wet weather and are abetted by unsanitary conditions, overcrowding, poorly ventilated quarters, improper diet, or recent visitations by wild waterfowl. Your local pathology lab can give a prescription for treatment after making a bacteriological analysis to determine if cholera is affecting your sick birds.

The second most common disease affecting waterfowl is duck plague, or more formally, duck virus enteritis. Rumor has it in avian pathology circles that the formal designation was created by commercial duck growers who were concerned that if the public heard too much about "duck plague" they would acquire bad associations with ducks and stop buying them in the market. The fancy name, though referring to the same disease,

241

is designed to sound so technical that it will go right over the layman's head.

Though the name specifically refers to ducks, all types of waterfowl are susceptible to this disease. Symptoms besides those already listed for disease in general include droopiness, watery or bloody diarrhea, swollen eyelids, and nasal discharge. Birds may lie about with their wings spread and are often unable to walk. Death may follow a period of convulsions. The virus is spread through contact with affected birds or their droppings, or through the drinking of contaminated stagnant or slow-moving water. The death rate is high and deaths occur within three or four days after the first symptoms appear.

Viral enteritis is a reportable disease, which means that it is a violation of the law not to report it to your local animal health authorities, who will promptly come out to quarantine your yard and kill your birds. Bureaucrats refer to this activity as "depopulation" of a yard. It is necessary because there is no known cure for duck plague, and until very recently there was no known vaccine. Depopulation is highly unpopular among flock owners, but it is really essential because of the danger that the disease may spread to other flocks, domestic or wild. In case your sense of civic duty is not sufficiently aroused by this pitch, we might point out that there is a hefty fine and jail term available to help convince you. At least the government pays you for the healthy birds they kill, and as for the others, well—have you checked with Lloyd's of London about their Duck Plague Insurance?

Luckily, this is not a common disease among domestic flocks and will undoubtedly become even less so now that a vaccine is available. However, because viral enteritis is fairly common among wild birds in this country, it is prudent to try to keep wild waterfowl away from your birds. Incidentally, you may be amused, as we were, to learn that the Fish and Wildlife Service regards outbreaks of duck plague among wild flocks as due primarily to their contact with domestic birds, whereas the Department of Agriculture blames wild birds for spreading the plague to domestic flocks!

15

Getting Started

Now that you are thoroughly acquainted with the habits and the needs of waterfowl, you are ready to begin thinking about acquiring your first birds. Much of the information in this chapter has been given elsewhere, but here we will direct it specifically toward getting started.

What kind?

The first decision to make is which breed or breeds to acquire, and there are a number of factors that will help you decide. First consider the purpose for which you will be raising waterfowl. If you desire weed control in the orchard, backyard guardians, tasty holiday meals for large numbers, or simply large ornamental birds, you may wish to choose from among the breeds of geese. On the other hand, if what you need is weed or insect control in your pond or drainage ditches, a bounteous supply of eggs, small-bodied meat birds, friendly pets, or a small breed to grace your pond, you might wish to choose from among the ducks.

If ducks are kept specifically for eggs, then best results will be obtained by raising a variety of Indian Runner or Campbell. For a meat-breed of duck, the choice is limited to those breeds that are full-bodied and fast-growing: Aylesburies, Muscovies, and Pekins all fit the bill. Among the geese, all are well suited for table use, the choice being simply whether a larger or a smaller breed is desired. If you want both meat and eggs, Campbells and the better strains of Muscovy are quite suitable, as is any breed of geese that strikes your fancy.

If you will be butchering green or junior birds, then you will definitely want to choose a white-feathered variety, since they make a better presentation at the table than the darker ones. If they will be plucked after full feathering, feather color is not as significant. Generally more than one breed is suited to each particular purpose. Among those to choose from are other less widely available breeds not listed in this book. If you learn about a breed that you like, try to find a breeder of that type to ask about its potential.

Your selection should reflect any limitations in your yard size. Obviously, Toulouse geese require more living space than Call ducks. Remember that roughly the same size yard will suit one goose, two regular size ducks, or three Call ducks, as described in Chapter 5. Geese can thrive largely on succulent pasturage, but ducks would require substantial supplemental nourishment. This will be a factor in the cost of keeping the birds, which may be an important consideration for you.

The size of the breed is usually directly related to its degree of activity, and it is important to match the disposition of the birds with that of their owners. The more active breeds make some people nervous, while others find the more sedate breeds lacking in spunk. The general rule is: The smaller the breed, the more nervous; the larger, the more sedate. Among the active birds are the Calls, Runners, Mallards, and Chinese. The calmer breeds include Aylesburies, Rouens, and Toulouse. Intermediate between excitable and phlegmatic are the Campbells, Muscovies, Africans, Embdens, and Pilgrims.

Another consideration is the amount of noise they will make. Some people like the noisier types, perhaps just because of fond childhood memories, or perhaps because they want their birds to inform them, by the tone of their voices, about all the news in the yard, from intruders to weather changes. Call ducks and Chinese geese tend to be the noisier breeds. For keepers who like waterfowl but don't care for the noise or fear that their neighbors might object, Muscovies are just the thing, as their voices are so soft and musical that it is hard to believe anyone could ever complain about them. We know many people who keep Muscovies in suburban areas where ducks are not allowed by zoning ordinance, and most of them get away with it simply because no one else knows they're there.

Adaptability to the local weather is another factor to keep in mind. Africans, Chinese, and Muscovies do better in the warmer areas, while Embdens, Toulouse, and the mallard-derived ducks are more tolerant of colder weather.

Those interested in raising and breeding waterfowl for show will want to be especially selective in choosing a breed. Consult the American Poultry Association *Standard of Perfection* or the American Bantam Association *Bantam Standard* before acquiring founding stock. It's a good idea to bring along a *Standard* when making a decision about acquiring any new waterfowl, as you can compare your potential purchase with the ideal.

Breeds of ducks and geese that have been raised according to the *Standard* are hard to find in many areas. Crossbred waterfowl are commonly seen in farmyard pastures. You may consciously choose to raise crossbred ducks or geese for their hybrid vigor or other characteristics, though, of course, you will have difficulty breeding from them with any consistency. But be aware that the accepted standards for show birds are not entirely arbitrary and not solely aesthetic: some have been found to correlate with the economic function of each respective breed. It is important to remember that in many cases the appearance is directly related to function—for example, large full-bodied white breeds are suited for meat, while small, tight-bodied birds are usually among the better layers. Seemingly irrelevant details like the uprightness of stance may have subtle but substantial bearing on more practical factors.

Obviously, then, it is important to learn to recognize the different breeds, and this recognition develops through acquaintance with birds in other people's backyards, at shows, and in books. Amazingly, some people keep birds for years and never know what breed they've got. One year we advertised in the papers for a pair of breeding Embden geese. An elderly lady called to tell us she had just the pair for us, and at a price we surely couldn't turn down. When asked what kind they were, she said she wasn't sure, but they were black and white

245

and red. "Lady," we said, "we'll be right over!" On the way we decided that these so-called "geese" could only be a pair of colored Muscovies, and on seeing the birds our suspicions were confirmed. Thus we acquired Hissy and Missy.

There are so many breeds and varieties to choose from that one is bound to fit exactly all of your practical requirements and tickle your fancy as well. As important as all of the other considerations are, choosing a breed that you enjoy having is at least of equal importance.

Eggs, young, or mature

Starting your first flock from eggs means you need to borrow or purchase an incubator to hatch them in, or to borrow a setting hen. You get the enjoyment of watching the birds grow from their very first moment of life. Once you have arranged for incubation, the starting investment is quite small. But not all of the eggs can be expected to hatch, and further, you can never really be quite sure what *will* hatch. Even if the eggs were purchased from a reliable breeder, the resulting hatchlings may not all be what you had expected due to the inevitable genetic fluctuations within any stock.

Waterfowl raised from eggs or from young birds will become very attached to their owners through the mechanism of imprinting. Some people find this one of the joys of raising ducks or geese. Those who raise young geese, though, justifiably worry that the adult birds will grow to have no fear of humans and will therefore likely attack during the mating season. This can be dealt with by maintaining a healthy respect for nesting birds.

When starting with young birds and following our advice in Chapter 11, "Bringing Up Ducklings and Goslings," there is rarely any reason to be concerned about loss. Ducklings and goslings can be brought home from the moment they fluff out and are fully dried. The precocial activity of these young birds totally amazes people who are familiar only with the young of dogs, cats, and robins, which must be carefully nurtured for several weeks by their parents.

Starting with mature waterfowl generally requires the most cash investment, but the least waiting, and you will never have any doubt as to what exactly you are purchasing. With patience, many older birds can be made friendly, although of course some never develop the rapport with their owners that younger birds do.

To a great extent the availability of waterfowl at any given stage of development depends on the season. Since spring is the time when the natural processes of setting and hatching take place in the wild, it is also the primary time when breeders hatch their young birds for the year. Hatching-eggs and hatchlings are normally available only in the spring months. Accordingly, you would expect to find that waterfowl offered for sale in the fall would generally be maturing, and mature birds available at the beginning of a season would ordinarily be nearly a year old.

How many?

The main thing to remember when trying to decide how many birds to get is that waterfowl are very gregarious birds and are never happy where just one is kept alone. Many beginners start with a trio—one male and two females. Most breeds will accept this arrangement, and it ensures each bird plenty of company. Though birds can be kept in pairs, for breeding purposes multiple matings are more efficient, since you get more breeding power for the price. Geese mate in pairs or trios, as do Mallards, but most breeds of ducks can be kept in larger groups of five or six females per male. The general rule is that the larger and less active the breed, the lower the ratio of females to males should be. Many people even keep the lighter breeds of geese in larger ratios than two to one and do not seem to be disappointed with the fertility rate. Of course, a male is not necessary unless you intend to do some breeding and hatching, but do get two or three birds anyway so that they can enjoy each other's company.

To decide on what number of ducks to keep for eggs, reckon how many eggs you want and, using the chart in Chapter 3, figure out how many birds of your chosen breed you will need in order to get the required number. Remember that there are seasons of plenty and seasons of want, so make allowances and either plan to store some of the surplus as described in Chapter 8 or else keep fewer birds and be reconciled to purchasing eggs during the off seasons.

For meat purposes some people simply eat whatever off-spring their ducks or geese produce, and thus keep the backyard population down. Others, with more deliberation, hatch a certain calculated number of eggs for meat production. Still others purchase the required number of young to raise each year so that their waterfowl-raising venture is strictly seasonal, concluding with the fall butchering. Remember that with proper care losses are minimal, so you need start with only a few more than the number you wish to put into the freezer.

When starting with eggs, remember that because of the many factors involved, hatching-eggs are not guaranteed to hatch, so it's wise to get a few extra. The percentage that will hatch is dependent on your skill with the incubator, the age and storing conditions of the eggs, and the health and vigor of the birds that laid them. If you are purchasing mature stock, you won't likely buy too many for the space available, but in buying eggs, or young, be forewarned against overcrowding. The explosive growth of ducklings and goslings is something that many beginners are totally unprepared for. A shoe box full of peeping down in April will fill the yard by July, and the clownish gosling that cuddles in your hand in summer will barely fit into the oven come Thanksgiving.

Selecting

When purchasing hatching-eggs, be sure to examine them for hatchability as carefully as you would your own eggs for hatching. We discussed some points to watch for in Chapter 10, "Artificial Incubation." Check for the correct color and size for the breed and for good hard shells with no cracks. When. purchasing mature ducks or geese look the birds over carefully before taking them home. Check for such problems as off-color, crooked backs or breastbones, and asymmetric pouches between the legs of geese. Don't be reluctant to examine eggs or birds for fear of insulting the seller. You will instead be showing him that you are a well-informed buyer. If you look like you know what you are doing, the seller may tell you things he might otherwise not have mentioned.

Ask about the age of the birds when purchasing ones that are full-grown. Though ducks and geese are generally long-lived, the laying ability of females and the fertility of males does begin to decline with age. Ducks are in their prime from one to three years of age, while geese reach their prime between two and five. Unfortunately, once a duck or goose is fully mature, its exact age is difficult to determine. You can hardly check their teeth, for example. A pliable upper bill, a flexible breastbone, and a softish windpipe are indications of a young bird. It is also useful to examine the tail feathers. Young birds will have squarish or blunted tail feathers where the down that was once attached has broken off. After the first full molt into adult plumage, the tail feathers will become the normal rounded feathers of the adult. For those who find these matters too subtle, we recommend acquiring ducks or geese that are nearly but not quite full-grown. That way you can be sure of the age, you get the advantage of the birds' full productivity, you avoid the hassles of raising young, and you know exactly what the mature bird will look like. If you opt for this plan, you will have to make your move in the summer or early fall months, since, as we noted, this is when the majority of domestic waterfowl are reaching the nearly full-grown stage.

It's also helpful to be able to tell the differences between the sexes. Most sellers can help you distinguish the males from the females, but a few honestly do not know how to tell. We must even admit that one or two scoundrels may deliberately try to mislead the unwary. Very young waterfowl are rarely sold sexed, so unless you want to get the older, more easily sexed birds, be content to get them unsexed and sort them out when more mature. By all means, do not expect to bring your birds back later and ask the seller to trade you for the sex you wanted. A better plan is to get a few extra to be sure of the proportions you desire, and then serve the surplus males for Christmas dinner.

Cost

It is impossible for us to say what you will have to pay to acquire the birds you want. The prices vary so widely from place to place and from year to year that it is practically impossible to keep track ourselves. You may even be lucky and get them free. Prices are directly dependent not only on feed costs, but also on the season and on supply and demand of each breed in your local area. The quality of the birds in general also has bearing on the price: a person who has invested years of carefully selected breeding will naturally ask more for his birds than someone who has an autonomous band of birds roaming the fields. Naturally, eggs will be cheaper than young birds, and young birds less expensive than mature ones. The best way to find out what you will have to pay is to shop around: check feed store bulletin boards, call advertisers in the want-ads, and visit local breeders.

The costs of maintaining a flock are also difficult for us to estimate for the same reasons. We can suggest that once ponds, brooders, and other equipment have been provided, virtually the sole expense is the feed. If you multiply the estimates on feed consumption for your breed, given in Chapter 7, by the cost of feed in your area, you will have a good idea of how much it will require to support one modest bird. Depending on how fancy you want to get, you can make your flock comfortable with a minimum of expense for facilities. By thoroughly reading Chapters 5 and 6, and by becoming familiar with the functions of the various necessities, you can easily save money by putting to use items that would otherwise be discarded.

Sources

There are lots of places from which to buy waterfowl. You can often get them through a local hatchery or feed store. Many areas have special waterfowl farms where birds can be purchased. These are sometimes listed in the Yellow Pages of the phone book or newspaper classified ads. Breeders can also be found through local poultry fanciers clubs or the county fairs and other poultry and waterfowl shows.

If you have difficulty finding what you want locally, you can purchase by mail-order from individuals or through general suppliers of poultry and waterfowl. Many mail-order dealers advertise in *Poultry Press* (listed in Chapter 16, "Resources"). You should be aware, though, that there are substantial difficulties involved in ordering birds by mail. One is the risk inherent in shipping anything fragile, especially hatching-eggs or live birds. It is impossible to ensure that eggs will travel under the proper conditions for good hatchability. Our experience is that whatever kind of eggs are ordered, they always arrive scrambled. In shipping live birds there is some danger of death or injury. You should by all means have a clear understanding with your supplier in advance as to who bears the risk.

Another problem is that you don't get to inspect firsthand the supplier's full operation. There are always a few disreputable dealers, of course, but even when your mail-order supplier is perfectly honorable there are disadvantages. Purchasing from a local breeder offers several advantages: you can see what you're getting and check for type, health, and vigor among the parents; locally bred birds will already be used to your climate; and you have a secure source of advice or answers to questions that might come up later on. If it becomes necessary to purchase from out of the area, do so only from someone you know or whom satisfied customers have recommended.

Whether local or mail-order, the supplier should be a reputable breeder as opposed to a dealer. Dealers who merely buy and sell waterfowl but do not raise them often cannot attest

251

to the breeding history or the health of the birds they trade. A breeder, on the other hand, knows exactly what he is selling and will generally be able to answer all of your questions about the birds.

Bringing home the birds

First-time waterfowl owners are often concerned with how they should go about acquainting birds with their new home. As long as feed, water, and protection have been properly arranged, it's an unnecessary concern: waterfowl will make themselves perfectly at home wherever conditions are suitable. You needn't confine them to a shelter, but it is helpful to ground flying breeds until they become familiar enough with their new environment to want to stick around. The section on pinioning in Chapter 4 tells you how to go about seeing that the birds cannot fly.

Ducks and geese in your backyard

You now have all the information you need to start your own backyard bevy of ducks or gaggle of geese, the knowledge to keep them healthy and happy, and the words to sound like a pro at it. Though this book is coming to an end, we hope you will find yourself rather at a beginning—a beginning of a lifelong enjoyment of waterfowl keeping.

Watching ducks and geese as they go through their life cycles affords even the most urban-bound the opportunity to observe firsthand the habits and customs of waterfowl. Some people become so fascinated with the activities of waterfowl that they enthusiastically and deliberately attract wild ducks and geese to their ponds. Conservation-minded individuals, who wish to create mini-wildlife refuges where migrating birds can find sanctuary from the confusions of modern civilization, keep domestic birds as year-round assurance to their wild brethren flying overhead that here is a safe and satisfactory place to land.

While domestic waterfowl have developed some quirks not exhibited in the wild, and on the other hand have lost certain

SIDNEY QUINN

characteristics that were once instinctive, they nonetheless provide a handy starting place in the study of the behavior of wild waterfowl. Learning to recognize the sounds and habits of domestic birds during their social interrelations leads to appreciation of the same characteristics in wildfowl or even birds in lakes at local city parks. You will grow accustomed, for instance, to the remarkable waterfowl habit of sleeping while standing on one foot! You will see a bird wake suddenly and indulge in a lazy and contented stretch by extending its free foot and neighboring wing gracefully backward like a ballerina on skates. You will learn that there's no such thing as a quiet romance among geese, for they characteristically make their sexual activities a community affair. The entire gaggle will celebrate a mating event by encircling the happy pair with a dreadful din of honking, holding a real old-fashioned shivaree. These self-appointed chaperones of the barnyard will even rush over to supervise whenever the ducks are fashioning the wreath of bliss.

Activities that once seemed peculiar and mysterious become a source of understanding and empathy, and you will soon find yourself inadvertently wrapped in the interest and intrigue of pond-side society. Don't be surprised if on occasion you suddenly come to the conscious realization that the day has been slipping away while you've sat meditatively, absorbed in the fascinating lives of your new feathered friends. Don't be surprised, either, when you find yourself deliberately contriving to include in your day a special time to share the company of the ducks and geese in your backyard.

16

RESOURCES

FURTHER READING

(USDA publications are updated periodically and given new numbers, but if you include the title in your request you should be able to track down the current version.)

Hatching.

The Avian Embryo, Emil Malinovsky. Cooperative Extension Service, The Ohio State University, Columbus, OH 43210.

From Egg to Chick, Northeast Cooperative Publications, NE1. Available through cooperative extension service offices throughout the northeastern states.

From Egg to Chick: A Guide to the Study of Incubation and Embryonic Development, S.F. Ridlen and H.S. Johnson, 1964. Cooperative Extension Service, University of Illinois, Urbana, IL 61801.

A Guide to Better Hatching, Janet Stromberg, 1975. Stromberg, Pine River, MN 56474.

How to Identify Eggs and Early Dead Embryos, University of California Division of Agricultural Sciences. Publication 4032. Publications, University of California Division of Agricultural Sciences, 1422 South Tenth Street, Richmond, CA 94804. (Color poster)

Ponds.

Garden Pools, Fountains and Waterfalls, 1965. Sunset Books, Menlo Park, CA 94025.

Butchering.

Home Canning of Meat and Poultry, 1970. Home and Garden Bulletin 106. USDA, Washington, DC 20250.

Home Freezing of Poultry, 1970. Home and Garden Bulletin 70. See address above.

Showing.

Bantam Standard, American Bantam Association. PO Box 610, North Amherst, MA 01059.

Standard of Perfection for Domesticated Landfowl and Waterfowl, American Poultry Association, Inc. P.O. Box 70, Cushing, OK 74023.

Poultry Press. PO Box 947, York, PA 17405. (National monthly newspaper for exhibitors of poultry and waterfowl.)

Sexing.

Sex Determination of Geese, Thomas H. Canfield. Bulletin 403. Cooperative Extension Service, University of Minnesota, St. Paul, MN 55101.

Sexing All Fowl, Baby Chicks, Game Birds, Cage Birds, Loyl Stromberg, ed., 1977. Stromberg, Pine River, MN 56474.

Disease and other perils.

Preventing Wing Deformities in Geese. Siwo R. deKloet, 1977. *American Game Bird Breeder's Federation Bulletin.* Convention issue.

Observations on 'Angel Wing' in White Chinese. D.W. Francis, R.H. Roberson, and L.A. Holland, 1967. *Poultry Science* 46:3.

Waterfowl Botulism Management. Brian F. Hunter and William E. Clark. Wildlife Management leaflet 14. The Resources Agency of California Department of Fish and Game, 1416 Ninth Street, Sacramento, CA 95814.

How to Avoid Freezing Feet in Waterfowl. H.M. Lackie, *American Pheasant and Waterfowl Society Magazine* 76-5:38-39.

Twisted Wing in Captive Waterfowl. Rick and Gail Luttman, *American Pheasant and Waterfowl Society Magazine* 77-8:10-12.

The Merck Veterinary Manual: A Handbook of Diagnosis and Therapy for the Veterinarian, Merck and Company, Merck, Rahway, NJ 07065

Wild waterfowl.

The Waterfowl of the World, vol. 1-4. Jean Delacour, 1956. Country Life, Ltd., London.

Raising Wild Ducks in Captivity, Dayton O. Hyde, ed., 1974. Distributed by International Wild Waterfowl Association. E.P. Dutton, New York.

Handbook of Waterfowl Behavior, Paul A. Johnsgard, 1965. Cornell University Press, Ithaca, N.Y.

Waterfowl of North America, 1975. Indiana University Press, Bloomington, Ind.

Waterfowl: Their Biology and Natural History, 1968. University of Nebraska Press, Lincoln, Nebr.

Ducks, Geese and Swans of North America, Francis H. Kortright, 1953. Wildlife Management Institute, Washington, D.C.

On Aggression, Konrad Lorenz, 1966. Harcourt, Brace and World, New York.

The Mallard, 1960. Olin Mathieson Chemical Corporation, East Alton, IL 62024.

General.

Managing a Small Duck Flock. Publication 1524. Agriculture Canada, 930 Carling Avenue, Ottawa, Ontario, Canada K1A OC7.

Pictures of Ducks. Publication 1349. Agriculture Canada, 930 Carling Avenue, Ottawa, Ontario, Canada K1A OC7.

Pictures of Geese. Publication 1345. See address above.

Raising Geese. Publication 848. See address above.

Ducks, Breeding, Rearing, Management, Reginald Appleyard. Poultry World Limited, Dorset House, Stamford Street, London SE1.

Practical Duck-Keeping, Leslie Bonnet, 1960. Malahi Breeding Project, Inc., PO Box 426, Greenhills Post Office, Rizall D-738, Philippines.

Raising Ducks in Small Flocks, W. Stanley Coates and Ralph A. Ernst, 1977. Leaflet 2980. Division of Agricultural Sciences, University of California, Davis, CA 95616.

What Makes Plumage Waterproof? Eric Fabricius, *American Pheasant and Waterfowl Society Magazine* 76-2:35-40, 76-3:21-23.

Modern Waterfowl Management and Breeding Guide, Oscar Grow, 1972. American Bantam Association, PO Box 610, North Amherst, MA 01059.

Domestic Geese and Ducks, Paul P. Ives, 1947. Orange Judd, New York. Out of print.

Raising Turkeys, Ducks, Geese, Game Birds, Morley A. Jull, 1947. McGraw-Hill, New York. Out of print.

Duck and Goose Raising, H.L. Orr, Publication 532. Ontario Department of Agriculture and Food, Parliament Buildings, Toronto, Ontario, Canada.

Successful Duck and Goose Raising, Darrel Sheraw, 1975. Stromberg, Pine River, MN 56474.

Raising Ducks, 1966. Farmers Bulletin 2215. USDA, Washington, DC 20250.

Raising Geese, 1972. Farmers Bulletin 2251. USDA, Washington, DC 20250.

Organizations

(These addresses change occasionally as responsibility transfers from person to person. Check a current edition of *Poultry Press* for more recent addresses. Check also for local or newly formed groups.)

American Bantam Association
PO Box 610
North Amherst, MA 01059.

American Pheasant and Waterfowl Society
Route 1
Granton, WI 54426.

American Poultry Association
PO Box 70
Cushing, OK 74023.

Associated Breeders of Campbell Ducks
7909 Lynch Road
Sebastopol, CA 95472.

International Waterfowl Breeders Association
Route 1, Box 211
Wheaton, IL 60187.

Supplies

Pond-building.

Beckett Company
2521 Willowbrook Road
Dallas, TX 75220.

Dutchman Fountains, Inc.
Mount Road
Lenni, PA 19052.

Fountains and Lighting, Imperial Bronzelite
1510 North Potrero Avenue
South El Monte, CA 91733.

General Fountain Corporation
264 West Fortieth Street
New York, NY 10018.

Hermitage Decorative Garden Pools
Box 361
Canastota, NY 13032.

Putnam's Rainbow Fountains
8011 Stockton Boulevard
Sacramento, CA 95823.

Rain Jet Corporation
301 South Flower Street
Burbank, CA 91503.

Van Ness Water Gardens
2460 North Euclid Avenue
Upland, CA 91786.

Incubators.

Brower Manufacturing Company
640 South Fifth Street
Quincy, IL 62301.

The Humidair Incubator Company
217 West Wayne Street
New Madison, OH 45346.

Leahy Manufacturing Company
Higginsville, MO 64037.

Lyon Electric Company, Inc.
3425 Hancock Street
PO Box 81303
San Diego, CA 92138.

Marsh Manufacturing Company
14232 Brookhurst Street
Garden Grove, CA 92643.

Butchering.

National Wax Company
3650 Touhy Avenue
Skokie, IL 60076.

Live animal traps.

Havahart
Box 551
Ossining, NY 10562.

Mustang Live-Catch Traps and Cages
PO Box 10947
Houston, TX 77018.

Tomahawk Live Trap Company
PO Box 323
Tomahawk, WI 54487.

Miscellaneous.

Burkey Company
PO Box 29465
San Antonio, TX 78229.

Marsh Manufacturing Company
14232 Brookhurst
Garden Grove, CA 92643.

National Band and Tag Company
Newport, KY 41072.

Rockytop Poultry and Pet Supply
PO Box 1006
Harriman, TN 37748.

Sidney Shoemaker
3091 Lincoln-Gilead Township Road 124
Route 3
Cardington, OH 43315.

Stromberg's Chicks and Pets Unlimited
Pine River
MN 56474.

Index

Page numbers in italics indicate illustrations.